RECIPES FOR LIFE
FROM THE FITONICS KITCHEN

RECIPES FOR LIFE

FROM THE FITONICS KITCHEN

Marilyn Diamond
with
Lisa Neuwirth

AVON BOOKS ■ NEW YORK

AVON BOOKS, INC.
1350 Avenue of the Americas
New York, New York 10019

Copyright © 1998 by FITONICS, INC.
Interior design by Rachael McBrearty
Visit our website at **http://www.AvonBooks.com**
ISBN: 0-380-97487-8

Library of Congress Cataloging in Publication Data:
Diamond, Marilyn
    Recipes for life: from the Fitonics kitchen/Marilyn Diamond, with Lisa Neuwirth—1st ed.
        p.   cm.
    Includes biographical references and index.
    1. Cookery.   2. Health.   3. Nutrition.   I. Neuwirth, Lisa.   II. Title.
TX714.D52   1998   97-44150
641.5'63—dc21   CIP

First Avon Books Printing: May 1998

AVON BOOKS TRADEMARK REG. U.S. PAT. OFF. AND IN OTHER COUNTRIES, MARCA REGISTRADA, HECHO EN U.S.A.

Printed in the U.S.A.

FIRST EDITION

QPM   10   9   8   7   6   5   4   3   2   1

*This book is dedicated to those who are looking for an easy and
practical way to fulfill two natural human desires:
the love of eating and the wish to be healthy.*

TO YOU!

To your happiness and good times in the kitchen!

To your health in its most joyous expression!

Acknowledgments

Our deepest gratitude to all who have eaten our food, expressed their delight and urged us to stay on this path. *Swamy, dearest beloved*, thank you.

Let thy food be thy medicine.
—Hippocrates

Contents

RECIPES FOR LIFE
FROM THE FITONICS KITCHEN

Introduction

PASSING THE TORCH TO YOU

The critical responsibility for the generation you're in is to help provide the shoulders, the direction, and the support for those generations who come behind.
—*Gloria Dean Randle Scott*

The shoulders I stand on are those of my mother Frances. She was the one who made the quality of the food on the family dinner table her most cherished responsibility. The aromas of her delicious, imaginative meals, prepared with so much care and love, warmed our home and drew me into the kitchen. There I would scrub and shine the pots and pans, just to be near her, in hopes of soaking up some of her talent. My mother passed on to me a family legacy, as she gave me a priceless education in feminine culinary nurturing that has dominated my life's work. I didn't know then that she'd handed me a torch. When I chose to carry it, I passed my philosophy on to millions; without my mother's influence, I would never have been able to do the work I do.

I can see now that I've ignited a similar passion for culinary nurturing in my own daughter Lisa. From a young age, her creative interests have mirrored my own and gone beyond, into the exciting world of restaurant cuisine, with professional training at the Culinary Institute of America. Her talent and innovation take the simple creative skills I learned from my mother, those I developed on my own, and the spirit of excellence in nurturing that has been our family tradition to a whole new level! One of my most cherished experiences has been the collaboration with her in the writing of this cookbook.

When my mother passed the torch to me, I found my calling to carry it in a way that would both draw from her example and seek solutions relevant to the nutritional concerns of my own generation. I was especially inspired by the needs of my children—who were being raised in a different environment, one far less secure than my own upbringing. The modern stresses on family life during the 1970s and 1980s required entirely new solutions to urgent new problems. Women were leaving their homes and children to enter the marketplace in record numbers. The resulting breakdown in family structure, the phenomenon of single parenting, and a national health-care crisis were all factors affecting my life and the message I was creating. My twenty-five years—a quarter century!—of research and development in alternative nutritional lifestyles, experimenting with a wide range of approaches to healing—from fasting to nutrient-supplementation—brought me to the balanced way of living articulated in *FITONICS* and demonstrated in *Recipes for Life*.

The predicament my generation faced first, which now confronts us all—to find the most healthful ways to maintain the continuity of home, hearth, and family—touched my life as it touched millions of others. My work reached everyone from teenagers to the elderly, but I was speaking primarily to my peers, the baby boomers. Today, more than ever, we look to solutions pioneered in the field of natural health for ways to avoid the apparently inevitable age-related illness that threatens our parents' generation. As I hone this message of balanced living and vital longevity for my peers, I am also more aware than ever of the concerns of my children's generation, whose hearts are seeking and whose voices are beginning to resonate with new solutions to suit the next phase of life on the planet. These beautiful young people are grappling with problems they had no role in creating. Collaborating with my daughter Lisa on writing this book has deeply inspired me and allowed me to bridge the gap and articulate solutions to a multigenerational quest.

As baby boomers, raised in more secure times, tend to wonder where the world is heading, I believe the younger generations are giving us reason to rejoice. What I hear and what I witness, through my own children and many others I find myself guiding, is a profound longing to return to real, old-fashioned, down-to-earth family-sustaining life. At the same time, many in this younger generation are searching for ways to make positive contributions to society. Their goals include a search for longevity and health in relationships, careers, and life, and turning back toward family heritage, tradition, or ancient spiritual teachings to find lasting solutions. Whatever the path, the longing is universal—to be happy, create a warm, secure family environment, and become more balanced human beings—in other words, to live life healthfully and wisely. Many want to know how to take care of themselves physically and spiritually, which I hope—in the next century—will bring about an end to the crisis of ill health that far too many in our population are experiencing.

The feeling I've put into *Recipes for Life* has afforded an environment for ritually passing the torch. Representing my own generation in the biologically encoded feminine role of nurturers of the species, I see myself passing my knowledge to those who find themselves gravitating toward natural living as the best path to enduring health and happiness. Understanding how to nourish and preserve humanity, long before the establishment of patriarchal organized medicine, was traditionally a feminine role each generation of women was required to fulfill. My concern is for the preservation of this role in these changing times for men and women alike, for if we lose the ability to nourish ourselves as a species, as well as to pass on the skills and secrets of how to do it from one generation to the next, how can we survive?

Recipes for Life supports the desire so many are seeking for greater well-being on all levels of existence. This well-rounded approach to living is particularly relevant to our needs in today's society. I have welcomed the far-reaching support, collaboration, and special contributions of my husband, Dr. Donald Burton Schnell, as he has helped me to articulate not only the message of health relating to food, but also to whole-food supplementation, as well as mental and spiritual health. His connection to the ancient and modern traditions and teachings for physical, mental, and spiritual well-being have enabled me to round out the repertoire of recipes

I have been able to offer here. His ability to articulate profound spiritual truth in a user friendly manner is, in a sense, a second passing of the torch, an awakening in my readers to the spiritual balance that makes life meaningful. Donald's input and guidance has been a source of deepest inspiration in my own life, and it allows this book to include recommendations for the highest nutrition on all levels of body, mind, and spirit.

So, dear reader, now the torch comes to you. As you turn the pages of this book, may you thoroughly enjoy the happiness and energy that are the inevitable result of the journey along the road to natural health.

A Fresh Start

⟨❦⟩

The connection between love of wholesome food and love of self is undeniable. A healthy appetite is a beautiful and wondrous quality. It reflects the passion of the soul. To trivialize or negate the natural human desire for food, to label that desire a disease, can contribute to serious eating disorders and the excess weight and ill health that so many are fighting as a result. Eating is one of the ways we sustain life! It's good to like to eat. So let's begin here with a clear and fresh start! Your love of food is what is normal about you, and we are here to direct that love in the most positive and satisfying way.

In this book you will find a fresh and lively design for eating that addresses the nutritional needs of your body, as well as the preferences of your palate. What a grand revelation to find that the two are synergistic rather than opposing pursuits. For food to truly nourish, it has to please your senses, which are the most individual aspect of your nature. For some people, a deliciously marinated filet mignon may be appealing; others would choose a colorful vegetable salad. The bottom line: *eating is a personal choice.* With that understanding in mind, we have provided on the pages that follow an eclectic collage of recipes designed to reflect the grand diversity of the American diet and all the wonderful healthful cuisine it offers. Be assured, there is something here for everyone.

Is your goal an increasingly healthier body and a consistently happier state of mind? Do you wish for those two qualities to endure well into old age? This has been our goal for decades, and we think we're on to something . . .

IT'S NOT JUST WHAT YOU'RE EATING

What you eat is only one factor that contributes to your state of health. Of course, the higher the quality of the food on your plate, the better the performance you can expect from your body (and remember, your brain is part of your body!). It has been our experience that choosing wholesome food actually brings more consistent opportunity for long-term happiness and success in life. So we begin by providing you with the ideas and recipes for ensuring that your food is of the highest quality. Our emphasis is on fresh food and pure ingredients, meals that supply your body with the energy it needs to thrive.

And, since *it's not just what you're eating, it's also what you're thinking*, we'd be remiss in our message if we talked only about recipes for the body. To support that idea, we'd like to offer some "food for thought" to help you make the shift to health and ideal weight. One of our goals is to add to your information bank and help you make better choices.

In the last few decades of heightened health awareness, our hunger for new information has centered predominantly on nutritional data, but in this era, a new hunger is manifesting. As we approach a significant turning point, the advent of a new millennium, more and more of us are finding satisfaction in the nurturing of our souls as well as our bodies. Since much of what you eat will be influenced by what you're thinking about yourself and the quality of your life, for best results, consider your spirituality and use it as you prepare your meals. The practice of high-minded thinking can actually help flavors to be richer and food taste better. Your optimistic, spiritual focus will pour good vibrations into what you're preparing, and they'll permeate your body. As you approach mealtime with heart opened, turning toward all the good in the universe, you'll find yourself and your world literally transforming.

SURROUND YOUR FOOD WITH LOVE

The environment in which food is prepared and eaten has a significant impact on the effect of that food on the body. The hot dogs and hamburgers at a down-home American Sunday barbecue, where friends and family gather to laugh and enjoy each other's company, can actually bring better health results than salad, brown rice, and steamed vegetables eaten in a hostile or unconscious environment with the nightly news blaring in place of warm and caring conversation. So many other cultures with less obesity and disease and far greater longevity than our own understand the importance of the social context of food. Isn't it time for us to learn that our tendency to minimize the dynamics around the food we're eating is having a serious impact on our health and the quality of our lives?

For example, in the Mediterranean countries, from France to North Africa, meals are not taken on the run or zapped in the microwave. Only in our language are there words for *TV dinner*. As we and other members of our family have traveled throughout the world, through Europe, Central and South America, the Middle East, and Asia, we have observed repeatedly that most people in other cultures, regardless of their social and economic stature, consider mealtime a coveted opportunity to recharge, gather, and socialize. For them, it's a warm and comforting time, a welcome break from work to relax and enjoy the art of eating. This merry atmosphere around food brings far more than social pleasure. It increases the healthfulness of the meal, and it actually facilitates digestion.

The time of business does not with me differ from the time of prayer, and in the noise and chatter of my kitchen, while several persons are at the same time calling for different things, I possess God in as great tranquility as if I were upon my knees at the blessed sacrament.

—Brother Lawrence

In Europe, we Americans are known as the culture driven by work, around which everything must revolve, especially the "grabbing" of a meal. Our dependency on fast and convenient food is pitied. We are the ones for whom food preparation and family life seem to be determined more and more by the demands of our careers, rather than the other way around. Many of us rarely find the time to gather with family and friends these days. American working women lament having to stop at the franchises or take-out counters for the dinner we must feed our families, but what can we do?

In Europe and Asia, on the other hand, the preparation of the family meal is a social priority. The female role of nurturer is prized and protected. A dear friend of ours from Jerusalem recounts, eyes moist with tears of nostalgia, the simple grandeur of humble meals prepared daily by his mother to maintain the health of her family of ten children. It's hard to find a single Italian who doesn't praise "mama" as the most talented cook in the entire world, and in Italy, as in many other European countries, time is set aside each day for a main meal at lunch and a rest thereafter. Yet in our country, we have so sacrificed quality of life that we "work through" lunch, that cultural time for recharge. Around the world, time is always set aside for this all-important daily ritual, and even among the poor, there is time to eat meals prepared from pure, natural, wholesome, and affordable ingredients. How poor we seem by comparison, rushing through our meals, leading the world in the manufacture of costly packaging containing nutrient-empty junk!

THROW OUT THE JUNK!

Many American families dine daily on nutritionally and spiritually impoverished junk. This book is a call to arms. As we march toward a new millennium, many of us are pausing to reassess our values and direction and improve not only our own health but also to come to the nutritional aid of our children. Many are seeking to spiritualize the choices we are making in our lives. Where we should start is in our own kitchens. The simple, lively meals we're proposing in this book will work for you as well as your children.

When the editor of *FITONICS* was nearly finished with her work on the manuscript, she told us one day that she had gone home and thrown out every bit of diet food, fat-free junk, packaged "stuff," and soda on her shelves. She was reconnecting to her Mediterranean roots, wanting to fill her refrigerator and pantry with the fresh, full-of-life foods that made up her diet as a young girl of Greek heritage. She wanted fresh eggplant and zucchini, vegetables in flavorful stews, bright red, juicy tomatoes, fresh feta cheese, olives, lamb, and the seafood of the islands. She craved the grapes, melons, and figs of her origins.

What was she telling us, essentially? Exactly what we've found to be true for ourselves as we researched the cultures healthier than our own. Where obesity, cancer, and heart disease are less prevalent, people eat *real* food, and they focus on local foods of their regions. They eat them fresh, from the farms, and in the seasons when they are naturally available. Rather than paying for artificial ingredients and slick packages of chemical-laden junk, they bring flavor and hearty aromas to simple, inexpensive fresh ingredients with fresh herbs, garlic, olive oils, and spices. We can do the same. We have our meats, soups, and root vegetables in cold climates. In warmer regions and seasons, we have an abundance of fresh fish, fruits, and vegetables to enjoy.

A particularly inspiring model is the Okinawans, the longest-lived people on Earth. Although they eat pork and drink beer, the majority of their diet is composed of fresh, enzyme-rich fruits and vegetables. They don't eat dairy products, yet they have strong bones. They eat a fair amount of fat, but in its natural form, in whole foods. The Okinawans would feel very much at home with the FITONICS plan.

So where do we start? The logical place is at the market.

First, we can make the effort to cut down on foods containing all the recent developments in artificiality. We can avoid butter "subs," margarine and olestra, and use a little real butter now and then, if a recipe calls for it. We can avoid the low- and nonfat dairy products that are missing the fat, but brimming with fattening sugar or artificial sweeteners. If we want sweet yogurt, we can do like the French and add a little pure honey, or if our palate wants a fruity flavor, why not add the real fruit without all the sugar?

We can toss out fiberless grains, cereals, and white breads and go for whole grains. If you had at your disposal all the white flour in the world, nutritionally you would still be a pauper. Pop-Tarts and frosting on cereal flakes are examples of how our diets have deteriorated in the past several decades. So is spongy, nutritionally-empty white bread. Toss the sugar-coated cereals. There's more nutrition in the box! Buy cereals like old-fashioned whole oats or shredded wheat with bran that have 4 to 8 grams of fiber per cup.

When possible, buy fresh, rather than canned fish, fresh rather than cured meats, and seek out organic meats as well as organic produce and grains. Explore the many uses of tofu. Avoid empty, overcooked canned vegetables and syrupy fruits. Buy fresh produce whenever possible, or frozen rather than canned, if you're in a climate where fresh produce is not abundant. Fruits and vegetables eaten fresh give you fiber and enzymes; they're the "soap and scrub brushes" for the inside of your body.

It's time to turn away from all the diet foods loaded with aspartame (NutraSweet, Sweet'n Low, Equal), which addict you and force you into the vicious cycle of artificially sweetened product consumption. Artificial sweeteners are chemicals, not food, and they cheat your body, pushing it to hunger for more food, as they promise nutrition but deliver none.

The trend is a movement away from fattening refined sugar toward healthful whole food sweeteners, such as honey, Sucanat, date sugar, and sorghum. Rich in minerals, vitamins, and fiber, they nourish, rather than fatten the body. Sugar is a nutritionally empty food that destroys the body's enzymes and precious B vitamins, and it forces perfectly good nutrition to be stored as fat. Unless you're seeking medical care for your children, it's time to avoid all the candy, loaded with sugar, artificial colorings, and flavors. If you tossed this stuff in the garden, your plants would wither and your cat would yawn and look the other way. Vote with your dollars against the junk

Human Life Is More Important Than Shelf Life

food industry's conspiracy to pervert your children's concept of what is and is not food!

THE POLITICS OF FOOD

The greatest discovery of any generation is that human beings can alter their lives by altering the attitudes of their minds.
—*Albert Schweitzer*

Why Choose Organic?

You've certainly noticed the burgeoning bins of organic produce in upscale super-markets. What may surprise you is that corporate giants—even Heinz the catsup king—are jumping on this trend. According to *Walking* magazine, the number of natural food supermarkets more than tripled in the five years from 1989 to 1994. So it's become increasingly easy to buy organic, and we strongly recommend that you do, if it's within your budget.

Remember, fruits and vegetables are the heart of the FITONICS kitchen, and you want them to be as delicious and nutrient-dense as possible. Studies have shown that organic produce has more nutrients, especially minerals, and of course it doesn't contain pesticides. In some states where the laws are very strict, such as California, it may not be possible for small farmers to comply completely with the standards—in which case, you'll see their produce marked "pesticide-free," another good choice. If you have a local farmers' market, it will supply you with seasonal produce from your area that's either organic or raised with a minimum of chemical fertilizers. Although it's fun to buy out-of-season exotics from faraway lands, those fruits and vegetables are frequently contaminated with the very chem-icals that are now banned in our food.

Animal products too have no national standard, though growth hormones are not allowed in pork, lamb, or poultry. Antibiotics are allowed across the board, however. Because toxic substances like pesticide residues are stored in fat, it seems like a particularly good idea to buy organic meats, eggs, and dairy products.

Children are especially vulnerable to hormones, antibiotics, and pesticides. In the July 26, 1996, issue of *The New York Times*, Senator Edward Kennedy laments, "Cancer kills more children under age fourteen than any other disease. Brain can-cer and leukemia [in children] have increased by 33 percent in the last two decades, so it's no time for Congress to loosen restriction on cancer-causing chemicals in the food supply, especially on baby food." (Parents wanting to prepare pure foods for their children might wish to take a look at *MOMMY MADE—and Daddy too! Home Cooking for a Healthy Baby and Toddler* by Martha and David Kimmel, Bantam Books, 1990.) According to Mothers & Others, a strong lobbying group in the organic food movement, it's hard to tell which fruits and vegetables are most contaminated—it depends on the soil and the carefulness of the grower. But in general, keep these foods on your organic buy list: strawberries, bell peppers, spinach, cherries, peaches, cantaloupe (from Mexico), celery, apples, apricots, green beans, grapes, and cucumbers.

Don't forget this is a political issue. Every time you buy food, you're voting. The greater demand we consumers create, the greater will be the supply, and soon the prices will come down. It costs a little more now, but you'll be part of the big wave that's sweeping the country and demanding healthier food for all of us. If you can, join us—the trend is extremely positive!

CITIZEN ALERT!

Food Irradiation: A Modern-Day Travesty

As spokespeople for pure food and natural health, we have been campaigning against food irradiation since its inception. So far, our efforts combined with the many other concerned citizens and practitioners in the natural health field have kept this insidious attack against the integrity of our food supply from becoming a universally accepted practice, but we can never drop our guard where this issue is concerned. We're facing a strategic campaign mounted by huge and powerful forces concerned with profit, not our health, and they're not going to go away quietly.

Food irradiation is not, as you might think, an outgrowth of the farming or food industries. It comes to us *directly* from the Department of Energy in its efforts to find a commercially viable destination for the nuclear waste our defense industry has created. In short, it's the ultimate solution to nuclear waste: Make it profitable. The idea was to sell it to private facilities that would then use it—with precious little government supervision—to treat the food destined for our dinner tables. To quote James Michael Lennon, the director of the American Natural Hygiene Society, food irradiation is "technology in search of a use. It creates a mushrooming of toxic waste sites, and the unmonitored transporting of contamination of our neighborhoods and communities." The process of food irradiation can never be environmentally safe. Radioactive materials are hazardous where they are produced, hazardous as they travel, and hazardous in exposure to any living thing. The risk of nuclear accidents escalates as each irradiation site is opened.

The FDA, which has no program to monitor food irradiation, nonetheless declares that it is safe! This judgment of safety was made after studying only 5 out of 441 studies on potential toxicity. Two of the studies were declared flawed. In a third, animals fed irradiated food experienced weight loss and miscarriage. One possible cause: the vitamin E deficiency induced in irradiated food. In the fourth and fifth studies, lower levels of irradiation were measured than those currently approved by the FDA for our food.

The argument is that food irradiation *preserves* our food, guaranteeing a longer shelf life. The admitted damage to our food created by food irradiation is declared "acceptable." In fact, every change in the intrinsic nature of food is harmful, and the foods that would be harmed the most by food irradiation are the fresh fruits and vegetables we rely on for health. Even cooking destroys essential nutrients in these foods, such as the life-enhancing enzymes. The idea that food irradiation preserves food is misleading, since the process simply *changes* how food spoils, carrying with it new risk factors such as reduced levels of certain vitamins and bacterial contamination. All the supposed benefits that are attributed to the process are already obtainable from other less expensive, far less dangerous processes. These foods are *damaged*, not preserved.

Germany, Sweden, Denmark, New Zealand, and Australia have all banned irradiated foods to protect their citizens. Japan does not import any foods that have been irradiated. In creating an industry around our nuclear waste, we are actually putting at risk our ability to export food to many important foreign markets. All of these countries rate far ahead of the United States in longevity. Clearly, national policies that protect the food supply of a country have a significant effect on the health of its citizens.

The good news is that to date, New York, Maine, and New Jersey are protecting their 36 million citizens by banning the sale of irradiated foods within their borders. Five additional states are presently considering the same ban. There has been support in the past in the U.S. Senate and House of Representatives for the prohibition of the sale of irradiated foods. But the food industry, which would benefit from extended shelf life of lifeless foods and the Department of Energy that needs to legitimize the dumping of toxic waste into the private sector, are not letting this campaign die.

What can you do? Make a copy of the following letter and send it to the President of the United States, and to your senators and representatives.

President of the United States
1600 Pennsylvania Avenue
Washington, DC 20500
FAX (202) 456-2461

Dear Mr. President,

I am deeply concerned about the degradation of American food through the process of food irradiation. A country's food supply is the most significant barometer of its future survival. For my health, the welfare of American children, and the future of the United States of America, *please present a program to Congress for legislation to ban food irradiation in the United States.*

Sincerely yours,

How to Convince Your Children to Eat More Fruits and Vegetables

Always go with the river of life. Never try to go against the current, and never try to go faster than the river. Just move in absolute relaxation, so that each moment you are at home, at ease, at peace with existence.
—*Bhagavan Shree Rajneesh*

The truth is, *it is not so hard to convince children to eat fruit! (Vegetables are an altogether different story.)* Up until the teenage years, most children love fruit. That is not to say they love *all* fruits, but they usually do have at least one or two favorites. Berries are most frequently adored by small children. So are cherries. It makes sense. For them, these fruits are the perfect size. They're finger foods they can handle all on their own. Some children absolutely adore bananas, oranges, or watermelon. Usually they love plums or peaches. I always tell moms to understand that children don't have to eat all fruits. And if you want them to eat any fruit at all, give them the ones they love. Generously!

And by all means, eat the ones you like in front of them. Do it subtlely. As you core an apple for yourself, carve off thin little slices and absentmindedly hand them to your child. Don't ask if an apple is wanted. Just eat and share. Or make a ceremony out of it. "Look, Johnny, Mommy's going to sit down to a great big bowl of tangerines. I wonder how many I'll eat? Oh-h-h, they're so-o-o sweet! Here, taste this little baby section I found just for you!" When you're watching television with your children, bring out a beautiful platter of fruit, and begin to eat it, even if they don't. Much unconscious eating goes on in front of a television set. Make the fruit available.

When a child asks for fruit, allow that fruit to be eaten as soon as possible and until the child is satiated. It is better to buy two pints of strawberries, rinse them as soon as you get home, put them in a pretty bowl, and let your children sit down and fill their tummies. If that fills them up, and they're less interested in the next meal you're planning on serving, that's okay. Or, you can make a meal out of the strawberries by adding a bowl of sour cream and a bowl of date sugar for dipping.

Children Need "Cleansing" Too

An occasional fruit meal will do your children as much good in terms of cleansing and energizing as it will you. The fruit meal they will probably not be attracted to regularly is the fruit breakfast. Which makes sense, since fruit breakfasts are ideal for adults who are wishing to lose weight and build their energy, but are less critical for energetic children who wake up hungry and may not thrive in the schoolroom if their stomachs are too empty. One fruit breakfast I have found that children (and adults) of all ages love is the fresh fruit "cereal" or fruesli on pages 81 and 86, which is mixed with nuts and nut milk.

A successful strategy for enticing children to eat fruits is to make a colorful "paint box" fruit salad. Let them help you decide what colors to put in the salad. Cut all the fruit up in small pieces so their flavors will blend, and to involve them in the process, you can let them help with their own small, dullish knives. Children love to cook. They love to play meaningful roles in the kitchen, and cutting up fruit is a great way to introduce the art. Add raisins or currants for sweetness. Make a beautiful pink strawberry-banana sauce in your blender with some fresh orange or apple juice and sit and eat this fruit salad with them. If there isn't much fruit in season in your area, make fresh applesauce in your blender with some orange or apple juice. Add cinnamon, a little honey or maple syrup, and a dash of nutmeg. You can soak raisins and blend them right into the apples for sweetness. Again, let your children help. It's fun to show them how you peel an apple, making one long strip of peel. Make a game out of it. Children also usually like dried fruit, such as raisins, figs, dried apple rings, or pineapple rings. All of these can be chopped and added to a fruit salad. Be sure you buy sun-dried fruit. In my experience, one can have a serious stomachache from eating sulfur-dried fruit.

Fruit Snacks Before Supper

If your children are hungry, waiting for supper, start them with a fruit platter or fruit salad. You can also make a fruit and cheese platter with squares of cheese and fruit cubes on toothpicks and encourage them to snack as you are preparing the meal. With a concentrated protein like cheese, the use of juicy fruits that are 95% water, such as apples, oranges, grapefruits, strawberries, peaches, and grapes will supply important enzymes and rich and nourishing water to help in digestion. Use teriyaki skewers to make fruit kabobs. To add enzymes to a traditional childrens' food, cut thin slices of banana and make them one of the layers of a peanut butter and jelly sandwich. On family outings that children look forward to, take fruit for snacks, and in the summer, be sure to make a special outing of going to the roadside farmers' stands where you can purchase the fruits and vegetables of the season.

Tricks with Vegetables

As much as children like fruit, they will be less attracted to vegetables in the early years. Still, I have found there is usually some vegetable they will enjoy, and that is what you will have to concentrate on serving. Most children like corn on the cob. Make it fresh when it is in season. Use corn as a basis for soup (Summer Corn Chowder, page 228), in a casserole, or added to salads. Suggest that they try it raw (and you try it with them). Uncooked corn is sweet and milky. If your children love string beans, that is what you should make. Frequently I find that if you camouflage vegetables, they will be more attractive to the younger set. Adding corn to a Nacho Casserole (page 153) or an assortment of chopped vegetables to a pasta sauce can bring some positive results. Children will usually be receptive to vegetable soups with pasta in them. Cook the vegetables well, so they aren't crunchy. A great trick is to puree a vegetable soup into a cream soup.

Salads are not the favorite of most young children. When my children were younger, I added fried potatoes, tortilla chips, or pasta to salads, which they loved. A salad with a cheesy dressing can attract a resistant salad eater. I also find that children will eat a salad that is chopped and contains a lot of other goodies, such as cheese and meats they like. Serve salads with hot garlic bread or muffins as a first course. The salad bar, where they can make their own salads, is a good family outing any time of day, if your children need a snack. Serving raw vegetables and a dip when your children are doing their homework or waiting for supper is a good idea. When my children were young, I relied so heavily on this trick that, in true Martha Stewart fashion (not only for my children, but for entertaining and in the workshops I was teaching), I learned how to carve vegetables into flowers and multi-shaped leaves, and I made beautiful baskets of raw vegetable flowers with dips. I sliced jicama thin and cut it into hearts or butterflies with cookie cutters and bought zigzag cutters for carrots and zucchini. It was amazing to watch the neighborhood children avidly dip and eat a vegetable that wasn't shaped like a vegetable.

Grow an Indoor Sprout Garden

Finally, make it a project with your child to sprout the seeds your family eats. Alfalfa sprouts are the easiest to grow. The procedure is simple. Sprouting jars can be purchased at most natural food stores, or simply cover a large mayonnaise jar with mesh or cheesecloth held tightly in place by a rubberband. Place a few tablespoons of alfalfa seeds to soak for a few hours in the sprouting jar. Rinse and drain well and then store them inverted on a folded paper towel (so any water runs out) in a dark cabinet. Rinse them once or twice a day for three days or until the sprouts are about an inch long. Place them in daylight, (but not necessarily direct sun), to green for 24 hours, pull them from the jar and place in a bowl of water. The seed hulls will come to the surface of the water. Skim them off, drain the sprouts well and store in a covered plastic bowl in your refrigerator. As soon as the sprouts are ready, you and your children can make sandwiches and eat them!

Vegetable eating is taught by example. If they always see you eat a salad, if there are always vegetables on your plate, the idea of eating vegetables will become ingrained in your children in spite of themselves. Even if they don't eat them readily yet, they are learning by your modeling, and later in life, when they are on their own, they will begin to copy your actions. Modeling is the most important tool you have when your child enters the teen years. For many teenagers, those are the years when food can become the issue around which the battle for independence is fought. Many teenagers are now gravitating toward a vegetarian regimen, but that is not always the healthiest choice for them if all they eat are refined foods and if they satisfy their blood's call for nutrients by eating sugary foods. With teenagers, it is important to keep a well-stocked refrigerator, with plenty of nourishing foods you have cooked that they can grab on the run. For growing teenage boys, cooked meats, such as barbecued chicken or a robust chili, packaged veggie-burgers, or tofu or turkey dogs. Teenage girls will appreciate having on hand slenderizing cooked vegetables that they can nibble with cottage cheese, or yogurt or add to salads.

One word of advice. It won't get you anywhere to allow yourself to become tense or unhappy over your children's eating habits. Provide plenty of nourishing food, remove as much sugar as possible from their diets, and, above all, make dietary changes first and foremost for *yourself*. Too many parents preach what they do not practice, and therefore, because children are observant, the parents never make any headway in pushing a more healthful diet. If your diet is nutritionally sound, your children ultimately, sooner or later, follow suit. *Your example* of health is the best gift you can give them.

THE FITONICS PRINCIPLES: YOUR TOOLS

The guidelines that follow will automatically allow you to eat an abundance of pure, whole foods and fresh fruits and vegetables. Please understand that our recipes support these guidelines as tools, rather than rules. They're designed to be flexible, since we have learned the hard lesson ourselves, through excess denial and fanaticism, that rigidity toward food in any way brings a loss in health. (The only "rules" we advise you to take into the kitchen are "Praise the Lord!" and "Don't worry, be happy!") As you use these principles from day to day, you'll find excess weight falling off and an increase in energy and well-being that others will reflect to you as they exclaim, "You look great!"

I. KEEP THE COLON CLEAN WITH FRESH JUICES, FRUIT, VEGETABLES, AND HIGH-FIBER GRAINS AND LEGUMES.

A clean colon is the key to better assimilation of nutrients and a major factor in efficient weight loss. Most people are carrying around at least 15 pounds of waste in their colons.

II. TO KEEP ENZYME SUPPLIES HIGH AND ENERGY ABUNDANT, AND TO SUPPORT WEIGHT LOSS, EAT ONE LIVE FOOD MEAL EVERY DAY, CONSISTING SOLELY, OR PREDOMINATELY OF FRESH FRUITS OR VEGETABLES.

The ideal is a fruit meal in the morning, or a salad and fruit meal at lunch or dinner. The "tonics," fruit meals, and Super Salads are ideal live food meal choices. For permanent weight loss, a dramatic increase in vital energy and an end to that blocked, dragged-down feeling, make every effort to eat no more than two cooked food meals a day. (Note: Adding some plain yogurt to a fruit meal or having some cheese or bread with your salad does not entirely negate this principle. Be comfortable while eating as much live food as you can!)

III. TO IMPROVE DIGESTION, AND GET THE MOST FROM FOOD, WE TAKE ENZYME SUPPLEMENTS WITH EVERY COOKED MEAL.

Enzyme supplements replace the enzymes that are invariably destroyed when food is processed or cooked at temperatures above 118 degrees. Cooked food must be broken down solely by your own digestive and metabolic enzymes—manufactured by your body in a diminishing supply as you age. Choose to facilitate digestion and lighten the drain from your body's enzyme capacity with regular use of enzyme supplements. Supplements help conserve your body's enzyme supply, which can lead to rejuvenation and better health.

IV. TO LOSE WEIGHT AND INCREASE ENERGY, AVOID <u>ROUTINELY</u> MIXING PROTEINS AND STARCHES. A SIMPLE WEIGHT-LOSS AND ENERGY-ENHANCING GUIDELINE IS TO HAVE PROTEINS WITH SALADS AND NONSTARCHY VEGETABLES AT LUNCH (THE POWER LUNCH) AND STARCHES WITH VEGETABLES AND/OR SALADS AT DINNER (THE SOOTHING SUPPER).

Protein is a stimulating food. It will digest more quickly and efficiently when eaten with enzyme-rich salads and juicy fruits, rather than with starches, such as potatoes, bread, pasta, or rice. Protein is an ideal lunch choice, if you need your energy to be high during the afternoon. Starches cause the brain to secrete serotonin, which makes you sleepy. They are best eaten at night, when peace and calm are appropriate. A starch meal can help you have a good night's sleep. Proteins eaten on their own with salads take approximately 4 hours to leave the stomach. Starches eaten on their own with vegetables take approximately 2 hours to leave the stomach. Proteins and starches eaten together at a meal can take 8 hours or longer to break down, which results in your valuable energy being wasted.

V. TO KEEP BODIES HEALTHFULLY ALKALINE, ENJOY A FUNDAY AS OFTEN AS POSSIBLE, EATING ONLY <u>F</u>RESH, <u>U</u>NCOOKED, <u>N</u>ATURAL FOODS SUCH AS FRUITS, VEGETABLES, SPROUTS, SUN-DRIED FRUITS, RAW NUTS AND SEEDS, AND FRESH FRUIT AND VEGETABLE JUICES.

A FUNday is a cleansing day. It's a day guaranteed to bring weight loss, radiance, and a dramatic increase in energy. (Note: On any FUNday, a steamed vegetable meal to "warm the tummy" will not negate overall cleansing benefits.)

VI. THINK TWICE BEFORE USING REFINED SUGAR AND ARTIFICIAL INGREDIENTS.

They destroy your body's enzymes, suppress the immune system, weaken the bones, exhaust valuable vitamin and mineral supplies, increase stress and contribute to excess weight. Substitute whole food sweeteners, such as those recommended in the Basic Shopping List (pages 26–29).

And, since the message of FITONICS emphasizes that health is so much more than just the food on your plate:

VII. TO ENSURE HEALTH AND HAPPINESS, MAKE AN EFFORT, ESPECIALLY FIRST THING IN THE MORNING, TO MENTALLY SET THE TONE FOR THE DAY.

Have an attitude of gratitude as you count your blessings and focus on the good in your life, and resolve that you will see the good in the people and situations that arise in your personal "theater" throughout the day. Using prayer, or other time-honored spiritual techniques, be confident that no matter what the stress or circumstance, you will consciously attempt to make each moment a rewarding experience.

VIII. TO FIND PEACE AND HARMONY, TAKE 5 TO 20 MINUTES EACH DAY TO DEEPLY RELAX BODY AND MIND.

Honor your spiritual essence. Pray before starting. Close your eyes. Breathe deeply and relax completely, focusing your attention on the third eye region of your forehead, using Hypno-Meditation* to count yourself down into a deep meditative state. When you count yourself up, consciously remove old programs that may not be serving you and visually create the reality you wish to experience. Regular meditation practice and prayer such as this will bring joy to your heart, focus, and tranquillity to your mind.

IX. CLEANSE AND FEED ALL THE MUSCLES OF YOUR BODY EVERY DAY BY SPENDING 12 TO 20 MINUTES IN AN ACTIVE SPINE-BASED ROUTINE.

BODYTONICS† is the active routine we recommend every morning to oxygenate your blood and tone all the muscle groups. Muscles you don't use, you lose.

---

*See Marilyn Diamond and Dr. Donald Burton Schnell, FITONICS for Life (New York: Avon Books, 1996), pp. 187–209.

†Ibid., pp. 213–54.

MINDTONICS

THINGS TO DO TO ADVANCE SPIRITUALITY

1. Today focus your awareness on the seat of higher consciousness, the space between your eyebrows and the center of your forehead, and feel your spirits lift.
2. Make a list today of all that you like about yourself. Read it and add to it daily for the rest of the week.
3. See the good in others. It's there. Just take a moment to notice.
4. You have 24 hours each day. Train yourself to spend your time in positive and constructive emotions. When you switch gears, be careful not to allow yourself to drop below neutral.
5. God helps those who help themselves. Help yourself today to plenty of fresh fruits and vegetables.

FITONICS Eating In a Nutshell

Morning meal: A nutritious tonic, fruit cereal, or fruit salad

Midday meal: Protein, salads, and juicy fruit

Evening meal: Carbohydrates and vegetables or fruit and grain cereal supper

How to Use This Book

Fresh fruits and vegetables, eaten in their uncooked, *live* state carry within them the enzymes that are destroyed when food is cooked. When you eat a healthful balance of sweet and succulent fresh fruits; crispy, colorful vegetables; and all the revitalizing juice blends that can be made from these basic ingredients, you're eating an enzyme-rich diet. Enzymes are the life force in your body, your body's labor force. If you focus on these foods in your diet in substantial amounts and take enzyme supplements with all cooked meals, you'll find your energy increasing, excess pounds melting away, and a light, vital feeling that brings peace and harmony to your life as you add vitality to your body. Fresh raw produce appears throughout this book, but especially in the first two chapters, Tonics and Fruit Meals. If you're unsure of what you want to eat and cooking seems too much of an effort, look there first. These suggested meals are designed to maximize your intake of life-giving enzymes and provide you with steady energy throughout the day and peaceful rest at its end.

On the pages that follow, we offer recipes that fit into three categories of meals.

1. Tonics and Fruit Meals (Our Recommended Breakfasts)
    Tonics and Teas
        Breakfast Tonics
        Anytime Tonics
        Herbal Teas and Infusions
    Fruit Meals and Breakfast Foods
        Satisfying Breakfasts
        FUNdays

2. Power Meals (Our Recommended Lunches)
   High-Protein Power Meals
      Fish and Seafood
      Poultry and Meats
   High-Protein Vegetarian Meals
      Tofu and Legume Entrees
      Super Salads
      Sauces and Dressings
3. Soothing Meals (Our Recommended Suppers)
   Pasta Dishes and Salads
   Grains in Pilafs, Salads, and Casseroles
   One-Dish Potato Meals

Beyond these major meal categories there are accompaniments, chapters on small salads and vegetables, hot and chilled soups, sauces and salsas, and breads and sweets. Remember, the FITONICS meal plan isn't rigid; if you feel like a soup, bread, and fruit for supper, that's what you should have.

The *Tonics* are concentrated meals in a glass, frequently fortified with natural, whole, and superfood supplementation. All are pure, easily assimilated, delicious sources of energy. If your goal is weight loss, an end to constipation, or detoxification, try beginning each day with a cleansing tonic. Many of them will appease your sweet tooth and keep your satisfied for hours. Your energy level will be consistently high, and your mind will be tranquil (as opposed to jittery, from the usual morning coffee habit). And you will be delighted to discover how easy the tonics are to make. They take only a few minutes of your precious morning time.

The *Fruit Cereals* magically give the fullness and satisfying texture of cereal, but they're made entirely from blends of fruits, nuts, and milks. Cleansing and energizing, they will leave you feeling happily nourished for hours. Make a quantity in the morning. After a high-protein and salad Power Lunch, you may want to have more fruit cereal for dinner. When you do, you'll sleep like a baby, and the pounds will just melt away.

An array of *Power Meal* ideas are presented in the fish, poultry, and meats chapters, as well as a vegetarian option. They are suited to those who have the opportunity to take lunch in restaurants or the leisure to cook at home, and they are some of the quickest and easiest meals to put together. High-protein choices are stimulating, mental foods that keep you even and "up" throughout the afternoon. They are particularly delightful and digestible accompanied by a salad.

Soothing Meals appear here in the form of delicious high-carbohydrate vegetarian entrees, complemented by soups and stews, Super Salads, fresh baked breads, and healthful sweets. In many spiritual traditions, these soothing, vegetarian choices are specifically recommended for those seeking more peace and higher consciousness in their lives. Vegetarian choices are recommended in the evening, to support the brain's adequate secretion of serotonin, and the good night's sleep it induces. You'll easily prove this to yourself. A high-carbohydrate meal in the middle of the day can put you to sleep, then you need a coffee break. But at night, a simple vegetarian meal can be "just what the doctor ordered." In all fields of health, natural and medical, the whole-food vegetarian choices we propose (as opposed to nutritionally empty *refined* vegetarian foods) are also viewed as health-promoting options. Increased health carries with it natural, comfortable weight loss.

Although we recommend this way of eating throughout the day, it's completely flexible. You might want just a tonic for dinner. Always consider the option for a fruit, vegetable, or salad meal when you feel you need a break from heavier food. Recipes for fruit, basic soups, simple salads, and vegetables can always be light meals on their own, rather than side dishes. This new way of thinking about food is one of the ways you can bring your body a feeling of lightness. *The willingness to eat simple, energizing meals, fewer courses, and to "mono-diet" on fruit or vegetables greatly enhances well-being of body, mind, and spirit.* It's a brand-new attitude about food for a healthy new millennium. Mono-dieting is a weight loss tool. For a given period of time you eat only fruit, only vegetables, or only live food.

In our experience, the best way to eat to compete in this mentally demanding information age is to blend the very new with some of the old-fashioned ideas. Tonics are very new, and those which contain an array of whole-food supernutrients are mental fuel and filling morning meals. There was a simpler time in our history, when dinner was eaten at midday. That is still the case in much of the rest of the world, where health and longevity exceed our own and quality of life remains high. And it makes sense! Why eat your largest meal in the morning? Your appetite at that hour is attenuated because you're burning stored calories from your evening meal. By mid-day however, you've worked up an appetite, you need a break to recharge and you still have the bulk of the day ahead of you. You need adequate nourishment and fuel to keep you going in an even-tempered way. For this reason, proteins are an excellent choice for lunch. They keep the blood sugar level even throughout the afternoon, and they stimulate brain activity. With enzyme-rich raw vegetable salads and juicy fruits, they're high-energy foods.

Most people overeat at supper because their food intake during the day has been too low. A large meal in the evening will interfere with a good night's rest. Traditionally, the evening meal is lighter around the world, wherever the lunch hour is truly honored as a break from work and a time for adequate nourishment of the body. A soothing carbohydrate meal, of soup and bread or some grain with vegetables, will allow for a relaxing evening and sound sleep. Again, for weight loss and health, when lunch has been ample, the fruit cereal or a fruit meal makes a wonderful meal. For entertaining, this is a guideline you might want to put aside, unless a vegetarian meal would appeal to your guests.

AT THE MARKET

What You'll Need to Get Started

You don't have to run out and buy everything at once. Just replace a few pantry items each week, as you use them up.

The Basic Shopping List

Apple cider vinegar, unfiltered. A natural antibiotic and toner for the arteries, high in potassium, aids in the digestion of protein. Use as a morning fortifier and in salad dressings and cooking.

Apple. For juice, snacks, and cooking. Golden delicious make the sweetest juice.

Bananas. A must. The good mood food. Keep a dozen on hand for use in tonics and cereals. Use before they are heavily spotted, which indicates that enzymes have already converted the starches to sugars and are now in the skin working to break it down. Freeze after peeling in an airtight container. (But remember, freezing destroys enzymes.)

Bragg's Liquid Aminos. A light alternative to soy sauce, tamari, and sea salt; made from water and soy beans.

Brewer's or nutritional yeast. Rich in the all-important B vitamins, which ensure mental acuity, energy, and calm. High in protein and chromium, which helps control craving for sweets. Use in tonics.

Broths, canned. Buy the organic variety at the natural foods store.

Broths, powdered. Vegetable, chicken-flavored, and beef-flavored. Add to soups for richer flavor. Useful for sauces and salad dressings. Bouillon in these flavors is also useful.

Butter, sweet organic. Fresher than salted, which has salt added as a preservative. Organic is good, since pesticides, hormones, and antibiotics are stored in animal fat.

Carob. A nearly fat-free substitute for chocolate; aids in digestion and conditions the bowels. Purchase powder to use in tonics and chips for baking.

Carrots. For juice, snacks, and cooking. Keep a 5-pound bag on hand. Buy organic.

Cayenne pepper. Aids in blood circulation, digestion, and elimination. Use sparingly in tonics and as a seasoning.

Celery. For soups or juice.

Cereals, dry. Buy an assortment of high-fiber dry cereals and create your own designer blend for a quick, soothing supper with banana and soy milk.

Dates. Excellent snack food; also great in tonics.

Dijon mustard. Important for salad dressings and sandwiches.

Eggs, organic. A fine, pesticide-free, hormone-free source of protein. Good brain food. Hard-boiled eggs are great for brown bagging, sliced into salads, or as a quick high-protein Power Lunch.

Garlic. A natural antibiotic and detoxifier. If you love it, *use it!* In tonics, salads, *everywhere!*

Ginger. Increases blood circulation to the stomach, stimulating digestion. Use in tonics, juices, teas, and cooking.

Herbamare. A flavorful seasoned salt from Switzerland; greatly enhances simple dishes.

Herbs. Start with dried basil, thyme, bay leaf, oregano, chili powder, dill, and tarragon.

Honey. A good natural substitute for refined sugar; high in vitamins, minerals, and amino acids alkaline; will not rot teeth or leech minerals from the body like refined sugar does. A natural sedative, honey contains both glucose, which enters the bloodstream rapidly, and fructose, which breaks down slowly, so it doesn't disrupt blood sugar levels. Use sparingly.

Lemons. For everything from tonics to salad dressings. You'll be adding lemon juice to juices and squeezing it over vegetables and fish. Keep a basket of lemons on your countertop.

Maple syrup. Delicious rather than nutritious, wonderful in oatmeal. Buy pure rather than maple-flavored, which is usually only 3 percent real maple syrup.

Miso. An alkaline soup base made from brown rice, barley, or beans. Lowers the acidity in your blood and makes you feel instantly refreshed. Mellow white or yellow miso is the least salty and best tasting. Found in refrigerated dairy section. Keeps indefinitely in the refrigerator.

Oatmeal. Buy whole oats for added fiber. A great soothing supper, cooked with cinnamon, raisins, bananas, or pears.

Olive oil, extra-virgin. Stimulates liver and detoxifies. Purchase in dark bottle if possible and keep in dark place to maintain freshness. Use in all raw preparations and specialty dishes. Virgin olive oil may be used in cooking.

Onions. For everything. Important enzyme food.

Raisins. Organic raisins have excellent flavor and texture. Important snack food and for cereal suppers.

Red peppers, roasted. Oil or water-packed in a jar. Wonderful sandwich fillers. Avoid if packed in vinegar.

Sea salt. Salt from New Zealand is extracted from clean seas; it's unrefined and contains natural trace elements.

Soy lecithin. Helps emulsify fats, regulate cholesterol, and absorb nutrients in the bloodstream. Use in tonics.

Soy milk. Vanilla flavored or plain, this "milk" is great for tonics, cereals, and baking. Buy in vacuum packs for long pantry storage. Wonderful in brown bag lunches.

Spices. The basics are cinnamon, curry, ginger, and nutmeg. Cardamom and coriander give a nice exotic spiciness. Replace jars at least once a year.

Sucanat. A whole food sweetener made from dehydrated cane juice. Great for creating a healthy sweet. Substitute for fattening, mineral-draining refined sugar whenever you bake.

Tofu. An alkaline protein source made from soy beans. Inexpensive and easy to prepare and digest. The most useful form with the best flavor and consistency is "firm," found in water-packed containers in the refrigerated section of your market—either in produce, meat, or dairy cases. Tofu keeps for five to seven days. Once opened, keep immersed in fresh water.

Tomato paste. Keep tubes of imported tomato paste on hand to season salads, dressings, soups, sauces, and stews. Look for tubes of sun-dried tomato paste for variety in flavorings.

Whole wheat pastry flour. The most versatile whole-grain flour. For thickening and baking. Finer than whole wheat. Includes germ and bran.

Whole wheat tortillas. For "wraps" of all varieties. Heat to soften on a dry skillet and roll around your favorite salad, sprouts, and steamed vegetables for a filling and nutritious weight-loss supper. Keep on hand in the freezer.

With the Seasons as Your Guide

It is always healthier to eat locally grown foods when they are in season. Food can be seen as a link with our external environment, and when the food comes from our region, we feel grounded to the place where we live.

Certain foods, like summer fruits, have a cooling effect on us and are therefore inappropriate, even unhealthy, when consumed in winter months or in cold climates. Tropical fruits probably should not be a staple in your kitchen if your home is in the Northeast, for example, when it's bitter, cold, and snowing. In the same way, a hearty beef stew won't leave you with that light feeling you require in hot weather.

In temperate to cool climates, your supermarket will stock a wide variety of root vegetables, such as potatoes of all varieties, carrots, turnips, beets, parsnips, and rutabagas. These dense vegetables will "stick to your ribs" in cold weather. Good quality leafy greens may be more difficult to find in cold climates however, in California and other warmer regions, you will be able to choose from multiple varieties of leafy greens. There will always be delicious spinach, chard, kale, and exotic lettuces that are costly, not so fresh, or unavailable in colder regions.

The more you eat according to what's in season, and what's available locally, the more in tune with your environment you will feel. It's confusing, because we can get just about anything anytime from anywhere in the world. On occasion, the imported foods can add a spark to your meal planning. However, to stay in tune with your geographical environment, and also within a comfortable budget, seek out the produce that is most available and economical in your region. Check out your local farmers' market, which always has the best local produce at the best prices.

IN THE KITCHEN

The most beautiful thing we can experience is the mystery.
—*Albert Einstein*

Cooking with Soul

Love of body and love of self are intricately related and inseparable, and both will affect your attitude toward food and cooking. For a better life, for a sounder mind and body, prepare your meals from the widest range of foods available to you, healthfully and enthusiastically! Avoid the idea of limitation of choices.

Food for Thought:
THE BIG CHILL

The freezer only slows down the process of age and decay of food. It doesn't actually halt or freeze the breakdown of foods. Generally, well-wrapped meats can be kept about 3 months in the freezer, at 0 to 5 degrees, a month for bread and vegetables. Of course, if a food is frozen, it no longer has the life force of fresh food. It's better to purchase food as frequently as possible.

Avoid philosophies of deprivation! Learn to cook the foods you enjoy that are real foods, including meats of your choice, fish and poultry, whole grains, plenty of vegetables and fresh fruits, fresh juices, pure dairy foods, and wholesome, comforting desserts. Make the move away from fake foods and engineered substitutes. Reach for the pure, natural food our species has relied upon through the ages. As a species, we are naturally disposed to build strong bodies with unadulterated nourishment, the same natural food that was used by our powerful ancestors, who were able to withstand hardship and challenge beyond anything we modern Americans, steeped as we are in technology, can imagine.

Embrace the old-fashioned choices of your family's tradition and resurrect old family recipes. These are the comfort foods that will nourish your heart and soul. Prepare what you love to eat in the freshest, most healthful form possible! Buy fresh food and make it yourself as often as you can, enjoying the simple recipes we have devised to help you.

Creating Heart Space in the Kitchen

Before we begin to make a meal, we frequently light some incense and a candle—especially after a stressful day. Bring a happy or tranquil spiritual dimension to your kitchen through music. Create the special atmosphere that rests your soul or makes it want to dance. On one occasion this may mean an old Nat King Cole love song, on another, a Strauss waltz, or a pulsing, hot-blooded Latin rhythm. All music has some spiritual quality. Chose whatever uplifts you most. We find there is a noticeable resulting peace and harmony that comes from creating an environment of higher consciousness around the food we are taking in to the "temple of the soul."

You may wish to play sacred music, songs, or chants that uplift your spirits while you are cooking (see Sources). If you sing along, notice the change in the energy of your home. If you have children, they may gather to fill their hearts with the nurturing love you are sending their way. If you're alone, you will be filling your home with a spiritual presence that will feel cozy and inviting and begin to draw others to you. By the time you've made that pot of soup, nothing could be better for you or taste better to you. By the time you've baked your own bread pudding or muffins or whatever sweet you covet, you'll have earned the right to enjoy dessert. Brimming with pure ingredients and all the loving energy you've poured into it, such dessert can have a powerful positive effect.

Being a good cook is far more dependent on attitude and energy than it is on actual technique, and we can share some subtle strategies for creating a new approach to your work in the kitchen. (1) Try changing into relaxed kitchen clothes before you start, leaving behind you the stresses of the workday. (2) Before you start, do a few repetitions of some of the BODYTONICS—for example the bear swing, woodchopper, or the thigh and calf shapers—to ready yourself for activity. The oxygenated blood you pump through your body will curb your fatigue and give you the energy to enjoy your time in the kitchen. You may also be inspired to make the food just a bit healthier.

Welcome change! The stressful standards of how we should look and, therefore, how we should eat are no longer more relevant than how we feel about ourselves. Happiness matters. Our bodies are all different and therefore our choices must all be different as well. As you relax about food, you'll discover how easy it is to shed excess weight and how wonderful it is to feel temperamentally even and able to focus on all the good in your life. As you bring the spiritual dimension to your dinner table, we speak from our own and the experience of many we have known when we promise you that your life will begin, in the most beautiful way, to transform.

MASTERING THE BASICS

If you've never had extensive kitchen experience, you may feel overwhelmed by the thought of playing a more active role in the preparation of your meals. Being a cook who prepares healthful and delicious meals may seem beyond the realm of the possible to you. One of the most frequent excuses we hear from those who don't cook is "I don't have time!"

In fact, the best cooks spend very little time in the kitchen. They plan simple meals that can come together in less than an hour, and even if actual cooking time requires more than an hour, preparation time involves far less. The key to enjoying cooking is to make sure you embrace this idea first: *Food that tastes good and is good for you does not take a long time to prepare.*

Food for Thought:

THE GURU'S BOWL

The Guru's Bowl is a one-dish meal inspired by the monastic tradition of eating small, simple meals out of a deep wooden or ceramic bowl. In the East, chopsticks are used. In the Middle East and India, a spoon or piece of flat bread, such as a chapati, tannour (Middle Eastern flat bread, usually made from whole wheat, resembling a thick, chewy tortilla. Available in Middle Eastern groceries.), or pita, is used to scoop the food from the bowl into the mouth. Many of our recipes, from the fruit cereals and Super Salads to pastas to soups and stews, lend themselves to the Guru's Bowl concept. The idea is to change the vessel from which you are eating to raise consciousness at your meal.

Have a special bowl for yourself and each member of your family that can be used when you wish a change of pace that will allow you to eat a little more consciously. It is also a wonderful way to limit your portions. Since the average stomach will hold between 3 and 4 cups of food, and you would always wish to leave a space for the food to turn, fill your bowl with no more than 2½ to 3 cups of food. You can savor your food slowly, especially if you are using chopsticks, and bring an added element of spirituality to the eating experience. We've been using the Guru's Bowl concept on and off for more than two decades, and we've noticed that children respond to a healthy meal when it is placed in their own special bowl and eaten with a special spoon or fork. There is an energy savings that makes this idea relevant for our busy times. Fewer dishes are used, the clean-up is a breeze, and children can help more easily!

This ancient practice, grounded in the pursuit of a more spiritual life, returns us to a simpler time for our species and carries with it the basic qualities of peaceful, social interaction that so greatly enhance the healthfulness of the foods we are eating.

How do you learn to be quick and efficient in your kitchen, as you prepare the foods that will enhance your life? Begin by mastering the easy steps that follow.

Plan a Simple Meal

If you're powering up with protein, you may wish only to make an interesting salad to accompany your entree. On the other hand, if your focus is on calming carbohydrates, you may be looking forward to a chunk of that fresh, whole-grain bread you just bought, or you may feel like baking muffins or yams. In that case, all you'll need for a comforting cold-weather meal is a pot of hearty soup. In hot weather, the ideal accompaniment to fresh bread, muffins, or yams is an energizing main course salad, enhanced by a variety of innovative additions that make a salad special.

When you first begin to prepare your meals regularly, start by making authentic foods that leave you feeling satisfied. For example, for beginners, a quick and easy high-protein Power Lunch might include scrambled or poached eggs sliced tomato, cottage cheese, and blanched asparagus tossed in olive oil and lemon juice. Or what could be easier than steaming a piece of fresh salmon along with some cabbage and cauliflower? An easy Soothing Supper for novices might be broad egg noodles tossed with blanched broccoli, sautéed mushrooms, and a tablespoon or two of crumbled feta cheese in a lemon and olive oil sauce spiked with tomato paste and a touch of garlic. The easiest Soothing Supper, after a busy day and a good-size Power Lunch, is a bowl of steaming cinnamon-spiced oatmeal, full of juicy cooked pears and raisins, sweetened with maple syrup. Like oatmeal, all one-dish pasta meals can be served in an oversized Guru's Bowl. This same approach works well for rice and vegetables. A nice touch with oatmeal: a glass of hot soy milk. With pasta: a glass of red wine. With rice and vegetables: an aromatic herbal

MAKE SURE YOU GET YOUR ENZYMES!

Bringing added health to the meal is easy. Before you prepare anything else, make yourself a tall glass of fresh fruit or vegetable juice, brimming with energizing enzymes, which you can sip while you're cooking. Any juice containing ginger, such as an apple-ginger-lemon juice or a carrot-beet-ginger juice will facilitate digestion. Or slice up raw vegetables or fresh fruit to replace a salad, which you can share with your family as a "pick-me-up" hors d'oeuvre while you cook. As you do this regularly, you'll learn first-hand that such effort on your own behalf brings rewards far greater than you can imagine. The fresh juice and fruit nourish the spirit as well as the body. You'll feel better as you cook, and your time preparing meals will be enhanced enormously by this simple energizing choice. In addition, the fresh juice or full-of-life fruits and vegetables prior to your meal will give your body the nourishment it is craving. You'll find yourself eating less cooked food, as you take the edge off your appetite with the healthiest possible before-meal snack.

tea. A simple steamed or blanched vegetable, tossed hot in olive oil and lemon juice, makes a lovely warm salad, and it's an ideal companion to any savory entree. Baked fruit is a lovely way to enhance a cereal or muffin supper.

You'll find as you simplify your meals, making only one or two dishes, you'll truly begin to relish, not only the cooking experience, but also the beauty of simple, fresh, well-prepared food.

1. Create an organized workplace.

Select the knives, measuring spoons, cups, work bowls, cooking utensils, salad bowl, garlic press, and other items necessary for the recipe you are choosing to prepare. If you are using a food processor, blender, or hand mixer, have it on hand, if possible. Have a "discard bowl" for trimmings and other unusables. Place all these items near your stove—near your cutting board when appropriate.

2. Prep all your raw ingredients.

Wash fruit or salad greens. Dry greens in a salad spinner. Wash the vegetables you plan to steam or cut for soup or casseroles. Rinse fish, chicken, or cuts of meat and pat dry with a paper towel. Make sure to wash hands thoroughly after handling fish, poultry, or meats. Bring all your prepped raw materials in colanders, bowls, or on plates, along with herbs, oils, spices, garlic, and other seasonings, to your work area.

3. Start with the dish that will take the longest to cook.

This idea seems obvious, but it's a pitfall for beginners. If you are sautéing fish, potatoes, or chicken, which will then be finished in your oven, if you are cooking rice or pasta, or grilling a steak, have that underway first before you put your salad together or steam or sauté vegetables. Ideally, once your main dish is cooking, you will have 15 to 20 minutes to make the quicker vegetable dish and set your table. If you are preparing a simple meal of salad with a cheese and fruit platter, you will only require preparation time for the salad.

EASY TECHNIQUES

Use the One-Bowl Method to Assemble a Salad Quickly

Start with a big salad bowl. Measure basic dressing ingredients, such as olive oil, lemon juice, crushed garlic, seasoned salt, Dijon mustard, and yogurt directly into the bottom of the empty bowl and use a whisk to whip them into a smooth cream. Tear washed and dried greens in bite-size pieces or, for a chopped salad, chop them finely on your cutting board with a knife. *If you're having protein as your entree,* you can enhance your salad by adding sliced tomatoes, or any juicy fruit, such as oranges, grapefruit, strawberries, ripe papaya, or kiwi. You might add finely shredded vegetables, such as carrots, cabbage, or thinly sliced radishes, onions, cucumbers, or bok choy. Leafy sprouts, sliced olives, or roasted red peppers; sliced sun-dried tomatoes; artichoke hearts; cooked kidney, navy, or garbanzo beans; crumbled, grated, or sliced cheeses also enhance a salad of greens and fruit that you will serve with protein. Cooked beans in a salad served with protein add extra fiber to the meal.

Ideal salads to serve with starches could contain starchy fruits, such as sliced figs, dates, bananas, mangoes, or blueberries, as well as finely shredded or chopped vegetables. Or, for a more savory flavor, you would add sliced or grated raw vegetables with sliced olives or artichoke hearts. With starches, a small amount of cheese or other protein is also an option as a salad garnish.

Whether your entree is a protein—such as meat, chicken, tofu, fish, or cheese—or a starch—such as bread, potatoes, rice, or pasta—you can always streamline and simplify your meal preparation by tossing into your salad steamed or sautéed vegetables, such as cauliflower, green beans, peas, broccoli, asparagus, zucchini, corn, or chard. If your entree is a protein, you can add steamed tofu cubes to your salad, to help lower the cholesterol taken in from the meats.

If your entree is a starch, you can add cooked, cubed potatoes, cooked rice, sautéed garlic bread cubes, or cooked pasta to your salad. A rule of thumb is to limit salad ingredients in a simple side-dish salad to three or four items, plus dressing. Once everything is in the bowl, simply toss well and serve. You will find wonderful ideas for many unusual and exciting side-dish salads in Simple Salads and Vegetables on the Side.

The easiest one-dish meal is the main course salad, or Super Salad, which contains the greens, cooked or raw vegetables, and proteins or starches of your choice. Everything is flavored by the dressing. The possibilities are endless. The preparation time and cleanup are minimal. The benefits to your energy and weight-loss goals are incomparable, as the focus of your meal is enzyme-rich, energy-enhancing raw food. Recipes for main course salads abound throughout this book.

The Art of Quick Protein Preparation

Fish fillets are easily prepared by sautéing or steaming, and a quick preparation for chicken is to first sauté it until lightly browned in olive oil, and then finish it by baking in a medium oven for 10 to 30 minutes, depending on size and cut. Sautéing allows you to season first and change the flavors of the dish according to your choice of seasonings. You might dip chicken breasts in chili powder for a Tex-Mex flavor, and then top them with smoked mozzarella and a lemon-tomato glaze. Fish fillets might be sautéed and then topped with a salsa or steamed and served with a raita of cucumber, dill, and yogurt. These simple preparations for protein give you just enough time to prepare your salad or vegetable while the steaming, sautéing, or baking is completed. See pages 105–107 for some quick-fix fish techniques.

The Simple Art of Soup

There are unlimited possibilities for making delicious creamy soups with vegetables. The basic technique is always the same. A mirepoix of chopped garlic, celery, and carrot is first sautéed in olive oil. Then small chunks of the vegetable are added and sautéed with the herbs of choice. Vegetable or chicken stock is then added to cover the vegetables. Cooking takes from 15 to 20 minutes, and then the soup is blended into a cream. The seasonings for the soup determine its flavors. A French cream of cauliflower soup will have thyme as its main seasoning. It can be turned into an East Indian soup by adding curry instead. A cream of carrot soup can be spiced with cinnamon and coriander or made savory with a lot of fresh basil. There are a wide range of garnishes to choose from, including yogurt, chutney, sour cream, chives, shaved Parmesan, finely grated carrot, shaved fennel, garlic croutons, minced red onion, grated cheese, tortilla strips, cubed cooked chicken, petite pois, or sautéed mushrooms.

A lighter, clear soup with remarkable health-promoting properties can be made from miso. Water is boiled and sliced vegetables, such as bok choy or other cabbages, onions, shiitake mushrooms, peeled and seeded tomatoes, and sea vegetables are added, along with cubes of tofu, small chunks of fish or shrimp, or thin slices of chicken breast or pork. After only a few minutes of cooking, ½ cup of the water is removed in which the miso paste is dissolved. The dissolved paste is then returned to the soup without further cooking.

Clean as You Go

All professional chefs know this secret, and home cooks who have mastered it find kitchen time more pleasant. Nothing is more discouraging than sitting down to a meal with the knowledge that you have left a holocaust to clean up when you've finished eating. And trying to clean when you've completed preparation ensures that you'll be eating a cold meal. The remedy is to wash work bowls and implements as you finish using them. Return ingredients to the refrigerator or pantry as soon as you no longer need them. Place the few items you have used for your final preparations in the sink, and when you've finished your meal, you will have only dishes and a few preparation tools to wash.

Observe Basic Rules of Hygiene

One of the important techniques to learn when you are preparing food for others is the correct way to taste what you are preparing. Often a novice cook will taste from a spoon or fork and then return that implement to the food, a definite health no-no. Once you have tasted from a spoon, put it in the sink, and don't use it again without washing.

Change your kitchen towels daily. Replace sponges every few days, and dish scrubbers or brushes every few weeks. Wash plastic cutting boards and brushes regularly in the dishwasher or soak them in the sink in a weak Clorox solution.

SAVOR YOUR MEAL

As you learn the art of preparing all the healthful food you love to eat, teach yourself as well to spend time over your meal, savoring the flavors, the textures, and thoroughly celebrating your efforts and the art of eating. Light a candle, play soft music, enjoy conversation, a glass of wine. When the meal is over, sit for awhile, over a cup of spicy herbal tea. Allow your body to adjust to food in the stomach before you bolt from your chair and rush off to the next activity. Take your time. Reflect on the day and the goodness in your life. Send the food to your cells in the best of spirits, and know that this joyful mentality is at least as important as the quality of the food you've prepared.

MAKING IT EASY: TECHNIQUES

How to seed a cucumber. Slice the cucumber in half lengthwise. Using a small spoon, simply scrape the seed from the fruit in a downward motion. You'll have a little valley down the middle of each half. Discard the seeds. Use this technique for cucumbers in salads and soups.

How to roast a bell pepper. Preheat oven to 400°F. Place peppers on a baking sheet. Bake peppers in the oven about 45 minutes. Remove from the oven and place in a paper bag to steam (and cool slightly) for another 15 minutes. Peel the skins away by gently rubbing the peppers. Discard skin, slice open peppers, and discard seeds and core. These keep for about a week. Make a batch of six or more, layer slices in a glass storage container, cover with olive oil, if desired, and store, tightly covered, in the refrigerator. To store longer, freeze without added oil in an airtight container.

How to clean and chop leeks. Remove dark green leaves and root end of leek. Slice leeks in half lengthwise. Slice both halves crosswise into half rounds. Plunge in a large bowl of water and separate individual half rounds with your hand, allowing the sand to wash out. Drain in a colander and rinse well.

How to select and prepare a pineapple. Look for golden brown fruit with a pleasant sweet, not fermented, aroma. Check for soft or rotten spots. Pull an inner leaf from the top. If it releases easily, the pineapple is ripe.

Although there are gadgets for peeling and coring pineapples, the job can easily be done by hand. Cut leaf top from fruit with a sharp or serrated knife. Stand fruit on cut end and slice skin from fruit from top to bottom, taking care to cut deeply enough, while at an angle, along fruit to remove the bristly eyes. Cut bottom end from pineapple. To core, cut pineapple lengthwise in quarters. Cut a triangular piece from top to bottom, removing hard center. Slice fruit lengthwise or crosswise, in spears or chunks.

How to make matchstick cucumbers. Peel cucumber. Slice into ¼-inch rounds on the bias, at about a 45-degree angle, to create ovals. Then slice each oval lengthwise into thin, even strips.

How to ripen fruit. Ripen bananas, pears, mangoes, and papayas in a brown paper bag at room temperature. This will trap the ethylene gas given off naturally by the fruit to speed the ripening process. This same approach will also work for tomatoes, avocados, and fruits with pits.

How to use a vanilla bean. Using a sharp paring knife, slice the bean down its length. Press the pod open. Using the point of the knife, scrape out the seeds to use as flavoring. Discard the pod or use it to impart a vanilla flavor to dry sweetener or to steeping or poaching liquids.

How to oil and flour a baking pan. Douse a paper towel or piece of wax paper with a light oil, such as sunflower or safflower oil, which are bland in flavor and do not smoke at high temperatures. Rub the baking dish well with the oil. Sprinkle the baking dish or pan with a handful of all-purpose unbleached flour and tap the dish on the counter on all sides, distributing the flour as much as possible. Shake off any flour that does not stick.

PART ONE

Tonics
and Teas

Food for Thought:

APPLE CIDER VINEGAR

The destructive element in white vinegar, wine vinegar, and even the most expensive balsamic or berry vinegar is the acetic acid. Acetic acid rapidly destroys red blood cells and can lead to anemia. It interferes with the efficient breakdown of food in the body by retarding digestion and preventing proper assimilation. Acetic acid acidifies your body. Remember, an acid body is an aging, irritable, stressed body.

Few people realize that raw, unfiltered apple cider vinegar, a naturally fermented vinegar made from apples and usually aged in wood barrels, is a *health-promoting* vinegar.

Apple cider vinegar is a rich source of potassium, which is to the soft tissue of the body what calcium is to the bones. Potassium can be called "the mineral of youthfulness." It keeps the arteries flexible and resilient. In my experience, a teaspoon a day in 8 ounces of water peps you up the way water perks up a wilting plant. But be careful, more is *not* better.

Your health depends on your *internal cleanliness.* According to Dr. Patricia Bragg, in *Apple Cider Vinegar: Miracle Health System*, apple cider vinegar is an internal toner, a natural antibiotic that fights bacteria and viruses and purifies the body by drawing out toxins from organs, tissue, intestines, and the lymphatic system. It has been used topically to shrink varicose veins. Mixed with clay and used as a facial, it draws impurities out of the skin and tightens pores. A cup can be poured into baths to draw toxins from the body and establish a healthy pH for the skin. When there is a deficiency of hydrochloric acid in the stomach, resulting in incomplete digestion of proteins and high blood pressure, apple cider vinegar has been used (1 teaspoon diluted in a glass of water) during the meal to normalize digestion and lower blood pressure. Three leading natural health pioneers, Drs. N. W. Walker and Paul and Patricia Bragg, praised apple cider vinegar for its myriad uses and repeatedly emphasized its importance in maintaining homeostasis (internal harmonious chemical balance) in the body and ensuring what they called "body competence."*

Apple cider vinegar has a neutral, versatile, clean flavor. Use it in water with honey as a tonic pick-me-up, in juices, sauces, and dressings. Look for unfiltered cider vinegar at the natural foods store and keep this fortifier within easy reach in your refrigerator.

*Dr. N. W. Walker, Fresh Vegetable and Fruit Juices (Prescott, Ariz.: Norwalk Press, 1970), pp. 71–72.

$\backsim\!\!\backsim$

ACV TONIC, AT DAYBREAK OR ANY TIME

Take this tonic in the morning upon arising before your daily BODYTONIC exercise routine* as a way to ensure a youthful *inner* body. Remember, both unfiltered apple cider vinegar and honey are high in potassium, which keeps the arteries and soft tissues of the body supple. The ACV tonic can also be a refreshing drink over ice any time of the day. Historians believe that a vinegar and water beverage consumed when wine was unavailable contributed to the stamina and fortitude of the ancient Roman army.

1 teaspoon honey
8 ounces pure water
1 teaspoon unfiltered apple cider vinegar

1. Dissolve the honey in the water. Add apple cider vinegar and stir.

SERVES 1

---

*Marilyn Diamond and Dr. Donald Burton Schnell, FITONICS for Life *(New York: Avon Books, 1996).*

CHAPTER ONE
Breakfast Tonics

SEA-GREEN TONIC

This is a basic cleansing breakfast that's a form of nutritional insurance. Even though you may take vitamins, minerals, and enzymes, and even though you may eat plenty of live food, you still need a regular infusion of the whole-food nutrients this tonic contains. Keep a lot of bananas on hand for your daily tonic, and use fresh orange or apple juice, depending on the season. You can always add a pear, some berries, or a peach to your tonic along with the banana if you want more fruit.

Let's look at a few of the benefits of the cleansing tonic. The fresh orange juice is rich in vitamin C, enzymes, and antioxidants. It detoxifies naturally. The fresh apple juice is rich in enzymes, malic acid, potassium, and pectins that act as solvents in the body, softening and removing debris from the gallbladder and other organs. Bananas are high in potassium, enzymes, fiber, and natural sugars to fuel the brain. They add body to this tonic to help you feel satisfied for several hours.

The cold-pressed flax seed and sunflower oils are readily usable vegetarian sources of the essential fatty acids we need for myriad processes in our bodies, from healing and repair to regulating cholesterol levels in the bloodstream to strengthening the immune, respiratory, digestive, and neural systems. These fatty acids are relatively unavailable in this era of hydrogenation and in the average diet of highly processed food.

A super green-food powder can be a highly nutritious blend of nutrient-dense algaes, such as chlorella and spirulina, along with wheat grass, hydrilla, barley leaves, alfalfa, and clover. Such whole-food powders are rich in chlorophyll, which acts as liquid sunshine in the body, "shedding light" in the form of oxygen on the cells. The more oxygen within, the more health!

Lecithin is necessary in our bodies for the emulsification of fats, regulation of cholesterol, and the absorption of nutrients. Soy lecithin is an excellent daily supplement, since lecithin is removed through processing from most of the foods we eat.

Brewer's yeast is a rich natural source of B-vitamins and protein. Regular intake at up to one tablespoon a day is known to be good for skin problems. Work up to this amount over 2–3 weeks.

Vitamin C keeps you young! Instead of taking it throughout the day in capsule form, it's a nice switch to use the powder form in your tonics. The buffering makes powdered C easier on the stomach.

3 cups fresh orange or apple juice

2 bananas

2 tablespoons cold-pressed flaxseed oil

2 teaspoons cold-pressed sunflower oil

2 tablespoons super green-food powder

2 tablespoons soy lecithin

2 teaspoons Brewer's yeast (optional)

2 teaspoons buffered Vitamin C

1. Blend all the ingredients in a blender for approximately 1 minute. Drink slowly. This is a meal, not a beverage.

SERVES 2

AM FLOWER POWER

We use this building tonic on days before heavy workouts or if supper the night before was light and cleansing. Add soy lecithin granules, a natural antioxidant, for a nutritional boost. Soy lecithin gives tonics and smoothies a natural malted vanilla flavor. It also plays an emulsifying role, assisting the body in the breakdown of animal fats and cholesterol in the bloodstream. It can actually break up the deposits of fat in the liver into tiny particles.

We are particularly partial to brewer's yeast grown on beets or molasses as a natural food supplement, as opposed to yeasts that are by-products of the fermenting of hops to make beer. This nutritional yeast is a particularly rich natural source of easily assimilated whole-food B vitamins for high stress tolerance. It's also a fine source of readily usable protein, providing a full spectrum of amino acids, as well as vitamins and minerals.

Bananas are a good mood food. They are high in potassium, enzymes, fiber, and energizing natural sugar. Many natural health pioneers understood the role of bananas in building body strength. (Think of the banana-dominated diet of the powerful silverback gorilla, whose digestive tract most closely resembles our own.) The natural bodybuilder, Charles Atlas, ate bananas for breakfast every morning, and in his nineties he was doing 250 push-ups a day. Bananas and soy milk are described by Jack LaLanne as a quick weight-loss meal when there's no time for food prep and you need something filling and nutritious. Carob aids in digestion. This is essentially a meal replacement formula, and it will keep you satisfied for several hours.

3 cups vanilla soy milk or nonfat lactase-enriched milk

2 bananas

1 teaspoon to 1 tablespoon Brewer's yeast

2 tablespoons soy lecithin

2 tablespoons cold-processed flaxseed oil

2 teaspoons cold-processed sunflower oil

4 teaspoons carob powder

2 teaspoons buffered vitamin C powder

1. Blend all ingredients thoroughly for 30 to 60 seconds in a blender.

SERVES 2

Variation: Replace each banana with ½ cup strawberries.

Food for Thought:

THE B VITAMINS AND YEAST

Whole-food B vitamins, such as those found in brewer's or nutritional yeast grown on whole-food sources like nuts, are the stuff of nutritional miracles in this era when such miracles can and should be everyday occurrences. There's a story behind the B vitamins. Long before holistic medicine became accepted, Drs. Abram Hoffer, Humphrey Osmond, and Linus Pauling created the field of orthomolecular medicine in pioneer studies to explore the effect of nutrients on mental health. Linus Pauling actually originated the term "orthomolecular." In documented case after case, long-standing problems of schizophrenia, depression, and intolerance to stress—in fact, nearly every mental illness—cleared when substantially large amounts of the B vitamins, far greater than the RDA mandates, were administered.* Since vitamins were relatively inexpensive and offered minimal profit to pharmaceutical companies, the public was instead presented with Prozac, Valium, lithium, and the litany of mood elevators or antidepressants. Our medical doctors were receiving their solutions from the sales representatives of pharmaceutical companies, who were pushing the high-ticket antidepressants. Research papers on nutritional cures using the B vitamins, which documented the absence of any side effects other than better health, were not accepted for publication in medical journals. If you have a problem which can be remedied by B-vitamins taken daily, why not do so?

Today, more than ever—with so many people suffering from mental imbalances—we must take a closer look at our options for nutritional, rather than chemical solutions. In our experience, B vitamin supplements, particularly in digestible whole-food form, solve many of the debilitating problems caused by stress, insomnia, and emotional imbalance.

There are plenty of other benefits to keeping the concentration of B vitamins high in our bodies. Nutrition pioneer Adele Davis believed, as we do, that the best vitamin choices are those that come directly from food sources, rather than from the chemical laboratories, because of the inherent synergy of elements in a whole-food product. Once she implemented a daily regimen of brewer's yeast, her gray hair returned to its natural, dark color, and grew shinier, thicker, and healthier than ever before. In the show animal industry, trainers and veterinarians dealing with horses, dogs, and cats knew that large doses of B vitamins will provide the glamorous coats that win blue ribbons. Remember, if your hair or skin is healthy, that's a reflection of the overall health of your body.

Soviet athletes and American bodybuilders have known since the 1950s that the secret to having more energy and better muscle tone is to take B vitamins. The average population now needs to understand its relevance to better health. Regular B vitamin supplementation, particularly of a whole-food nature, brings about increased athletic potential and greater mental well-being.

There is confusion about the ingesting of yeast and its relationship to yeast infections such as *Candida albicans*. According to Dr. William Cook, author of the best-seller *Candida: The Yeast Connection*, there is no connection between the yeast you ingest in baked goods or yeast supplements, and *Candida albicans*. Since brewer's yeast is high in the B-complex vitamins, it may actually help control the B-vitamin deficiency that is often one of the causes of *Candida albicans*.

Another benefit from brewer's yeast is that it is high in chromium, which helps control cravings for sweets. With 1 tablespoon packing a walloping 18 to 20 grams of pure, usable protein, it is an excellent, low-fat source of all the amino acids and natural RNA and DNA. Research by Dr. Benjamin S. Frank, in his book *No-Aging Diet*, indicates that whole-food sources of RNA and DNA can slow the aging process and give you a younger, more vital appearance. Need we say more?

---

*Alternative Medicine: The Definitive Guide, (*Puyallup, Wash.: Future Medicine Publishing, 1993), p. 398.*

ISLAND TONIC

What is it that makes us yearn for a tropical vacation? Why do we associate islands with inner peace and sanctuary? Aren't tropical flavors and climates therapeutic to body and soul? This pure fruit tonic is a tropical vacation in a glass, sure to elevate you to a sunny mood.

Natural health practitioners have found that the enzyme bromelain in fresh pineapple juice is beneficial for those who suffer from arthritis or other disorders involving inflammation. If you have a fruit and vegetable juicer, slice the skin from the pineapple and juice the whole fruit, core included. If not, substitute bottled unsweetened pineapple juice.

1 cup unsweetened pineapple juice, fresh or
    bottled

1 mango, pitted, peeled, and sliced

Juice of ½ lime

1 teaspoon honey

1 banana

½ cup ice cubes

1. Combine all ingredients in a blender and puree until smooth.

SERVES 2

Variation: *Fresh orange or tangerine juice can be substituted for the pineapple juice.*

HI-PRO-TONIC

You'll swear it's a milkshake! And it has all the flavor kids love and the nutrients their bodies crave. The enzyme-rich presoaked almonds are rich in protein, vitamins, minerals, and heart-healthy free fatty acids. Keep peeled bananas in the freezer in a plastic container or bag so you can make this tonic on a moment's notice. It's a great way to break the chocolate habit for you and your children.

1 fresh or frozen banana

2 tablespoons unsweetened carob powder

2 pitted dates

¼ cup enzymized almonds or sunflower
    seeds (see p. 52)

2 cups soy or low-fat milk

1 tablespoon soy lecithin granules

Dash vanilla extract

1 tablespoon natural peanut or almond
    butter (optional)

1. Place ingredients in a blender and blend until smooth.

SERVES 2

Food for Thought:

HONEY

In addition to being a healthful alternative to refined white sugar, honey, one of the most commonly found medicinals in ancient cultures, is best known for its antibiotic properties. It's also used as an internal soothing agent, helpful in digesting spicy, peppery foods. (That's why honey appears in so many spicy Mexican delicacies.) Honey also has mild sedative qualities; a teaspoon of honey in herbal tea just before bed will help ensure sweet dreams and a deep sleep.

Because of its high mineral content, honey does not appear to decay teeth, unless it is made in an unnatural way from bees that are fed white sugar. To ensure that you are buying high-quality honey, choose local varieties or those that give the source of the pollen the bees have gathered—i.e., orange blossom, sage, Patagonia. Keep your eye out for raw unpasteurized honey, which contains the enzymes inherent in all raw, natural foods. Raw honey boasts the most exquisite, floral qualities, from the flower nectar the bees were sipping. Try it in recipes that don't require cooking, and you'll taste the difference. Raw honey can sometimes be found in fine natural food or gourmet stores. It is also frequently advertised in the mail-order sections of food magazines. All commercial honey found in supermarkets is pasteurized, but there are varying degrees of quality available even there.

Note: Avoid giving honey to infants under one year of age. It's too concentrated for babies, they need their sweets from mothers' milk and fruit.

ON A SPIRITUAL NOTE . . .

All food is God's gift to us, as sustenance for our lives. Honey has a long spiritual history, borne out in repeated Biblical references, two of which, from Proverbs, admonish against the overindulgence of honey.

> 25:16 *Eat to your satisfaction what honey you may find,*
> *but not excess or you will bring it up again.*

> 25:27 *It is not good to eat too much honey,*
> *Nor to seek for glory on top of glory.*

This is a food to be treated with respect, as so much energy is spent in its creation. Over 550 bees are required to gather only 1 pound of honey, and they must fly over 35,500 miles to do so, which is more than once around the world, according to Frank and Rosalie Hurd in their book *Ten Talents*.

Food for Thought:

ENZYMIZED ALMONDS

Though they're actually in the peach family, almonds are most appropriately called "king of the nuts." They contain 84 grams of high-quality protein for every pound, which means a 2 to 4-ounce serving can give you 10 to 21 grams of excellent protein. Almonds are also high in calcium, phosphorus, iron, and niacin so they are a healthy food for teeth and bones. And since they also pack a good dose of the B vitamins, they are one of those natural foods that help relieve stress, build healthy hair and nails, and keep you mentally sharp.

The key to making almonds a perfect food is a simple presoaking step. Soaking to remove enzyme inhibitors is recommended for all nuts and seeds with hulls, including hazelnuts, unhulled sesame seeds, and sunflower seeds. Just place them raw in purified water for 30 minutes to an hour, and then drain and allow them to dry naturally in a sieve. This releases the enzyme-inhibitors that Nature provided to keep them from sprouting until the rain comes. Soaking also converts the fats into readily usable free fatty acids.

Eat almonds with juicy fruits or raw vegetables for a wonderfully nutritious live meal, morning, noon, or night. Give them to your children for snacks and watch their health improve! For rich, nondairy almond milk, blend ½ cup enzymized almonds with 2 cups water and 1 tablespoon honey. Strain through a fine sieve.

Food for Thought:

CAROB

Carob is commonly known as Saint John's Bread in references in the Bible. Carob powder, which resembles cocoa, is a bowel conditioner that smooths digestion. It is good for babies, so it is good for us! Frequently compared to chocolate, carob has the advantage of being equally sweet and pleasing to the palate, but it contains 2 percent fat to chocolate's 52 percent! As opposed to chocolate, which is acidifying to the blood and therefore aging, carob is alkaline, and we can use it to offset some of the acid in our diets. Carob is also rich in minerals: calcium, potassium, phosphorus, magnesium, silicon, and iron. It is high in vitamin A and niacin, rich in natural sugars, and low in starch.

Use carob in smoothies, soy milk, and baking some of those coveted desserts that you would enjoy so much more if they were healthy! Three tablespoons of carob powder and two tablespoons of water equal one square of chocolate.

YOGI TONIC

The yogis call the combination of fruit and pure, natural dairy products *satthwic*. *Satthwic* is food for the nourishment of the soul and the purity of the body, and *satthwic* foods are highly recommended for meditators or those who wish to decrease the stress in their lives. This fruit and dairy combination will give you a milk and honey complexion. Acidophilus, the "friendly" bacteria found in natural yogurt (which contains live *Lacto bacilus acidophilus*, unlike other commercial yogurts that are fractionated, overly processed and frequently loaded with sugar) helps maintain the microbial balance of the digestive tract and aids in overall health and vitality. Live *l. acidophilus* is also a preventive for vaginal yeast infections. Make sure you use only yogurt cultured with live acidophilus. Papaya contains the natural digestive enzyme papain, and fresh pineapple juice contains the natural digestive enzyme bromelain. Both enzymes aid the digestion of the protein in the yogurt.

½ cup plain yogurt
½ papaya, peeled and seeded
2 pitted dates (optional for sweetness)

1 cup unsweetened fresh or bottled pineapple juice

1. Place ingredients in a blender and blend until smooth.

SERVES 1

ZEN TONIC

The Japanese lead the world in longevity and spend less than half what we spend on health care. The traditional Japanese breakfast always includes miso soup, a highly alkaline beverage, extremely rich in amino acids. Seaweed is rich in minerals. Ginger brings heat to the body and blood to the digestive tract, making it more efficient. Perhaps the Japanese live as long as they do because they start their day with alkaline miso instead of acid in coffee.

2 cups pure water   *1 tablespoon miso paste*
1½-inch piece fresh ginger

1. In a small saucepan, bring water to a boil. Remove from heat and squeeze ginger directly into water with a garlic or ginger press. Remove ¼ cup of water and dissolve the miso in it, stirring with a spoon.

2. Pour miso into ginger water. Do not reheat.

SERVES 2

Variation: To turn this into a more filling breakfast, add ½ cup tofu squares to water and boil briefly before adding other ingredients.

Food for Thought:

MISO

Miso is an alkaline staple ingredient in Asian cooking, popularized here through the Macrobiotic movement. Most natural food stores sell miso in dry packets or as a paste in vacuum packed pouches or in tubs resembling cottage cheese containers. Tightly wrapped, miso keeps forever in your refrigerator.

There are many varieties of miso, made from soy, brown rice, or barley. The soy can be quite salty, and it should be used sparingly. Brown rice miso is sweet, and barley miso has a slightly fermented flavor.

When using miso, use a heaping teaspoon per cup of water, or 1½ teaspoons per person. And please, try not to cook the miso when you're making soup. Cooking destroys miso's enzymatic value and gives the broth an off flavor. Simply remove ¼ to ½ cup of the hot soup water just before serving, and dissolve the miso in it. Add miso broth back into the soup *with the heat off*, and stir.

CHAPTER TWO

Anytime Tonics

LEMON ROSETONIC

Rosemary is used in modern herbology for just about every ailment imaginable, both physical and emotional. This superachiever herb is a stimulant, clears the mind, and offers a great pick-me-up. Like a walk in a pine forest, it soothes as it invigorates.

1 to 2 teaspoons honey
1½ cups pure water

Juice of ½ lemon
1 sprig fresh rosemary

1. In a small saucepan over medium heat, dissolve the honey in the water and lemon juice. Turn off heat, add rosemary, cover, and steep for 20 minutes.

2. Reheat to just before boiling. Remove the rosemary and sip hot. Or enjoy chilled over ice as a warm-weather refresher.

SERVES 1 TO 2

MINTED BERRYTONIC

Peppermint leaf is possibly the most commonly used herb in America. Not at all an ancient herb, it's actually a hybrid developed in England just three centuries ago. Few people realize that peppermint is high in calcium and therefore acts as an alkaline neutralizer of acids in the body. As it plays this important role, it relieves muscle tension, indigestion, nausea, sore throat and the general discomforts suffered after overeating acidic foods. Enjoy this thirst-quenching, slushy treat. And take advantage of a regular cup of peppermint tea, to keep your body balanced.

2 cups pure water
¼ cup fresh peppermint or spearmint
    leaves

3 to 4 teaspoons honey
1 cup ice cubes
1 basket fresh stemmed strawberries

1. Heat the water to boiling. Break up mint leaves in a heatproof bowl. Pour water over leaves, stir in honey, and steep about 15 minutes. Strain and discard leaves.

2. Cool the mint-infused water until it's at least room temperature. Combine with ice and strawberries in a blender. Process until smooth.

SERVES 3 TO 4

Food for Thought:
PEPPERMINT TEA

Food is your best medicine!
    In China, doctors prescribe peppermint to treat colds, headache, sore throat, and congestion. Hot peppermint tea is your ticket in cold months, when such ailments run rampant. American herbalists suggest a mixture of olderflower and peppermint, taken regularly (3 to 4 cups a day) with bed rest to quickly knock out symptoms of cold or flu.

SUNTONIC

This strong dose of chlorophyll will literally flood the body with light. It bears repeating that chlorophyll is liquid sunshine in the body. Many natural health pioneers drew their enthusiasm for green drinks from Dr. Bernard Jensen, who pioneered chlorophyll therapy. When you choose this tonic, you are preventing disease-promoting bacteria from taking hold in your body. Such bacteria cannot grow in sunlight, nor can they flourish in the oxygenated environment in your body after you drink something fresh and green.

A vegetable juicer is required for this tonic. It's wonderful to be able to juice the nutrient-rich green vegetables! The bell pepper adds vitamin C. Celery is a natural blood purifier. Dr. N. W. Walker, a centenarian who lived in Arizona, taught that on a hot day (or after a tough workout), celery restores the sodium you've lost through perspiration, replacing that "wilted" feeling with a more refreshed one. Green food formulas, made from blends of enzyme-rich superfoods such as algaes, wheat grass, alfalfa, and barley leaves are high in chlorophyll. Look for them in the natural foods store.

4 celery ribs, leaves removed, scrubbed
6 green apples, scrubbed, unpeeled and
quartered

1 green bell pepper, quartered, not seeded
1 tablespoon green food formula

1. Juice the celery and apples. Place juice and green food in blender, and puree until smooth.

SERVES 1

ALOE TONIC

A real blast of vitamin C, this tonic is also fortified with aloe vera, a desert plant with soothing medicinal properties when taken internally. Aloe, one of nature's best natural moisturizers, has been used for more than 3,500 years as a healing agent in every culture. Cleopatra used it to protect her skin against the damaging effects of the sun. Desert dwellers handle the wilting summer heat by drinking aloe vera juice. Aloe vera means "true medicine." A naturally rich source of minerals, it is also a natural laxative, with healing properties for the linings of the digestive tract.

1 cup freshly squeezed orange juice
1 cup freshly squeezed grapefruit juice

1 cup fresh or frozen strawberries, stemmed
3 tablespoons aloe vera juice

1. Combine ingredients in a blender and blend until smooth.

SERVES 2 TO 3

WALKER TONIC

Dr. N. W. Walker, who wrote the last of twelve books on natural health when he was 105, discovered that young men who were unable to qualify for the military owing to poor eyesight were able to improve their vision dramatically by adding carrot juice to their diets. Dr. Walker is the father of carrot juice therapy and the originator of the first vegetable juicer, the Norwalk Press. He healed his own near-fatal illness when he was in his twenties with carrot juice and raw food, and thousands have followed in his footsteps. For this healing juice, you will need a vegetable juicer.

This tonic is an antioxidant that will restore inner—and therefore outer—beauty. It is also a powerful weight-loss tool. Cayenne helps deliver vitamins to the bloodstream. If you live in a cold climate, cayenne can be a great help, since it promotes inner heat and improves circulation. It's so effective that it's actually used medicinally to treat ailments caused by exposure to extreme cold. Go easy when you introduce cayenne into your tonics. As time passes and your tolerance builds, you will be able to increase the amounts you use.

In Europe, beet juice is taken as an anticancer treatment. Beets help the body to resist illness and infection. They purify the blood. The alfalfa or sunflower sprouts introduce the powerful chlorophyll factor, oxygenating and cleansing the blood. The bell pepper is high in vitamin C.

5 medium carrots, trimmed and scrubbed

1 beet, trimmed and scrubbed

1 red bell pepper, quartered, not seeded

2 cups alfalfa or sunflower sprouts

Juice of ½ lemon

Pinch of cayenne

1. Juice vegetables and stir in lemon juice. Add a pinch of cayenne and stir well.

SERVES 1

Food for Thought:

GRAPES

Red grape juice has a powerful health-promoting quality. It is actually the grapes in red wine that help lower blood cholesterol. Oligo-proanthocyanidins are powerful anti-oxidants found in grape seed and pine bark. Present in both red grape juice and in red wine, OPCs protect the body against cardiovascular disease by preventing fatty deposits from building up in the arteries where free radicals have caused lesions. The antioxidant effect of OPCs is thought to be fifty times that of vitamin E.

Recent research from the University of Illinois at Chicago also indicates that a substance called resveratrol in grapes may also inhibit the formation and growth of cancerous tumors. Grapes are rich in boron, a mineral that not only helps the body assimilate calcium but also has been proven to contribute to healthy estrogen levels in women. Make fresh grape juice yourself using a vegetable juicer and seedless red flame grapes. (Grapes with seeds tend to yield a bitter juice.) Or look for bottled grape juice, not pasteurized and not from concentrate, containing no additives or sweeteners. Since some commercial grapes are heavily sprayed, organic is your best choice.

DR. EHRET'S REJUVENATION TONIC

Professor Arnold Ehret, who developed the revolutionary mucusless diet healing system in the 1920s and restored health to tens of thousands of his patients, believed in the cleansing properties of grape juice. Dr. August Rollier, of the well-known natural health spa in Switzerland, used grapes in his healing therapies as a way to restore vitality. All foods taken into the body must be converted to glucose for the brain to be able to use them as fuel. Grapes are the only fruit *containing* glucose, rather than fructose. They're the ideal brain fuel. Packed with vitamin C, Ehret Tonic is also high in naturally occurring iron, thanks to the grape juice. Lemon balm is therapy for the nervous system, said to renew youth and calm anxiety. This tonic is a pleasant substitute for iced tea. It can be enjoyed any time of day as a naturally sweet beverage to satisfy sweet cravings.

1 quart pure water
¼ cup lemon balm leaves (see Sources)

Juice of one lemon
2 cups unsweetened bottled grape juice

1. Boil the water and pour over leaves in a large teapot. Cover and steep 15 to 20 minutes.

2. Remove the tea leaves or strain them out and combine the tea with the remaining ingredients in a pitcher. Serve over ice.

SERVES 4 TO 6

OAXACA TONIC

Our editor, Fran McCullough, returned from a Mexican vacation in Oaxaca amazed that in a small village market she had been served a *tonic*! You'll need a juicer for this one.

½ fresh pineapple, peeled but not cored
2 oranges

1 teaspoon honey
½ basket alfalfa sprouts

1. Pass pineapple through vegetable juicer.

2. Juice orange by hand or with a citrus juicer, or peel, leaving pith, which contains vitamin C and bioflavinoids, and pass through vegetable juicer.

3. Combine juices, honey, and sprouts in blender until smooth and creamy.

SERVES 1

CREAMY CARROT TONIC

When you liquify sprouts, they have a surprisingly creamy, sweet flavor. This energizing and cleansing tonic is absolutely delicious!

4 medium carrots, trimmed and scrubbed
5 small golden or gala apples, quartered
¼ to ½ basket alfalfa or clover sprouts
½ to 1 tablespoon nutritional yeast

2 heaping tablespoons lecithin
1 teaspoon Ester C powder
1 tablespoon heart-healthy oil such as flax,
* borage, or sunflower*

1. Pass carrots and apples through a vegetable juicer.

2. Combine juices in blender with remaining ingredients and blend until smooth and creamy.

SERVES 1

FLU TONIC (MEXICAN LEMONADE)

Maybe you're feeling a little under the weather, or maybe you'd just like to do what you can to protect your immune system. Whatever the case, ginger is a great physical toner. It increases the blood flow to the stomach, discourages unfriendly bacteria, relieves nausea, aches, and pains, and also clears out congestion. Cayenne also increases blood circulation to the stomach, and it has antibacterial properties, as well as a high vitamin C potency. Use cayenne cautiously, adding it in small doses to determine your tolerance. Less is more in this case, as too much can literally "take your breath away!"

Echinacea, an herbal antibiotic (see Sources), is added to enhance medicinal benefits. This remedial tonic is particularly useful when you're feeling infectious, not as a daily drink.

2 cups pure water
⅛ to ¼ teaspoon cayenne
2 tablespoons honey or maple syrup

1 chunk fresh gingerroot, minced or squeezed through a press
20 to 30 drops echinacea extract

1. Place water, cayenne, sweetener, and ginger in a small saucepan. Bring to a boil and turn off heat. Cover and steep 15 minutes. Bring heat up again to warm but do not boil.

2. Strain liquid through a fine sieve, discarding any ginger pulp. Add echinacea. Drink hot.

SERVES 1 TO 2

IMMUNITY TONIC

A fruit and vegetable juicer makes this boon to your health possible. The investment in a good juicer may be more valuable in the long run than health insurance! The healing and medicinal properties of garlic (which is actually an herb) are astounding. It's a strong natural antibiotic and immune system strengthener. It purifies the blood naturally and lowers blood cholesterol. Dr. Norman Walker, author of twelve books on natural health who lived to be 109, claimed that garlic kills parasites in the intestines. He drank juices like this one every day. Be careful though—raw garlic can upset a delicate stomach. Spinach or the sunflower sprouts add a healing dose of chlorophyll. The importance of chlorophyll in the body cannot be overemphasized. It's the vehicle for oxygen, which wipes out deadly disease-causing anaerobic bacteria. At Hippocrates Health Institute in West Palm Beach, Florida, potent green juices, containing ginger and garlic, are consumed every day as part of the healing diet.

6 carrots, trimmed and scrubbed
1 tomato
2 celery ribs, scrubbed, leaves removed
1 red or green bell pepper not seeded
1 beet, trimmed and scrubbed

1 cup spinach leaves or sunflower sprouts
1 whole cucumber, scrubbed
1 to 3 garlic cloves, according to tolerance
½ lemon

1. Juice everything but the lemon in a fruit and vegetable juicer. Juice the lemon by hand, then stir it into the tonic.

SERVES 2

SUMMER TONIC

Melon, the quintessential weight-loss tool, is the most cleansing food available to us. *However*, for weight-loss, it carries with it a *cardinal rule. Always eat melons on an empty stomach.* The rich waters they contain can only flush our systems if they are allowed to pass through the stomach unimpeded. Use this tonic in summer as you play the monodieting game, eating only melon and nothing else for a whole day. Sip it slowly and savor the delightful sweetness. When you are monodieting, it's fun to *drink* some of the melons you are taking into your body.

2 cups watermelon, honeydew, or
  cantaloupe, seeds and rind removed,
  cut into chunks

1. Blend until smooth and frothy. Add a handful of fresh strawberries, if desired.

SERVES 1

GREEN AND CREAMY TONIC

For many people, the flavor of wheat grass is hard to take. This formula makes it palatable, even delicious. Look for 1-ounce containers of fresh wheat grass juice in your natural food or juice store. You'll need a vegetable juicer for this tonic.

8 golden delicious apples, quartered
One 3-inch piece fresh gingerroot, peeled
1 whole lemon, peeled
1 whole orange, peeled

3 tablespoons soy lecithin
2 tablespoons flaxseed oil
2 ounces wheat grass juice

1. Put the apples, ginger, lemon, and orange through a vegetable juicer.

2. Place juice blend, lecithin, oil, and wheat grass in a blender, and blend until green and creamy.

SERVES 2

VIKTOR'S TONIC

Viktor Kulvinskas, author of *Survival into the 21st Century* and pioneer in sprouting and wheat grass juice therapy, introduced us to this thoroughly pleasant wheat grass drink. Wheat grass has a strong flavor that's difficult for some people to tolerate; here it's well-disguised with apple, ginger, and lemon as accompanying flavors. You would do well to take advantage of this tonic, if you have a juicer and wheat grass juice is available to you, since chlorophyll-rich wheat grass is a powerful blood cleanser and blood builder. You can buy freshly made wheat grass juice in 1-ounce containers at your local natural foods store. According to Marcia Acciardo, a pioneer in natural health and author of *Light Eating for Survival*, "Chlorophyll cells are very similar to the hemoglobin blood cells of our bodies. Disease-producing bacteria cannot live in the presence of oxygen or oxygen-producing agents like chlorophyll. Green juices are the best health insurance one can find."

In our experience, shortly after taking wheat grass, the eyes are clear and shining. There is a feeling of energy and well-being as the body takes a giant step in a healthy direction.

8 to 10 golden delicious apples, quartered
One 2-inch piece of fresh gingerroot, peeled
1 lemon

1 to 3 ounces wheat grass juice, according to tolerance

1. Using a vegetable juicer, juice the apples and the ginger.

2. Hand juice the lemon or peel the yellow skin from it and pass it through the juicer. (The skin contains mustard oil, which is toxic. The white pith is very high in vitamin C, so leave it on when peeling.)

3. Stir in the wheat grass juice. Bottoms up!

SERVES 1

MERRY TONIC: A HEALTHFUL COCKTAIL

Bloody Mary, eat your heart out, and move over! It's the era for the Merry Tonic. This heart-loving cocktail is designed to help lower hypertension with its potassium-rich apple cider vinegar, enzyme-rich tomatoes and cucumbers, and tarragon—a natural diuretic that helps the body remove excess fluids. Lemon is a natural liver cleanser.

2 medium tomatoes, cut in chunks

½ to 1 hothouse cucumber, unpeeled and cut in chunks

1 cup pure water

1 tablespoon fresh tarragon, or 1 teaspoon dried

Juice of ½ lemon, or 1 tablespoon apple cider vinegar

Dash of cayenne

1 celery rib, scrubbed, leaves intact, for garnish

1. Place ingredients in a blender and puree until smooth or, if you have a vegetable juicer, put the entire cucumber through it, omit the water, and blend the tomatoes and other ingredients directly into the cucumber juice.

2. Pour in a tall glass and garnish with celery. Sip as a cocktail before your meal.

SERVES 2 TO 3

BEDTIME SNACK TONIC

Bananas contain tryptophan, which helps you sleep. Combined with sweet, alkaline soy milk, the resulting bedtime tonic is truly a comfort food. If you want to use the old hot-milk-before-bed trick, heat the soy milk until just before boiling, then blend. Sweet dreams!

1½ cups vanilla or plain soy milk
1 banana

Dash of cinnamon or cardamom

1. Blend until smooth and creamy in a blender.

SERVES 1

BEDTIME TONIC

This hot tonic is a cup of bedtime therapy. The scent of cinnamon has an extraordinarily soothing effect on the psyche. This spice was brought to the western world from Sri Lanka by the Portuguese, and is now cultivated all over the tropics. Medicinally, cinnamon is often used as a muscle relaxant, which is why it makes us feel so darn good! Chamomile is the happy tummy, calm spirit herb, which only adds more relaxing qualities to this bedtime beverage.

1 teaspoon honey
¾ cup pure water
1 cinnamon stick

2 teaspoons fresh lemon juice
1 bag chamomile tea

1. Place honey, water, and cinnamon stick in a small saucepan. Bring to a boil. Remove from heat and add lemon juice and tea bag. Brew 3 to 5 minutes.

2. Remove cinnamon stick and tea bag and stir. Take to your bath, and sip while you soak.

SERVES 1

BASIC JUICE FORMULAS

Use a vegetable juicer or citrus juicer to create these basic blends. It is not necessary to core apples. Recipes serve 1 person, 10 to 12 ounces. Or divide a recipe for two and serve in wine goblets. Drink all these juices when your stomach is empty. A perfect time to enjoy these juices is while you're preparing dinner.

CARROT BLUSH

8 carrots, scrubbed and trimmed
1 small beet, scrubbed and trimmed
One 2-inch piece of fresh ginger
Juice of ½ lemon hand squeezed (optional)

APPLE-LEMON CLEANSER

8 to 10 golden delicious or gala apples,
    scrubbed, stems removed
Juice of ½ lemon, hand squeezed

APPLE-CELERY-SUNFLOWER SPROUT ENERGIZER

A great pick-me-up on a sizzling hot day, since celery replaces sodium lost in perspiration.

8 apples, scrubbed, stems removed
2 celery ribs, scrubbed
1 cup sunflower sprouts

REAL EIGHT NUTRIENT INFUSION

6 carrots, scrubbed and trimmed

1 small beet, scrubbed and trimmed

1 tomato

1 red or green bell pepper, quartered, not
    seeded

2 celery ribs, scrubbed

1 garlic clove

½ unpeeled cucumber

Juice of ½ lemon, hand squeezed

WATERMELON BLADDER FLUSH

Without rind, watermelon juice is just sugar water. The rind supplies nutrients and chlorophyll. Be sure to take only on an *empty* stomach.

Juice ⅛ large watermelon, seeds and rind
    included

CHAPTER THREE

Herbal Teas and Infusions

TEA TIPS

With all the herbal teas on the market today, it's easier than ever to make a good cup of tea, and the tea industry goes the extra mile to help us understand which teas are relevant to our specific needs. You can purchase tea blends to help you sleep, calm you, soothe your throat, give you energy, or help you digest your meal. And they've even put those blends into tea bags, so very little work is left for the consumer. Here are some practical rules for getting the most from your tea:

- For herbal tea bags, boil the water, pour into the cup with the tea bag, and steep 3 to 5 minutes. Remove the bag before you drink the tea.

- For fresh herbs, measure 2 tablespoons per cup and break them into small pieces in a bowl. Bring water to the early bubbling stage before boiling, and pour it over the tea. The delicate essences of the herb will be lost to boiling water. Steep 15 to 30 minutes to infuse the water with herbal flavors. Reheat gently, for hot tea or pour over ice.

- For dried herbs of the leafy variety, such as peppermint, measure 1 tablespoon of dried herb for each cup and one for the pot. Place the herbs in a floating tea caddie or in the bottom of your teapot. Bring water to the bubbly, preboiling stage, and pour into the pot. Cover and steep 15 minutes and pour into teacups or mugs through a tea strainer, unless you have used the tea caddie.

- For dried roots or seeds, such as licorice or cardamom pods, place 1 teaspoon per cup in a small saucepan and add measured amount of water. Bring to a boil, remove from heat, and let steep for 15 to 40 minutes. Strain as you pour into cups.

- To prepare sun tea, make your favorite tea in a glass jar by placing tea bags in pure water and letting the mixture sit in the sun for several hours.

- To cool hot tea quickly, let it sit in the freezer briefly.

- Remember, sugar robs your body of nutrients and energy. Honey is calming and nourishing. Go for the sweet that will make you sweeter!

- To benefit from herbal teas, make a mental shift while you're preparing them. See yourself healing yourself, breathe, relax. Hold a picture of yourself vibrant and healthy and know that the tea is part of the picture. Take a few minutes to sit quietly while you drink your tea, and reflect on all the goodness in your life. Coffee breaks are usually fairly rushed and frenetic. Make your tea break a true break. Let it set your mood of well-being for the rest of the day.

THE EASY GUIDE TO HERBAL AND GREEN TEAS

HERB	BENEFIT	INFUSION	HINTS
Chamomile	Helps digestion disturbances; calming, soothing; mouthwash for minor gum irritations; safe for children.	Pour 2 cups boiling water over 1 heaping tablespoon of the flower heads and allow them to steep in a covered vessel for 10 to 15 minutes. Drink a cup three or five times daily between meals for intestinal disturbances. Very soothing to drink at bedtime.	Best quality teas are in the form of the whole flower head.
Echinacea	Immunostimulant, detoxifier, antimicrobial; promotes perspiration; antiallergenic, blood cleansing, anti-inflammatory, stimulates circulation. It is useful for those whose immune system is run down or deficient and who are prone to one infection after another.	2 tablespoons of herb to 1 cup boiling water, but because not all of the active constituents are water soluble, the herb in a tincture form added to tea is preferable.	For greatest benefit, internal or external, do not use for more than 8 successive weeks. Those allergic to members of the sunflower family may experience allergic reactions.
Ginger	Stimulates circulation; clears congestion; aids digestion;	Use commercial tea found in herbal tea section or prepare	Ginger can create a feeling of warmth and is not recom-

THE EASY GUIDE TO HERBAL AND GREEN TEAS *(cont.)*

HERB	BENEFIT	INFUSION	HINTS
Ginger *(continued)*	antioxidant; detoxifying; relieves nausea, relieves gas, promotes menstruation, relieves cramps, invigorates reproductive system; lowers blood pressure and cholesterol; relieves morning sickness; anti-inflammatory.	decoction from gingerroot: break root with a mortar and pestle, then place in pan with water, bring to a boil, cover, and simmer for 10 minutes and strain. Use a pint of water for each ounce of ginger.	mended for those who do not tolerate heat well or individuals with peptic ulcers or chronic gastritis.
Green Tea	Green tea is an antioxidant. It is widely drunk in Japan and is one of three major nonalcoholic beverages in the world.	Pour 2 cups boiling water over one heaping teaspoon of tea. Brew for five minutes. Prolonged brewing will result in a bitter tea.	Contains caffeine.
Licorice	Treatment of peptic ulcers; helps reduce fever; helpful during menopause; improves resistance to stress, natural pick-me-up; liver cleansing; acts as a mild laxative, soothing to the digestive tract; useful for hay fever, runny nose, and itchy eyes associated with allergies.	½ cup boiling water to 1 teaspoon herb, simmer the mixture for 5 minutes. Drink daily after meals.	Should not be consumed over long periods owing to possible toxicity. Not suitable for children or elderly people. Avoid during pregnancy.

THE EASY GUIDE TO HERBAL AND GREEN TEAS *(cont.)*

HERB	BENEFIT	INFUSION	HINTS
Peppermint	Eases gas cramps; digestive aid; good general tonic to recharge vital energy, calm anxiety and tension; cleansing to liver and gallbladder.	⅔ cup boiling water poured over 1 teaspoonful of herb. Steep for 5 to 10 minutes. Drink this amount three to four times daily between meals to relieve upset stomach.	Do not use peppermint oil for babies or young children. Spearmint is better to use for children.
Raspberry leaves (blueberry and blackberry have similar benefits)	Good for the treatment of digestive problems, including diarrhea, and problems of pregnancy such as morning sickness and labor pains.	Pour 2 cups boiling water over 1 to 2 teaspoons of leaves. Let steep for 10 to 15 minutes. Alternatively, soak plant material in cold water for 1 to 2 hours and then strain. A cup of the tea may be drunk up to six times a day to control diarrhea.	If a diarrhea condition lasts more than two or three days, it is probably not treatable by the use of astringent herbs.
Rose hips	High in vitamin C, digestive aid, and overall toner for the bladder.	Pour 2 cups boiling water over 1 tablespoon rose hips. Steep for 10 to 15 minutes. Strain, bring to a boil again, and serve.	

THE EASY GUIDE TO HERBAL AND GREEN TEAS *(cont.)*

HERB	BENEFIT	INFUSION	HINTS
Rosemary	Improves circulation to the brain, relieves menstrual cramps, acts as a decongestant. Also fights bacteria and relieves cold and flu symptoms.	Steep 2 sprigs rosemary in 2 cups boiling water for 15 to 20 minutes. Remove stems and heat liquid again. Sip warm.	To treat colds and congestion, try putting a few sprigs rosemary in a hot bath and soak for 20 minutes.
Thyme	Reduces fever, headache, and congestion. Healing to the entire respiratory system.	Use 1 tablespoon fresh thyme leaves or 1 teaspoon dried. Steep in 2 cups boiling water for 10 to 15 minutes. Strain off the leaves and sip warm with a teaspoon of honey added.	Look for lemon thyme at your supermarket or specialty food store. It is an exotic variety that is delicious as well as therapeutic.

PART TWO

Fruit Meals and Breakfast Foods

CHAPTER FOUR

Satisfying Breakfasts

APPLENUT CEREAL

This is an example of a "fruit cereal." The grated apples, chunks of banana, ground nuts, shredded coconut, and raisins create a wonderful cereal-like texture. The blend of sweeteners from fruit and syrup combined with spicy cinnamon create a flavor that reminds you of a lovely dessert. A meal of fruit cereal in the morning—or any time of day—is heavenly!

This beats any sugar-coated cereal in the supermarket.

1 large banana, quartered and sliced

2 large apples, coarsely grated

¼ cup enzymized raw almonds (page 52)

¼ cup shredded unsweetened, grated coconut

1 teaspoon maple syrup

½ teaspoon cinnamon

½ cup raisins or currants

¼ cup lactase-enriched low-fat milk, vanilla soy milk, or apple juice

1. Combine apple and banana in a medium bowl.

2. Coarsely grind almonds in a blender or food processor.

3. Sprinkle nuts and coconut over fruit. Combine syrup, cinnamon, and raisins. Toss together with fruit.

4. Spoon into bowls and top with milk or apple juice.

SERVES 2

FLORIDA FRUIT BREAKFAST

1 pineapple, peeled, cored, cut into ½-inch
*   cubes*
2 bananas, sliced into ¼-inch rounds
1 mango, peeled, pitted, and diced into
*   ½-inch cubes*
1 basket fresh strawberries, stemmed
1 orange

1 tablespoon poppy seeds
¼ cup plain yogurt
2 teaspoons honey
Fresh mint leaves for garnish

1. In a large serving bowl toss pineapple, bananas, and mango. Top with strawberries.

2. Grate enough zest off of the orange to make 1 teaspoon; juice the orange by hand. Combine orange zest and juice, poppy seeds, yogurt, and honey in a separate bowl. Drizzle over fruit and garnish with mint leaves.

SERVES 4

BREAKFAST GAZPACHO

Sometimes you just don't want to start the day with anything sweet. For those times, especially in summer, when you prefer a savory start, drink this slowly or eat with a spoon.

4 Roma (plum) tomatoes
1 handful spinach leaves
1 small cucumber, scrubbed
2 celery ribs, scrubbed

½ cup alfalfa sprouts
1 cup carrot juice (optional) or water
1 teaspoon fresh lemon juice
½ avocado, or approximately ½ cup

1. Place 3 tomatoes, spinach, cucumber, celery, sprouts and carrot juice or water in blender and puree.

2. Stir in lemon juice. Dice remaining tomato and the avocado, and stir into "soup."

SERVES 2

FIG PUDDING

6 black mission or Calmyrna figs, soaked
*   for 1 to 2 hours in 1½ cups water*
1 medium navel orange, peeled
2 teaspoons peanut butter
½ cup orange or fig juice, from soaked figs,
*   or combination of both*

½ cup raisins
1 teaspoon cinnamon
¼ cup rolled oats

1. Combine all ingredients and blend until smooth. Pour into goblets and serve.

SERVES 2

SUNNY SEED AND FRUIT MEAL

The amounts are for a family-sized salad. For one serving make one-quarter the amount. This makes a delicious soothing supper or a cleansing morning meal. Great with tea made from chamomile and ginger.

1 pineapple, halved, cored, and sliced (page 40)

1 pint hulled strawberries, sliced

2 oranges or tangelos, peeled, halved, and sliced

4 bananas, sliced

8 black mission figs, chopped, or 1 cup raisins

4 kiwis, peeled and sliced

2 cups enzymized hulled sunflower seeds (below)

1½ cups vanilla or plain soy milk

Juice of 2 oranges

Dashes of cinnamon and cardamom

1. Prepare fruit and combine in large bowl. Add sunflower seeds and mix well.

2. Spoon into large bowls. Combine soy milk, orange juice, and spices. Pour over individual servings.

SERVES 4

Food for Thought:

SUNFLOWER SEEDS

They used to be thought of as bird food, but hulled sunflower seeds have gained national popularity as a snack food—or an ingredient in meals—and rightly so.

Sunflower seeds are a good survival food because they are so rich in nutrients. They average 27 percent protein and are rich in calcium, iron, magnesium, phosphorus, and potassium. They are good sources of several B-complex vitamins and vitamins A and D. Soak them in pure water for at least an hour to remove the enzyme inhibitors and convert the polyunsaturated fats to usable fatty acids. Once enzymized, drain well and allow them to dry before storing in a covered container in the refrigerator.

Keep sprouted sunflower seeds on hand to add to tonics, fruit salads, vegetable salads and vegetable dishes. Sprinkle on top of casseroles before baking or add to muffin mixes and cookie doughs. Blend with 4 parts water, 1 tablespoon honey, and 1 part seeds to make rich Sunmilk.

BASIC BIRCHER MUESLI

Muesli is a raw cereal developed by Dr. Max Bircher-Benner at the world-famous Bircher-Benner Clinic in Zurich, Switzerland, founded in 1897 to pioneer the treatment of the "whole person" rather than "the disease." To this day, the Bircher-Benner Clinic treats a variety of illnesses through an enzyme-rich live food diet that supports the "inner physician." Traditional Bircher muesli is a combination of a raw grain, such as oatmeal, soaked in water or fresh raw milk or buttermilk, to which grated fruit and ground nuts are added. In Switzerland, where the citizenry is robust and active, Bircher muesli was eaten so often it was known as "the daily bread." If you are feeling "not quite whole," this is an excellent meal at breakfast, lunch, or dinner. The grain sauce can be made in quantity and stored in the refrigerator three or four days. Add the grated fruit and nuts shortly before serving. Keeping a bowl of muesli on hand is a way to ensure you can always have a quick, healthy meal. The following is Dr. Bircher-Benner's basic recipe, with our suggested variations. We recommend the rolled oats you get in your local natural foods store.

1 tablespoon rolled oats
3 tablespoons cold water
1 tablespoon lemon juice
1 tablespoon low-fat milk or soy milk

1 cored apple, grated
1 tablespoon ground enzymized hazelnuts
* or almonds (page 52)*

1. Soak oats in water for 12 hours. Add juice and milk and mix into a smooth sauce.

2. Grate apple directly into sauce. Stir immediately to combine with lemon juice and prevent oxidation of apple flesh. Add nuts and serve.

SERVES 1

Variations: Add any of the following: 1 tablespoon honey; substitute 3 tablespoons yogurt or cream for the milk; substitute mashed strawberries, raspberries, blueberries, blackberries, peaches, plums, apricots, or bananas for the apple; add soaked dried fruit.

APPLE-CARROT FRUESLI

This is a fruit cereal. Fruesli instead of muesli, since this one contains no grain. The carrot adds color, texture, and excellent fiber.

1 carrot, peeled and finely grated

3 medium apples, finely grated (leave peel for added fiber)

⅓ cup unsweetened, shredded coconut

¼ cup currants or raisins

¼ cup chopped, enzymized pecans or almonds (page 52)

½ teaspoon cinnamon

¼ teaspoon cardamon

1 cup soy or low-fat milk

1. Combine all ingredients except milk in a serving bowl and toss together.

2. Pour milk over each portion and serve.

SERVES 2

Food for Thought:

YOGURT

Only yogurt containing the *Lactobacillus acidophilus* and *L. bulgaricus* can be considered natural yogurt, which means several things. First, these are friendly bacteria; they aid in healthy digestion, are antibiotic, and support immune system functions in the body. Natural yogurt carries the enzyme lactase, thanks to its acidophilus and bulgaricus content. This helps digest lactose, the sugar which for many people is indigestible in dairy products. Rich in calcium and protein, yogurt is an ideal kid food and cooking food, for dressings, sauces, as a garnish for soups, in tonics and baking—plain natural yogurt appears as a staple in some of the healthiest cuisines of the world: Greek, East Indian, French, and some Middle Eastern countries.

Avoid the sugary presweetened yogurts, and look for labels that specifically list acidophilus and bulgaricus cultures. Any other kind of culture is not the same. If you like flavored yogurts, add natural fruit preserves, honey, maple syrup, or fresh fruit to plain yogurt.

MAPLE GRANOLA WITH POACHED PEARS AND YOGURT

Making your own granola is easy. Make a double batch; it will keep up to a month stored in an airtight container. This is a beautiful breakfast meal for special occasions when you want to serve something unusual and healthy.

1 cup raisins

2 cups hot water

4 cups rolled oats

1 cup chopped pecans

2 tablespoons safflower oil

½ cup water

½ cup maple syrup

¼ teaspoon sea salt

4 firm pears, peeled

2 cinnamon sticks

1 tablespoon whole cloves

1 vanilla bean, split in half lengthwise

¼ cup honey

1 lemon, quartered

2 cups plain yogurt or buttermilk

Fresh berries for garnish (optional)

1. Place raisins in a small bowl and cover with hot water. Set aside.

2. Preheat oven to 375°F.

3. Combine oats, pecans, safflower oil, water, maple syrup, and salt in a large mixing bowl. Stir well to thoroughly moisten the oats. Place on a baking sheet and put in the oven. Stir every 5 minutes, until dry and golden, about 25 minutes.

4. Meanwhile, place pears in a large pot of boiling water with cinnamon sticks, cloves, vanilla bean, honey, and lemon. Simmer about 15 minutes, until pears are tender. Remove them from liquid and cool slightly.

5. Gently slice pears into quarters and remove cores. Distribute granola among 4 bowls. Drain soaked raisins. Spoon ½ cup yogurt or buttermilk onto each and top with poached pears and raisins. Garnish with berries, if desired.

SERVES 4

EASY FRUIT AND DAIRY BOWLS

In India, the combination of fruit and dairy foods is traditionally seen as spiritual and soothing—or *sattwic*. This is not a combination to be ignored at supper, if you're looking for something easy to prepare. It's filling and delicious, and you'll awaken in the morning feeling light and happy. Accompany your fruit and cream meal with a fresh glass of carrot-ginger juice.

STRAWBERRIES AND CREAM

Place strawberries in bowl with a dollop of sour cream mixed with date sugar. Dip strawberries into cream.

PEACHES AND CREAM

Slice peaches and mix them with plain yogurt sweetened with honey.

BANANAS AND SOUR CREAM

Slice bananas, add a handful of currants or raisins, and mix with sour cream. Dust with cardamom.

BLUEBERRIES AND SOUR CREAM

Mix blueberries in sour cream until they break down. This is blue food for higher consciousness.

MARILYN'S PÊCHE MELBA

When I'm craving ice cream, I have it for dinner—with a lot of fruit! Why not? Simple meals are easier to digest. Why put ice cream in my stomach on top of cooked food? The fruit helps wash the ice cream through. I sleep like a baby after this meal. *Caution:* This is an occasional treat, not an everyday meal.

1 banana halved lengthwise

Sliced peaches (or strawberries, if peaches aren't in season)

1 hefty scoop of vanilla ice cream

1 tablespoon fruit-juice sweetened blueberry or grape jam, thinned with 1 tablespoon water

1 tablespoon ground enzymized almonds (optional) (page 52)

1. In the Guru's Bowl, arrange banana and peaches. Top with ice cream and jam. Dust with almonds. Sip tea and love your meal!

SERVES 1

Note: Look for Cascadian Farms vanilla ice cream sweetened with dehydrated cane juice instead of refined sugar.

CHAPTER FIVE

_F_resh _U_ncooked _N_atural Food, or "FUNdays"

One of the features in *FITONICS* is the optional "FUNday," when only Fresh Uncooked Natural food is eaten. FUNdays are particularly appealing in warm weather, when all the fresh fruits and vegetables are available. You can see them as spring cleaning, after a winter of eating heavier foods that have possibly added some unwanted weight. In warm regions FUNdays are year-round options.

When you eat only raw food, you flood your bloodstream with vital nutrients and enzymes, and you're saving your body's energy. How? Live food is so enzyme-rich it digests on its own, without requiring enzymes or digestive energy from your body. Since digestion takes more energy than anything else you do, you can see how a day of live food frees up quantities of energy that can be put toward other life-enhancing processes, such as rejuvenation, repair, and weight loss. Always remember, weight loss requires energy.

There are many ways to approach FUNdays that will allow them to be one of the easiest, most uncomplicated ways to eat local food. Here are some possibilities:

- You can spend the day drinking fresh fruit blends and tonics. To avoid cravings for heavier foods, start with a nutritious, thick, and frothy tonic in the morning, have your juices approximately 2 hours apart, and repeat with a thick, frothy tonic in the evening.

- You can eat only fruit all day long, having three, four, even five fruit meals. You might have a bowl of oranges or tangerines; a plate of sliced apples with grapes, figs, and raisins; or a melon platter of honeydew, cantaloupe, and watermelon.

- You can have a tonic in the morning; some peaches for a snack; and lunch of pears, celery, and enzymized almonds; and a large dinner salad with half an avocado.

- You can blend melon into a frothy soup in the morning, dip raw vegetables into salsa and guacamole at lunch, and roll a chopped vegetable salad in romaine lettuce leaves for dinner, followed by a banana for a snack before bed.

We have provided innovative recipes for tonics and fruit cereals in the last section, and there are recipes for simple salads in this section. When your energy is low, or a few extra pounds have managed to sneak on, the FUNday is one of the healthiest tools for weight loss and revitalization. *To add life to your body, eat food full of life.*

CLEANSING FRUIT MEAL

This tangy fruit salad is ideal on the morning after a heavy supper. The citrus juice dressing gives you that squeaky clean feeling. The fresh mint refreshes.

1 cup diced fresh pineapple
1 orange, peeled and diced
1 ruby red grapefruit, peeled and diced
1 pear, cored and diced
2 fresh mint leaves, julienned (optional)

DRESSING

Juice of ½ lemon
Juice of ½ grapefruit
Juice of 1 orange

1. Combine diced fruit in large bowl with mint leaves.

2. Pour citrus juices over salad and toss well.

SERVES 2 TO 3

PINEAPPLE SURPRISE

This meal is refreshing, filling, and ideal when avocados are in season. The tomato adds a good contrasting flavor to the pineapple, or the persimmon can add to the sweetness. Use fuyu persimmons, which are hard and tomato-shaped, rather than teardrop-shaped and soft. The julienned lettuce adds texture, fiber, and color. Don't be afraid to mix lettuce in fruit salads, even at breakfast. The effect is very pleasing.

2 cups cubed pineapple (page 40)
1 avocado, halved, seeded, peeled, and
 cubed

1 diced tomato or sliced persimmon
1 cup julienned lettuce
Juice of 1 orange

1. Combine salad ingredients and toss in orange juice.

SERVES 2

MORNING FRUIT PLATE

Sitting down in the morning to a platter of fruits with enzymized nuts gives one the most virtuous feeling. That sense of "being good" is rewarded *big time* by your body, as you sail through a most pleasant and energetic day. Don't take our word for it! See for yourself. Stress in your outer world comes from stress inside you. Fruit and nuts are the nonstressing foods. Unless, of course, you overeat the nuts!

   The celery may seem startling here but it has an acid-neutralizing role that we shouldn't ignore. It goes just as well with fruit as with a sandwich or dip.

1 Bosc pear, stemmed, cored, and sliced
Several large strawberries, sliced
Papaya or kiwi fruit

Some celery ribs
¼ cup enzymized almonds, hazelnuts, or
 sunflower seeds (pages 52 and 84)

1. Halve the papaya or kiwi to be eaten with a spoon.

2. Arrange the fruit on a platter with celery and nuts.

SERVES 1

WINTER FRUIT PLATE

Even when you have no time to fix something heavier, in cold climates it's hard sometimes to embrace a morning fruit meal. But try fruits that are concentrated and filling. This is the best time for dried fruit, which gives that extra energy needed to make it through the cold. Warm up the meal with a spicy cup of tea or hot vanilla soy milk, spiced with cardamom. Start with a glass of fresh orange juice.

1 banana

2 dates

2 black mission figs or a handful of raisins

A bunch of seedless black or red flame grapes

Celery or carrot ribs

1. Peel and slice the banana.

2. Arrange fruit attractively on a plate.

SERVES 1

Food for Thought:

EAT MORE FRUIT

According to Jean Carper, author of *Food—Your Miracle Medicine*, the most urgent advice for escaping pancreatic cancer has to be "Eat more fruit." In a study done in Louisiana, a National Cancer Institute research team found heavy pork eaters had a high incidence of cancer; however, heavy pork eaters who loaded up on fruit were no more likely to get pancreatic cancer than skimpy pork eaters.

According to a Johns Hopkins study, having low levels of lycopene in your blood can be an indicator of pancreatic cancer. Foods high in lycopene are tomatoes and watermelon, according to Carper.

BANANA-PEAR SALAD WITH ALMOND BUTTER

Almond butter is the only alkaline nut butter. Remember, alkaline foods help you keep your body chemistry in balance. It is also lower in fat than other nut butters and has an unusually mild flavor. Almond butter is available in natural food markets and specialty food stores. It can be a bit expensive, but you won't eat it every day, so splurge and enjoy.

2 bananas, peeled and thinly sliced

2 Bartlett pears, peeled and thinly sliced

⅓ cup raisins, soaked in ½ cup warm water (reserve)

Cinnamon to taste

Cardamom to taste

¼ cup shredded, unsweetened coconut (optional)

1½ tablespoons almond butter

1 teaspoon date sugar, or 1 soft pitted date (optional)

1. Toss sliced fruit and raisins with cinnamon and cardamom. Add the optional coconut, if desired.

2. Blend almond butter, raisin soaking water, and date sugar or date in a blender until creamy. Pour over fruit salad.

SERVES 2

FRESH SUMMER FRUIT WITH A TRIO OF MELON SORBETS

This fruit salad makes a lovely summer brunch when heavier foods would slow you down. When melons are abundant, freeze them—just peel, seed, and slice them into small chunks. Seedless watermelon makes the job easier. Keep the frozen fruit on hand or make this sorbet.

2 cups frozen honeydew chunks
2 cups frozen watermelon chunks
2 cups frozen cantaloupe chunks
2 kiwi fruit, peeled and sliced into ½-inch
    rounds

1 papaya, peeled and sliced into wedges,
    seeds scooped out
1 pint strawberries, stemmed
1 pint blueberries
2 peaches or pears, peeled and quartered

1. Puree each of the frozen melons separately in a blender or food processor until you have smooth, thick sorbets. Freeze again in separate containers for 1 hour. Or, if you have a juicer that turns frozen fruit into sorbet, freeze juicing mechanism for 30 minutes, then pass frozen melon through juicer. You will not need to refreeze.

2. Arrange sliced fruit on individual serving plates. Place one small scoop of each sorbet on each serving plate.

SERVES 4

ENERGY WRAPS

This is one of the best keys to making it through a FUNday when you eat Fresh, Uncooked Natural food. Have it for lunch or supper and surround it with fruit meals.

1 head romaine or salad bowl lettuce

1 large avocado, halved, seeded, and scooped from peel

1 tomato, diced

2 tablespoons diced red onion

Sprouts

¼ teaspoon chili powder, or a dash of cayenne

1. Separate lettuce into individual leaves.

2. Mash avocado and combine with remaining ingredients.

3. Spoon onto lettuce leaves, roll up, and munch.

SERVES 1 TO 2

Food for Thought:

MELONS AND MONODIETING

Have you ever heard of monodieting? It's the practice of eating only one food, or only one type of fresh food, such as fruit, juice, or raw vegetables, for a given period. Monodieting gives the body a rest while supplying it with a high concentration of enzymes and cleansing live food. Natural health pioneers, Drs. Paul and Patricia Bragg, gave us the melon cleanse. In summer, they would retreat to a secluded mountain cabin, rest, hike, and feast on nothing but luscious, sweet melons for a week or more. Having experienced numerous multiday melon fasts, we can heartily vouch for the spirit-raising, body-cleansing benefits. We have found that melon monodieting brings a radiance to the eyes, a "glow," and a rejuvenated appearance and feeling of well-being. If we look for evidence of the spiritual value of melons, we find that watermelon was one of the favorite foods of Mahatma Ghandi, who accomplished his long marches by frequently monodieting on watermelon.

If your energy is low, if you want to cleanse and raise your vibrations, or if you wish to lose some extra pounds, you can monodiet for a meal or a day. Melon is one of the best foods for monodieting. Grapes are another ideal monodieting option.

CUCUMBER WAKAME SALAD

Why not experiment with wakame and other sea vegetables? The result is always unusual and innovative and the benefit is significant, since sea vegetables contain minerals, vitamins, and proteins. Wakame is a delicate translucent green sea vegetable that is easy to use. It adds a decidedly Asian quality to this dish. Soba is a kind of Japanese noodle that is available in some supermarkets and natural food stores.

2 large hothouse cucumbers
Sea salt to taste
1 tablespoon sesame oil
1 tablespoon black sesame seeds
½ cup wakame shreds (see Sources)

1 tablespoon rice vinegar
1 teaspoon roasted sesame oil
Buckwheat soba

1. Cut unpeeled cucumbers diagonally in ⅛-inch slices. Then cut each disk into thin long strips. Sprinkle lightly with salt and place on a plate. Cover with a second plate and let sit 30 minutes, until cucumber releases juices. Add the tablespoon of sesame oil to a small skillet and heat it. Sauté sesame seeds in hot oil for 3 minutes. Set aside to cool.

2. Soak wakame in 2 cups water for 10 minutes. Drain and coarsely chop. Discard water. Squeeze juice from cucumber and mix with wakame. Toss with vinegar and reserved sesame seeds, roasted sesame oil, and oil from the skillet. Serve over bed of chilled buckwheat soba for a light summer meal.

SERVES 2

CHINESE COLE SLAW

A delightful salad to cut the intensity of Marinated Pork Chops with Black Beans for a true fusion meal.

¼ cup mung bean sprouts
¼ cup grated carrot
1 cup slivered fresh spinach
½ cup grated red cabbage
1 green onion (scallion), chopped
⅛ cup chopped fresh cilantro
½ teaspoon white or black sesame seeds

DRESSING

2 tablespoons vegetable broth
1 teaspoon roasted sesame oil
1 tablespoon fresh lime juice
½ teaspoon grated ginger
1 teaspoon tamari

1. Mix the salad ingredients together in a salad bowl.

2. Mix the dressing ingredients together in a small bowl and toss with the salad.

CREAMY APPLE-CARROT SLAW

Peeling of the apples and carrots is optional although this dish will be prettier if you do.

2 cups shredded carrots
1 apple, cored and grated
2 tablespoons pecan pieces or chopped enzymized almonds
¼ cup raisins, soaked in warm water for 15 minutes, drained (reserve water)

2 tablespoons sesame tahini or ¼ cup plain yogurt
¼ teaspoon cinnamon

1. Combine carrots, apples, nuts, and raisins in a bowl and mix well. In a separate bowl combine remaining ingredients with ¼ cup reserved raisin-soaking water. Mix well and pour over salad. Toss to combine.

SERVES 2 TO 3

WALDORF SALAD

Make a large amount of this salad and eat it for lunch or dinner. Watch the pounds melt away!

2 apples, cored and cubed

1 large or 2 medium celery ribs, finely diced

½ cup pecan or walnut pieces, coarsely chopped

2 tablespoons nut butter or tahini

Juice of 1 orange

2 tablespoons water

Cinnamon to taste

2 tablespoons chopped parsley

1. Combine apples, celery, and nuts.

2. Blend nut butter, orange juice, water, and cinnamon in blender.

3. Pour over salad. Add parsley and mix well. Chill for several hours, if desired, before serving.

SERVES 2

PART THREE

High-Protein Power Meals

How you combine foods will determine your energy levels. Combining proteins with vegetables or simple salads will yield maximum energy and weight loss.

BROWN BAG LUNCHES

Especially if you are having fruit or tonic breakfasts, lunch can be your main meal of the day. Take a well-earned break and have a substantial lunch. If you can't cook or go out to eat, bring any of the following to work:

- Yummy vegetarian sandwich on lightly toasted whole-grain bread with a thermos of soup, carrot and celery sticks, corn tortilla chips, and mango, banana, or pears. Here is a list of suggested sandwich fillings:

  1. Dijon mustard, roasted red peppers, Swiss cheese, thinly sliced cucumbers, and alfalfa sprouts

  2. Cream cheese, olives, sprouts, and shredded carrot

  3. Almond or peanut butter, honey, sprouts, and thinly sliced banana

  4. Hummus with sprouts, onions, and sliced cucumbers

  5. Avocado, roasted red pepper, jack cheese, mayonnaise or mustard, and lettuce

- Healthy crudités (a lot of raw vegetables) with hummus and pita bread chips, Apple-Carrot Slaw

- Hot soup in a thermos, whole-grain bagel, and an avocado to spread on it

- Apple-Carrot Slaw or Waldorf Salad—a big bowl for weight loss and energy

- Any pasta salad, bagel, and avocado

- An energizing and slenderizing live food lunch of avocado, red pepper, carrot, celery, cucumber, whole tomato, and the fruit of your choice

- Juicy fresh fruit and an assortment of cheeses

- Seasoned cold chicken, vegetable salad, kiwis, and strawberries

- A filling whole grapefruit, hard-boiled eggs, tuna salad, raw vegetables, and cherry tomatoes

- Enzymized almonds or sunflower seeds, apples, and celery

- Antipasto of cold meats, cheeses, olives, and artichoke hearts

- Slenderizing tortilla wraps of your choice with a thermos of soup:

  1. Steamed broccoli, avocado, barbecue sauce, sliced pickle, and plenty of sprouts

  2. Turkey and cheese, shredded raw vegetables, and mustard

  3. Mustard, avocado, goat cheese, sprouts, and sliced cucumber

  4. Chunks of chicken, sliced olives, lettuce, sprouts, cucumber, and dilled mayonnaise

Food for Thought:
A TOMATO TIP

When you're packing sandwiches for lunch, avoid using tomato as a filling. The acidity in the tomato will ferment the bread (in fact, its enzymes immediately begin to break down the cut tomato and the starchy bread). A good substitute for tomatoes on sandwiches is roasted red pepper. Pack whole cherry or Roma tomatoes instead.

~~⦿~~

CHAPTER SIX

Fish and Seafood

FIVE SIMPLE WAYS WITH FISH

1. Broiling

Broiling is best for fattier varieties fo fish, such as salmon or halibut but will work well for any cut that is at least ¾ inch thick. Rub the fillet with olive oil, season with salt and pepper, and place in a 400°F preheated broiler until the center is opaque and firm. Some varieties of fish, such as sea bass, may require slightly longer than salmon, for instance, because it is best when served on the well-done side.

2. Poaching

Poaching is traditionally done in a seasoned liquid called a court bouillon:

½ cup white wine

1 tablespoon apple cider vinegar

4 cups stock or water

1 tablespoon fresh tarragon, or
   1 teaspoon dried

½ onion, coarsely chopped

1 celery rib, coarsely chopped

Juice of 1 lemon or orange

Place all ingredients in a deep skillet. Bring to a boil, then simmer 30 minutes. Turn off heat and allow to cool. Court bouillon may be prepared in advance and stored, covered, in the refrigerator, for up to 4 days.

To poach the fish, place court bouillon in a deep skillet. Add your fillets to warm, *not hot*, liquid. (Adding them to hot liquid will cook the outside of the fish too quickly, and your result will be dry.) Bring to a boil, then simmer until the fish becomes opaque, but not rubbery. Remove from the liquid with a slotted spatula or spoon when the fish is just slightly underdone, as it will continue to cook after it is removed from the liquid.

3. Steaming

Place any assortment of herbs and spices in the bottom of a pot, with 2 inches of water to cover. Place vegetable steamer or bamboo steamer, if available, in the pot. Bring water to a boil, and gently arrange the fish, skin-side down, in the steamer. Steam the fish, covered, until firm and cooked to your specifications. Season with salt and pepper to taste, or ladle the steaming liquid over the fish for extra flavor. Practically any fish is ideal for steaming, which is the cleanest, most healthful choice for fish preparation.

Try these interesting herb and spice combinations, or make up your own:

- **Thai flavors:**
¼ cup fresh mint leaves	*1 garlic clove, sliced*
¼ cup fresh cilantro	*1 tablespoon sliced gingerroot*
A pinch red pepper flakes	*1 lime, sliced*
1 tablespoon honey	

- **Italian influence:**
2 garlic cloves, sliced	*1 teaspoon dried oregano*
2 plum tomatoes, sliced	*⅓ cup white wine*
1 sprig fresh rosemary	

Serve fish prepared with these seasonings with a green salad and some Italian olives.

- **Indian aromatics:**
  1 tablespoon curry powder   *1 scallion, coarsely chopped*
  1 tablespoon sliced gingerroot   *¼ teaspoon mustard seeds*
  1 garlic clove, sliced   *¼ teaspoon fennel seeds*

4. "En Papillote"

This French technique is perfect for cooking fish, because it allows the fish to steam in its own juices. It's also great for medallions or fillets.

All you do is wrap the fish, plus any fresh herbs you have on hand, in parchment paper and bake. Start by folding a large rectangle of parchment paper in half. With scissors, cut the folded paper into half a heart shape, starting at the top of the fold and cutting toward the bottom. Open the paper outward and place fish and herbs on the bottom half of the heart. Fold the top half over, then fold and crimp the edges all the way around, starting at the top of the heart and finishing at the bottom with a twist of the tail of the crimped paper. Don't fold the paper too close to the fish so that there will be enough room inside the packet for the steam to expand.

Place packet on a baking sheet and put into a preheated 400°F oven for 8 to 10 minutes. To serve, place a packet on each plate and slice or tear the tops open. Serve a wedge of fresh lemon or lime as a garnish.

5. Baking or Oven Roasting

Baking fish is ideal for finishing any fish dish after it has been seasoned, then sautéed or pan-seared. Brown one side of your fillets in a very hot, oiled skillet for about 2 minutes (3 to 4 minutes for thicker cuts, such as bass or tuna). Flip the fish over and place the entire skillet in a preheated 400°F oven, and bake until fish is opaque and firm.

You can also bake the fish completely, without any initial pan-searing. Place a baking sheet in the oven, then preheat it to 400°F. Add your seasoned fish directly to the hot sheet. Flip over after 3 minutes and continue cooking until fish is opaque and firm.

TANDOORI-STYLE SALMON WITH CUCUMBER RAITA

Tandoor is the name of the traditional Indian ovens used to bake bread and roast meats. The rub for this fish has a reddish tone reminiscent of Tandoori chicken. It is mild and unusual in flavor. Raita is the all-purpose yogurt sauce used to cool the palate in spicy Indian cuisine.

An excellent simple accompaniment to this dish is steamed or blanched asparagus, over which some of the raita can be spooned. Follow the meal, if desired, with fresh kiwi fruit or pineapple.

RUB

¼ teaspoon ground cumin
¼ teaspoon curry powder
¼ teaspoon ground coriander
¼ teaspoon paprika
⅛ teaspoon turmeric
⅛ teaspoon black pepper

Four 6-ounce Norwegian salmon fillets
2 tablespoons safflower oil
¼ teaspoon salt

RAITA

5 cups shredded cucumbers
3 cups plain yogurt
¾ cup minced fresh dill, or ¼ cup dried
¼ cup minced mint (optional)
1½ teaspoons ground cumin
1 cup seeded and diced tomato
Sea salt to taste
1 head Belgian endive
Fresh mint leaves for garnish

1. Preheat oven to 350°F. Combine all the ingredients in the rub in a small bowl.

2. Brush the salmon with oil, sprinkle with salt, and coat with spice mixture. Place on a parchment- or paper-lined baking sheet, and roast for 10 minutes.

3. Meanwhile, prepare the raita. In a mixing bowl, stir together all ingredients except for endive and garnish.

4. Arrange endive leaves, pointed tips outward, on serving plates. Place salmon fillets on endive. Top with raita, garnish with mint leaves, and serve.

SERVES 4

SPINACH SUPER SALAD WITH CHILLED POACHED SALMON IN CREAMY DIJON DRESSING

This is a marvelous spring dish when asparagus is in season. Use Pacific or Norwegian salmon steaks, if available. Serve with a first course of Chilled Broccoli and Watercress Soup with a dollop of crème fraîche.

1 teaspoon whole white peppercorns
1 shallot, chopped
1 cup white wine
2 cups water
2 salmon steaks
½ pound asparagus, trimmed
6 cups coarsely chopped spinach
1 tomato, diced

DRESSING
3 tablespoons extra-virgin olive oil
2 teaspoons balsamic vinegar
2 teaspoons fresh lemon juice
1 small garlic clove, pressed
2 teaspoons Dijon mustard
¼ cup buttermilk or plain yogurt
2 tablespoons snipped fresh dill
1 teaspoon dry mustard
Sea salt and freshly ground black pepper to taste

1. Place first four ingredients in a deep skillet over medium heat. When liquid begins to simmer and tiny champagnelike bubbles begin to form, gently place salmon steaks in poaching liquid. Do not boil. Allow salmon to poach for 4 to 5 minutes.

2. Remove from liquid with a slotted spatula and place on a plate, cover with plastic wrap, and chill. Place asparagus in liquid and cook until bright green and tender.

3. Remove asparagus from liquid and shock under cold water to stop cooking. Drain and set aside.

4. Whisk together dressing ingredients in a small bowl.

5. Place mounds of spinach on serving plates and top each mound with a salmon steak. Arrange asparagus over salmon, scatter tomatoes on top, and drizzle with dressing.

SERVES 2

PAN-SEARED YELLOWTAIL IN ROASTED TOMATO SAUCE

This sauce seems complicated, but it is really quite simple and well worth the effort. You can use it with grilled pork chops also. Start the meal with Chilled Cucumber Bisque with Dill and finish it with a simple green salad with gorgonzola cheese or steamed zucchini served in the sauce along with the fish. A perfect company dish.

SAUCE

1 tablespoon pure olive oil

1 tablespoon butter

2 garlic cloves, minced

1 red onion, roughly chopped

¼ cup cooking sherry or white wine

10 medium roasted tomatoes

1 tablespoon rinsed capers

1 seafood bouillon cube, dissolved in
    2 cups hot water

1 teaspoon saffron (optional), or
    ¼ teaspoon ground turmeric

1 tablespoon fresh thyme leaves

Sea salt and crushed red pepper flakes
    to taste

Four 6-ounce yellowtail fillets

Sea salt and pepper to taste

2 tablespoons extra-virgin olive oil

1. Preheat oven to 350°F.

2. In a medium saucepan over medium heat, warm the olive oil and butter. When they're hot, sauté the garlic until it gives off a sweet aroma. Add the onion. Sauté about 2 more minutes. Add sherry, sauté another 2 minutes. Add tomatoes, capers, and broth. Add saffron or turmeric. Cook uncovered 25 minutes, stirring occasionally.

3. To finish sauce, add the thyme. Pour entire contents of pot through a strainer, reserving the liquid. Puree pulp until smooth in a blender. Return pulp and liquid to pot and reheat. Season with salt and red pepper flakes.

4. Season fish with salt and pepper. Place a medium sauté pan over medium-high heat. Add olive oil and heat another minute. Sear yellowtail 2 minutes per side, then place on a lightly oiled baking sheet and roast 5 to 7 minutes, depending on thickness of the fillets.

5. To serve, ladle sauce into centers of plates and top with fish.

SERVES 4

SALMON ON WILTED GREENS WITH CUCUMBER RELISH

This is a nice option when company comes to lunch or supper. The relish is your salad, nicely disguised but nonetheless full of life, enzymes, and nutrition. Start the meal with Summer Corn Chowder. Serve the entree with white wine, if desired, and finish with a platter of Strawberries and Cream.

RELISH

2 cucumbers, peeled if waxed, seeded, and cut into ¼-inch cubes

½ red bell pepper, seeded and chopped into ¼-inch pieces

¼ cup roughly chopped fresh cilantro

2 avocados, peeled, seeds removed, cut into ¼-inch cubes

Juice of 2 limes

½ jalapeño, seeded and chopped

1 garlic clove, minced

1 tablespoon apple cider vinegar

1 tablespoon honey

1 tomato, chopped into ¼-inch cubes

Four 6-ounce salmon fillets

Sea salt and pepper to taste

2 tablespoons olive oil

GREENS

¼ cup olive oil

2 cups arugula

2 cups spinach leaves

Sea salt and pepper to taste

1. Preheat oven to 350°F.

2. Season salmon with salt and pepper. Set aside.

3. Make the relish: In a mixing bowl, combine relish ingredients and toss gently to mix well. Adjust seasoning and set aside.

4. In a medium sauté pan, sear the salmon in olive oil over medium-high heat. Cook 2 minutes on each side. Place in an ovenproof baking dish, roast in the oven for about 4 minutes, or if you prefer to save energy, cook 4 minutes longer in skillet. (The salmon will be slightly crustier skillet-cooked.)

5. For the greens, wipe out the sauté pan (or use a separate skillet) and add oil, arugula, and spinach. Sauté over high heat until greens are wilted, 2 to 3 minutes. Season with salt and pepper.

6. To serve, place a mound of spinach in the center of each plate. Top with salmon and then relish.

SERVES 4

SEA BASS WITH SWISS CHARD AND RED PEPPER SAUCE

Complement this dish with steamed broccoli or a green salad. Finish with sliced Comice pears in a nutmeg-flavored cream.

2 garlic cloves, minced

1 tablespoon butter

2 tablespoons olive oil

1 tomato, cubed and seeded

2 red bell peppers, put through juicer or blender

½ cube fish bouillon

¼ cup water

2 tablespoons fresh lemon juice

1 tablespoon chopped fresh mint

Four 6-ounce sea bass fillets

Sea salt and pepper to taste

4 cups chopped Swiss chard

Sea salt and black pepper to taste

1. Preheat oven to 350°F.

2. In a medium skillet sauté the garlic in butter and oil over medium heat until soft, about 1 minute. Add chopped tomato. Sauté 1 minute, then add red pepper juice, bouillon, and water. Cook for 5 minutes. Remove from heat. Stir in lemon juice and mint and adjust seasonings. Set aside.

3. Rub fillets with salt and pepper. In a sauté pan over medium-high heat, sauté fish in oil until browned on one side. Place in a baking dish in the oven and cook 6 minutes.

4. Wipe out the sauté pan and add the chard. Sauté 3 minutes and adjust seasonings.

5. Serve the fish on a bed of chard. Drizzle red pepper sauce around chard to create a red ring and serve immediately.

SERVES 4

OVEN-ROASTED SNAPPER WITH TOMATOES AND ASPARAGUS

Serve this elegant dish in the spring when asparagus is fresh and affordable. Serve with a classic green salad. For a first course, try Herbed Artichoke Soup with Kale.

4 snapper fillets
Sea salt and black pepper to taste
5 tablespoons olive oil
3 garlic cloves, minced
2 shallots, minced
Splash of white wine, if desired
¼ cup coarsely chopped fresh basil

4 plum tomatoes, diced
10 asparagus spears
1 fish bouillon cube, dissolved in 2 cups hot water
3 cups spinach leaves, chopped
Salt and white pepper to taste

1. Preheat oven to 350°F.

2. Season snapper fillets with salt and pepper. Put a large skillet over high heat and add 2 tablespoons of olive oil.

3. Sear on one side only, about 1½ minutes. Remove from skillet and drain on a paper towel.

4. Wipe out skillet and place over medium heat. Add 2 tablespoons olive oil, garlic and shallots. Sauté 2 minutes. Add wine, basil, and tomatoes. Add asparagus. Continue cooking another minute, then add the fish stock.

5. Arrange the snapper fillets, raw side down, in a baking dish. Roast in the oven for 8 minutes.

6. Meanwhile, add 2 cups water to a medium skillet and bring to a boil. Add spinach and cook for 30 seconds, then drain off water. Add remaining tablespoon olive oil to spinach and return to heat. Sauté 1 minute and season with salt and pepper to taste.

7. To serve, place a mound of spinach in the center of each plate. Place a piece of fish on top, season sauce with salt and white pepper, and spoon sauce and vegetables over the fish.

SERVES 4

GRILLED HALIBUT IN MANGO BARBECUE SAUCE

This Caribbean-inspired dish is one of those entrees that sounds complicated but is actually simple. It does take a little time, because the sauce must cook 45 minutes to reduce. Halibut is an elegant, special-occasion fish, and we think this recipe is perfect for just that.

Serve with Roasted Pepper and Corn Salsa and grilled zucchini, onions, and red peppers, which you can also brush with sauce.

½ *white onion, quartered*

2 *mangoes, peeled, fruit sliced from seed*

1 *whole jalapeño pepper*

2 *roasted red bell peppers (page 39)*

2 *tomatoes, quartered*

½ *tablespoon ground allspice*

½ *tablespoon ground cinnamon*

½ *tablespoon ground coriander*

½ *tablespoon ground cumin*

¼ *cup brown rice syrup*

¼ *cup molasses*

¼ *cup honey*

3 *garlic cloves*

1 *cup red wine vinegar*

4 *medium sized halibut steaks*

1. Place the onion, mango, and peppers in a heavy medium saucepan over medium-high heat. Cook, stirring occasionally, for 10 minutes. Add remaining ingredients, lower heat and cook 45 more minutes, continuing to stir occasionally.

2. Strain the sauce through a fine sieve and reserve liquid. Place half the pulp in a blender or food mill and puree until smooth. Repeat with remaining pulp. Add reserved liquid as needed to get the blender moving. Season with salt to taste.

3. Coat fish in barbecue sauce and grill each side 3 to 4 minutes, basting constantly with additional sauce. Season with salt and pepper to taste.

SERVES 4

SAUTÉED SHRIMP IN SWEET CORN PUREE

Serve with Mesclun Salad with Sun-Dried Tomatoes and Oil-Cured Olives or a simple steamed green vegetable over which you can ladle the sauce for a heavenly one-dish meal.

SAUCE

1 tablespoon butter

1 tablespoon extra-virgin olive oil

1 garlic clove

½ red bell pepper, seeded and diced

¼ teaspoon cayenne

3 ears cooked corn, kernels removed, or 1½ cups frozen corn kernels

1 cup chicken or vegetable broth

½ cup buttermilk

2 tablespoons chopped fresh Italian parsley

Juice of 1 lime

1 tablespoon honey

Sea salt and pepper to taste

SHRIMP

1 pound shrimp, peeled and deveined

Sea salt and black pepper to taste

2 tablespoons butter

½ tomato, seeded and diced

1 tablespoon chopped fresh Italian parsley

1. In a heavy medium saucepan, melt butter with the olive oil over medium heat. Add garlic and sauté 1 minute. Add pepper and cayenne, and cook for 1 minute. Add corn kernels, broth, and buttermilk. Cook for about 20 minutes, stirring occasionally. Turn heat to low and add parsley, lime juice, honey, and salt and pepper. Place the sauce in a blender and puree. Return puree to the pot.

2. Season shrimp with salt and pepper. In a medium skillet melt the butter over medium heat and add shrimp. When shrimp are pinkish, after about 1½ minutes, add tomato and parsley. Stir together, then remove from heat. Serve the shrimp on individual plates on top of sweet corn puree.

SERVES 4

Food for Thought:

WHICH FISH SHOULD YOU BUY?

The following list comprises not only fish that is advisable to eat, but fish choices that are highest in omega three fatty acids and are generally caught from the purest and cleanest waters (including farmed fish). Because of the predominantly low fat and low cholesterol content of these seafoods, there are only traces of toxic residues, if any at all. Enjoy these seafoods liberally, of course, avoiding fried versions.

- dover sole
- dungeness crab
- flounder
- grouper
- halibut
- mahimahi

- orange roughy
- monkfish
- salmon
- red salmon
- sea bass
- shrimp

- snapper
- yellowtail
- trout
- tuna
- canned tuna

Because the following choices often come from unclean waters and/or are infected with parasites, they are not desirable choices for optimum health. If you do go for these fish once in a while, be sure they are farm-raised or as fresh as possible, and not fried.

- freshwater bass
- catfish
- cod
- lobster

- shark
- swordfish
- perch
- eel

- clams
- mussels
- scallops

SPICY SHRIMP QUESADILLAS

Serve this delectable dish with warm Zucchini and Spinach Salad. It also makes a lovely accompaniment to any cream soup. Always cook shellfish the day you buy it, even if you refrigerate it a day or so before eating it. It has a very short shelf life.

6 ounces large shrimp

2 tablespoons olive oil

1 teaspoon minced garlic

1 teaspoon minced jalapeño, seeds discarded

3-ounce ball of fresh mozzarella, sliced in ⅙-inch rounds

Four 10-inch corn tortillas

1 tomato, diced

2 tablespoons chopped fresh cilantro

¼ teaspoon ground cumin

2 tablespoons fresh lime juice

Sea salt and pepper to taste

1. Butterfly the shrimp by slicing an opening along the outer spine, from top to bottom. Rinse out the dark vein and pull off the tails.

2. In a small skillet, heat 1 teaspoon olive oil and sauté garlic briefly. Add jalapeño and cook another 2 minutes, then add shrimp. Cook 2 more minutes, or until pink. Remove shrimp from skillet and coarsely chop.

3. Assemble quesadillas by placing the cheese and shrimp pieces between 2 tortillas. In a fresh skillet, heat half the remaining olive oil and sauté the first quesadilla on each side, for 2 minutes, until cheese is melted and tortilla is crispy. Repeat with second quesadilla. Slice each quesadilla into quarters.

4. Combine tomato, cilantro, cumin, and lime juice in a small bowl. Season with salt and pepper. Drizzle over quesadillas and serve.

SERVES 2

CHAPTER SEVEN
Poultry

HOT MAMA'S CHILI CHICKEN

Sometimes the inspiration for a certain dish will just come in a flash, and all the flavors will absolutely work! At times like these, a cook can truly feel gratified and say "Hot Mama!" This recipe takes less than 30 minutes to prepare.

4 tablespoons chili powder

1 teaspoon onion powder

Seasoned salt to taste

4 boneless skinless chicken breasts, pounded to one-inch thickness

2 tablespoons olive oil

4 thin slices smoked mozzarella

2 teaspoons chicken-flavored bouillon granules dissolved in ½ cup water

Juice of ½ lemon

1 tablespoon tomato paste

1 teaspoon ground cumin

1. Preheat oven to 375°F.

2. Combine chili powder with onion powder and seasoned salt in a pie plate. Mix well.

3. Dip chicken breasts into seasonings on both sides to coat.

4. Heat olive oil in a large sauté pan. Add chicken breasts and brown over medium heat on both sides, 3 minutes per side.

5. Arrange browned chicken breasts in shallow casserole. Top each with a slice of smoked mozzarella.

6. Deglaze pan drippings by adding chicken broth and lemon juice. Bring to a boil over high heat, whisking in tomato paste and cumin. Allow to boil to reduce by one-third and thicken. Drizzle over cheese-topped breasts.

7. Bake in oven for 15 minutes.

**SERVES 2 TO 4, DEPENDING ON SIZE OF CHICKEN BREASTS.
RULE OF THUMB: TWO BREASTS PER MAN, ONE PER WOMAN.**

HOT MAMA'S VINEGAR AND CHILI CHICKEN WINGS

This variation of Hot Mama's Chili Chicken will please all wings lovers. They're just spicy enough, battered enough, and tangy enough to win a prize. Serve as a main course with Warm Cauliflower and Olive Salad. Everybody will love you!

4 tablespoons chili powder

¼ cup whole wheat pastry flour

1 teaspoon onion powder

1 teaspoon ground cumin

1 teaspoon salt

2 dozen chicken wings, preferably the drumettes

4 to 8 tablespoons safflower oil

¼ cup apple cider vinegar

2 tablespoons tomato sauce

2 teaspoons chicken-flavored broth dissolved in ½ cup water

1. Place chili powder, flour, onion powder, cumin, and salt in a plastic bag. Add chicken wings and toss aggressively to coat thoroughly. Refrigerate for several hours or cook immediately.

2. Preheat oven to 375°F.

3. Heat oil in a large Dutch oven. Add chicken wings in batches, and brown until crispy, removing to a paper towel to drain when well browned. Add more oil as needed.

4. In small saucepan, combine vinegar, tomato sauce, and broth. Bring to a boil, and reduce by one-third until it thickens.

5. Place drained chicken wings in shallow casserole. Coat well with vinegar sauce. Bake in oven for 30 minutes.

SERVES 3 TO 4

COUNTRY CHICKEN WITH
ROOT VEGETABLES AND MUSHROOMS

What a wonderful winter meal! With this on your stove, who cares if "the weather outside is frightful." Instead of salad, sip a fresh Carrot-Blush as you prepare this meal and munch on raw vegetables.

1 turnip, peeled and cubed

2 carrots, peeled and cubed

2 celery roots, peeled and cubed

3 parsnips, quartered

1 onion, coarsely chopped

1 leek, rinsed and chopped

1 sprig rosemary, or 1 teaspoon dried rosemary

2 tablespoons fresh thyme, or 2 teaspoons dried thyme

1½ cups chicken broth

1 free-range chicken

Sea salt and pepper to taste

2 tablespoons olive oil

1 shallot, chopped

1 cup sliced fresh shiitake mushrooms

½ cup sliced button mushrooms

1 teaspoon crushed red pepper flakes

2 tablespoons butter

1. Preheat oven to 400°F.

2. Place the root vegetables, onion, leeks, herbs, and ½ cup broth in a roasting pan with a lid. Season chicken with salt and pepper. Place the chicken on vegetables. Place in the oven, partially covered, and roast 1 hour.

3. In a large saucepan over medium flame, heat olive oil. Add shallot and sauté 1 minute. Add mushrooms and sauté another minute, then add remaining broth. Cook about 5 minutes. Add red pepper flakes. Adjust seasoning. Remove from the stove and whisk in butter.

4. Remove chicken from oven. Add any juices from the chicken to the mushroom sauce.

5. Cut up the chicken and serve with the vegetables family-style, in large bowls, ladling the mushroom sauce over each portion.

SERVES 4

CHICKEN BREASTS WITH MOROCCAN SPICES

A different ethnic flavor for chicken. Serve with jicama slaw.

4 boneless, skinless chicken breasts

3 tablespoons fresh orange juice

1 teaspoon honey

2 teaspoons ground cumin

2 teaspoons ground coriander

1 teaspoon ground ginger

½ teaspoon turmeric

1 teaspoon mild or hot chili powder (or a combination)

½ teaspoon cinnamon

½ teaspoon sea salt

1½ tablespoons safflower oil

1. Wash chicken breasts and pat dry. Pound to ½ to ¾-inch thickness with a mallet.

2. Combine orange juice, honey, and spices and salt in a small bowl and mix to form a paste. Cover the chicken breasts with the spice paste, cover, and refrigerate for 30 minutes.

3. Heat a dry skillet over medium heat, then add oil. When oil is hot, add chicken breasts and sauté 5 minutes per side, turning frequently. Paste will brown and caramelize slightly. Add a little water as needed if spices begin to burn.

SERVES 4

TURKEY CHILI

A modern cowboy dish, our turkey chili has robust Southwestern flair. Cole slaw rounds out the meal and calms the palate. The applesauce adds moisture to the meat. This recipe is best when simmered for a long time over low heat. If you are rushing, 30 minutes will do.

1 onion, chopped

1 tablespoon safflower oil

2 garlic cloves, minced

1½ pounds lean ground turkey

1 tablespoon tomato paste

One 16-ounce can Italian tomatoes

½ cup unsweetened applesauce

1 tablespoon Worcestershire sauce

1 tablespoon chili powder

2 teaspoons ground cumin

1½ teaspoons Tabasco sauce, or to taste

1½ teaspoons sea salt

½ teaspoon freshly ground pepper

1 teaspoon dried oregano

½ teaspoon crushed red pepper

2 ounces canned green chilies, drained and chopped

16 ounces cooked kidney beans

1 cup chopped fresh cilantro leaves

1. In a large pot, sauté onion in oil over medium heat until soft. Add garlic and meat. Cook, stirring constantly, about 3 minutes.

2. Stir in remaining ingredients except cilantro. Cover and cook over low heat about 2 hours, stirring occasionally. Garnish with cilantro before serving.

SERVES 4 TO 6

⌒

TURKEY CUTLETS

Ask your butcher for turkey tenderloin. This delicious cut lends itself to a breaded preparation like the following one. Serve after a first course of Opa Schnell's Favorite Italian Vegetable Soup and accompany with Three of Hearts Salad.

2 cups buttermilk

2 teaspoons Worcestershire sauce

2 teaspoons dry mustard

2 teaspoons powdered chicken or vegetable broth

½ teaspoon cayenne

1 teaspoon onion salt

1 teaspoon garlic powder

2 cups turkey tenderloin or boned turkey breast, cut in six ⅓-inch cutlets

Sea salt and freshly ground pepper to taste

1 cup whole wheat bread crumbs*

Canola or olive oil spray for the pan

1. In a shallow casserole, combine buttermilk, Worcestershire, dry mustard, powdered broth, cayenne, onion salt, and garlic powder.

2. Add turkey cutlets, cover, and marinate in the refrigerator for several hours or overnight.

3. Drain cutlets and discard marinade. Put the bread crumbs in a soup plate and season with salt and pepper. Dip the turkey cutlets in the seasoned bread crumbs on both sides and set aside on a plate. Spray a large nonstick skillet with oil. Heat skillet to hot, add the cutlets, and sauté for 3 minutes per side.

SERVES 6

---

*To make your own whole wheat bread crumbs, blend or press dry whole wheat bread into crumbs.

SOUTHERN-STYLE TURKEY STEW

Saucy, rustic, and hearty turkey stew—a feast. The vegetables, lima beans, and black-eyed peas add alkalinity and fiber.

2 tablespoons olive oil

½ turkey breast, bone in

Sea salt and pepper to taste

1 tablespoon minced garlic

½ cup frozen pearl onions

3 cups parsnips, cut into 2-inch pieces

4 carrots, sliced into 2-inch pieces

3 cups shredded green cabbage

3 celery ribs, in 2-inch slices

1 leek, white part only, well rinsed and chopped

⅓ cup frozen lima beans

¼ cup frozen black-eyed peas

1½ cups okra, chopped in 2-inch pieces

1 tablespoon fresh thyme, or 1 teaspoon dried

1 tablespoon fresh rosemary, or 1 teaspoon dried

2 cups chicken broth

1. Preheat oven to 400°F.

2. In a large skillet, heat 1 tablespoon olive oil over medium-high heat. Rub turkey with salt and pepper, and sear, flesh side down, for 10 minutes, being careful not to burn. Remove from skillet and set aside.

3. Add remaining oil to a large soup pot, and sauté garlic until soft. Add onions, parsnips, and carrots. Cook 8 to 10 minutes, stirring occasionally. Add remaining ingredients except for salt and pepper. Place turkey on top of vegetables, cover, and roast in the oven 45 minutes. Season with salt and pepper to taste.

4. To serve, spoon vegetables into individual bowls. Slice the turkey meat, lay it over the vegetables, and ladle broth on top. Serve immediately.

SERVES 3 TO 4

GARLICKY CHICKEN SAUTÉ WITH ARTICHOKES AND CARROTS

This chicken and vegetable dish has the flavors of Provence. Serve with FITONICS House Salad as a first course. A light red or chilled white wine will complement the meal. You can make this several hours ahead and finish cooking 30 minutes before serving.

2 tablespoons olive oil

3 pounds chicken breasts, legs, and thighs

Sea salt and freshly ground pepper

One 10-ounce box frozen artichoke hearts, thawed

2 carrots, peeled and cut in chunks

1 medium onion, coarsely chopped

10 garlic cloves, sliced

¼ teaspoon dried thyme

1 cup dry white wine

Juice of ½ lemon

¼ cup chopped Italian parsley

⅓ cup pitted and halved brine-cured black olives

1. Heat olive oil in large nonstick Dutch oven with a lid. Season chicken with salt and pepper and add to skillet, skin side down, sautéing over medium-high heat, turning once until well browned. Transfer breasts from skillet to a shallow serving dish after 10 minutes. Transfer legs and thighs after 15 minutes.

2. Pour off all but 2 tablespoons of fat from sauté pan. Add artichoke hearts, carrots, onion, garlic, and thyme. Sauté over medium-high heat, stirring frequently, for 15 minutes, or until vegetables begin to brown slightly.

3. Stir in wine and lemon juice and bring to a boil. Cook until the liquid has been reduced to a glaze, approximately 10 minutes.

4. Return chicken to skillet with vegetables. (To this point, the recipe can be prepared ahead and stored in refrigerator for several hours. Bring to room temperature before continuing.)

5. Cover the skillet and cook over medium-low heat for 15 minutes until breasts are cooked through. Remove breasts and continue cooking thighs and legs for 15 minutes longer. Return breasts to pan. Sauté entire dish for 5 minutes over high heat to brown. Stir in parsley and olives. Cook 2 minutes longer.

SERVES 6

CHICKEN MEDITERRANEAN

This easy stovetop preparation gives the impression you slaved all day in the kitchen. If you're looking for a heavier meal that will stick to the ribs for hours, serve over linguine.

2 tablespoons olive oil

One 3-pound chicken, cut in serving pieces, or 2 breasts and 2 legs, and 2 thighs, skinned

2 garlic cloves, minced

¼ pound mushrooms, cultivated or wild (shiitake, oyster), cut in half

1 large tomato, peeled and chopped

¼ cup chopped fresh basil, or 1 teaspoon dried

¼ cup chopped fresh parsley

½ teaspoon dried thyme

¼ teaspoon dried tarragon

¼ teaspoon dried rosemary

¼ cup pitted French or Italian olives

¼ cup white wine

Sea salt and pepper to taste

1. Heat oil in deep sauté pan with a lid. Add chicken and brown over medium-high heat on both sides, 10 to 15 minutes total. Add garlic and mushrooms, and sauté 2 minutes. Stir in tomato, herbs, and olives, add wine and salt and pepper. Stir gently. Cover and simmer 10 to 15 minutes over medium-low heat.

SERVES 3 TO 4

LIME-MARINATED GRILLED CHICKEN WITH AVOCADO-TOMATILLO SALSA

This Southwestern creation makes a perfect summer outdoor feast. Serve with Grilled Corn on the Cob. Instead of salad, snack on crudités and yogurt while chicken grills.

LIME MARINADE

Juice of 3 limes

2 tablespoons olive oil

1 tablespoon minced scallions

1 tablespoon chopped fresh cilantro

1 tablespoon fresh rosemary or 1 teaspoon dried

1 teaspoon sea salt

¼ teaspoon cayenne

1 garlic clove, minced

SALSA

1 jalapeño pepper, seeded and minced

½ white onion, chopped

12 tomatillos, papery husk removed

2 tablespoons extra-virgin olive oil

2 tablespoons chopped fresh cilantro

½ teaspoon sea salt

1 avocado

1 tablespoon fresh lime juice

6 chicken thighs

6 chicken legs

3 chicken breasts, halved

1. Make the marinade: Combine the ingredients in a small bowl. Arrange the chicken in a flat-bottomed dish and cover with marinade, turning the pieces to coat them. Cover and refrigerate at least 1 hour or up to 24 hours.

2. Preheat oven to 350°F. Arrange chicken pieces (remove from marinade) in roasting pan and pre-roast for 15 minutes. Remove from oven and set aside.

3. In a medium saucepan, bring 4 cups of water to a boil. Add the jalapeño, onion, and tomatillos. Boil about 7 minutes, or until tomatillos are tender and skin begins to pucker. Remove vegetables from water with a slotted spoon and chill in a small bowl for 15 minutes.

4. Place chilled tomatillo mixture in a blender with olive oil, cilantro, and salt. Blend until pureed but not totally smooth. Cut the avocado in ¼-inch dice and combine in a mixing bowl with the tomatillo mixture. Stir in lime juice and adjust seasoning. Chill.

5. Cook the chicken: Remove it from the marinade, drain, and grill about 4–7 minutes on each side, depending on the heat of the grill and thickness of the meat.

6. To serve, place chicken on individual plates and serve with a dollop of the salsa.

SERVES 4

QUICK FAJITA "WRAPS"

This quick sauté for "wraps" makes a fun family feast. Vegetarians can substitute cubed tofu or cooked potatoes for the chicken. Wraps are easiest to eat when folded envelope-style. Place filling in a line in the center. Fold up one side to catch the juice, and then roll.

1 yellow or red bell pepper, seeded and
   sliced in thin strips

1 large red onion, thinly sliced

2 tablespoons olive oil

¼ teaspoon cayenne

2 garlic cloves, minced

¼ teaspoon dried oregano

4 boneless skinless chicken breast halves,
   sliced in ½-inch strips

¼ cup chicken broth

Juice of 1 lime

Sea salt to taste

1 avocado, peeled and cut in thin wedges

1 large tomato, cut in thin wedges

¼ cup fresh cilantro, chopped

4 large flour tortillas

½ cup plain yogurt or sour cream, if
   desired

1. Sauté the bell pepper and onion in 2 teaspoons olive oil in a medium skillet over high heat until tender, about 5 minutes. Add cayenne, garlic, and oregano, and sauté another minute.

2. Add the chicken strips and broth. Stir thoroughly and continue to sauté until chicken is cooked and liquid has reduced significantly, about 4 minutes. Remove from heat, season with lime juice and salt, and spoon chicken mixture onto a serving platter. Surround with avocado and tomato slices and garnish with chopped cilantro.

3. Heat tortillas 45 seconds on each side in a very hot skillet. Serve the hot tortillas on the side and let each person make their own wrap. Roll chicken and vegetables in tortillas, adding a dollop of yogurt or sour cream before rolling, if desired.

SERVES 4

SESAME CHICKEN SALAD

This salad is a kid pleaser because it's fun to eat and "tastes like Chinese food."

8 wooden skewers

4 whole boneless, skinless chicken breasts, split

DRESSING

3 tablespoons safflower oil

2 tablespoons rice vinegar

1 tablespoon fresh orange juice

1 tablespoon toasted sesame oil

1 tablespoon soy sauce

¼ teaspoon dry mustard

1 garlic clove

1 tablespoon minced fresh gingerroot

2 tablespoons olive oil

2 cups julienned Chinese cabbage

8 ounces snow peas

8 ounces shiitake mushrooms, steamed

2 cups julienned fresh spinach

4 Kirby cucumbers, peeled and cut in matchsticks (page 40)

2 tablespoons toasted sesame seeds, for garnish

1. Soak skewers for 30 minutes. Slice chicken into ½-inch strips and thread equal number of strips onto each skewer. Arrange in a baking dish.

2. Combine dressing ingredients in a blender, puree, and pour one-quarter over chicken to marinate. Cover, and refrigerate for 30 minutes to 2 hours.

3. In a large stove-top grill pan over medium heat, brown the chicken strips in 1 tablespoon olive oil. Turn to cook evenly, 2 to 3 minutes to a side. Remove chicken and set aside. Stir in cabbage and cook 2 minutes to soften. Remove and set aside. Add remaining tablespoon olive oil to a skillet and sauté mushrooms and snow peas for 2 minutes.

4. Place warm vegetables, spinach, and cucumber in a large mixing bowl. Toss with remaining dressing and place on individual serving plates. Top each salad with 2 chicken skewers. Garnish with sesame seeds and serve.

SERVES 4

SHREDDED CHICKEN SALAD

An exotic chilled salad. Apple adds sweetness and lends a subtle hand to help digest the protein.

6 grilled, baked, or sautéed chicken breast
   halves
1 tablespoon minced green onion
   (scallions)
1 tablespoon minced celery
1 teaspoon dried chervil
½ teaspoon dried basil
1 tablespoon minced fresh parsley
2 tablespoons chopped pecans

½ cup chopped apple
¼ cup shredded, unsweetened coconut
2 teaspoons extra-virgin olive oil
2 teaspoons fresh lemon juice
3 tablespoons yogurt
1 tablespoon mayonnaise
½ teaspoon ground coriander
Herbamare and pepper to taste

1. Shred cooked chicken into strips along the grain, and place in a mixing bowl.

2. Add onion, celery, chervil, basil, and parsley. Add pecans, apple, and coconut.

3. Whisk together remaining ingredients in a small bowl and combine well with chicken.

SERVES 4

Food for Thought:

APPLES

The star player here is the pectin. The equivalent of two large apples a day causes a 16 percent drop in cholesterol levels, attributed to the high pectin levels in the fruit. Pectin forms a sort of gel in the stomach that prevents total absorption of the fats in foods.

THAI LEMON CHICKEN SUPER SALAD

This one-dish Super Salad presents the traditional Asian combination of noodles, vegetables, and a small amount of chicken. It makes a delightful lunch or dinner on a warm day. The black sesame seeds are elegant in this dish, but if your Asian specialty food store doesn't have them, just leave them out or substitute white sesame seeds. Serve with a cold ginger-spiced herbal tea.

8 ounces udon noodles

2 cups snow peas, trimmed

2 cups paper-thin slices savoy cabbage

1 boneless skinless chicken breast, split

2 tablespoons safflower oil

2 teaspoons minced garlic

Juice of 1 lemon

½ teaspoon lemon zest

1 teaspoon black sesame seeds

2 tablespoons tahini

2 tablespoons water

1 tablespoon minced green onions (scallions)

2 tablespoons rice vinegar

2 tablespoons soy sauce

2 teaspoons honey

½ teaspoon minced Thai pepper, or ⅛ teaspoon cayenne

Sea salt to taste

1. Cook udon noodles according to package instructions and drain well.

2. Steam snow peas and cabbage 5 minutes, until tender but not mushy. Remove from vegetable steamer and set aside.

3. In a large skillet over medium heat, sauté chicken breasts in 1 tablespoon oil and 1 teaspoon minced garlic for 2 minutes. Add lemon juice, lemon zest, and sesame seeds. Turn chicken to cook evenly another 8 minutes or so, until it releases clear juice when pressed with a spatula. Remove from heat, reserving cooking juices.

4. In a small bowl, combine remaining oil and all other ingredients except the salt. Add cooking juices to dressing and taste for seasoning.

5. In a large bowl, toss noodles, chicken, and vegetables with dressing to coat well. Serve at room temperature.

SERVES 2

〽️

CURRIED CHICKEN SALAD

This delicious salad comes together in just a few minutes. You can make it even faster by using takeout organic roast chicken.

1 Belgian endive
3 whole boneless chicken breasts, split
2 tablespoons olive oil
¼ cup halved seedless red grapes
Sea salt to taste
2 to 3 cups torn lettuce

DRESSING

1 tablespoon safflower oil
1 tablespoon curry powder
1 tablespoon mayonnaise
¼ cup plain yogurt
1 tablespoon minced green onion (scallions)
2 tablespoons finely chopped Italian parsley
Sea salt to taste

1. Cut off core at base of endive and discard. Slice endive into ¼-inch rings, separate pieces, and place in a large mixing bowl.

2. In a nonstick skillet over medium heat, sauté chicken breasts in olive oil 5 to 7 minutes on each side, or until juice from the meat runs clear when pressed with a spatula. Remove from heat and chill. When the chicken is cold, cut into ½-inch cubes.

3. Make the dressing: Heat oil and curry powder in a small skillet over medium heat for 2 to 3 minutes. Cool slightly and stir into mayonnaise in a small bowl. Add yogurt, onion, parsley, and salt, and mix well.

4. In a mixing bowl, combine grapes, chicken, and dressing with chopped endive and mix well. Season to taste with salt. Serve on a bed of lettuce.

SERVES 4 TO 6

CHICKEN CAESAR SUPER SALAD

This may be one of the easiest ways to help your teenager enjoy a salad.

DRESSING

1 anchovy fillet (optional)
1 garlic clove
1 teaspoon balsamic vinegar
1 teaspoon fresh lemon juice
1 teaspoon Worcestershire sauce
½ teaspoon dry mustard
¼ cup extra-virgin olive oil
¼ cup grated Parmesan cheese
3 tablespoons buttermilk

2 boneless, skinless chicken breasts, split
1 tablespoon olive oil
¼ teaspoon sea salt
Freshly ground pepper to taste
Juice of ½ lemon
1 garlic clove, minced
4 cups romaine lettuce

1. Combine dressing ingredients in a blender and process until smooth. Set aside.

2. Rub chicken with oil, salt, pepper, lemon juice, and garlic. Sauté in a large non-stick skillet over medium heat about 7 minutes on each side, or until the meat releases clear juice when pressed with a spatula. Add a little water if needed to keep the chicken from burning. While chicken is cooking, toss greens with dressing in a large mixing bowl and arrange on individual serving plates.

3. Remove chicken from heat and slice each piece diagonally, into 4 sections. Fan over salad and serve warm.

SERVES 2

CHAPTER EIGHT

Meats

MARINATED PORK CHOPS WITH BLACK BEANS IN A MILD CHILE SAUCE

Spicy, protein-packed he-man food with a Cuban twist. This dish asks for a salad on the side.

MARINADE

Juice and zest of 1 orange

Juice and zest of 2 limes

½ onion, chopped

1 teaspoon dried oregano

1 teaspoon dried coriander

1 teaspoon ground cumin

Four 8-ounce loin pork chops,
    approximately ¾-inch thick

BEANS

2 cups cooked, rinsed, and drained black
    beans

1 tablespoon olive oil

1 teaspoon dried marjoram

Sea salt and ground pepper to taste

SAUCE

2 tablespoons safflower oil

1 white onion, chopped

3 garlic cloves, chopped

4 mild green chilies, seeded and chopped

*5 Roma (plum) tomatoes, peeled, seeded
    and chopped*

1 cup raisins

½ teaspoon ground cloves

1 teaspoon ground cumin

2 tablespoons maple syrup

5 cups chicken broth

2 corn tortillas, quartered

1. Combine the ingredients for the marinade in a shallow baking dish. Add meat, turn in the marinade to coat all sides, cover, and refrigerate. Marinate for at least 6 hours, or up to 24 hours.

2. In a large bowl, combine the beans with the oil, marjoram, and salt and pepper. Set aside.

3. Preheat oven to 350°F.

4. Make the sauce: Place a tablespoon of safflower oil in a medium saucepan over high heat. When the oil is hot, add the onion. Sauté about 30 seconds and add the garlic. Continue to sauté until the onion is golden, another 2 minutes or so. Add the chilies. Cook for another 2 minutes. Add remaining ingredients except for tortillas. Cook, uncovered, over medium heat 30 to 35 minutes.

5. Place tortillas in sauce. Cook another 5 minutes. Remove saucepan from the heat and puree everything, including tortillas, in a blender. Strain through a semi-fine strainer. The sauce should have a thick consistency. Discard the pulp. If the sauce is too thin at this point, return to medium heat and reduce further, another 4 minutes or so.

6. In a medium ovenproof skillet over medium-high heat, sauté pork chops 3 minutes on each side. Place the skillet in the oven and cook until chops are done, 20 to 25 minutes, depending on thickness.

7. To serve, ladle sauce onto 4 plates, adding a generous portion of beans. Top with pork chops.

SERVES 4

ROAST LOIN OF PORK WITH SPICED APPLES, ASPARAGUS, AND BROWN GRAVY

A Sunday lunch menu idea for entertaining those who love the most traditional foods. Serve with FITONICS House Salad.

LOIN OF PORK

One 3- to 4-pound loin of pork

2 large garlic cloves, sliced

2 teaspoons ground sage

Sea salt and freshly ground pepper to taste

SPICED APPLES

5 apples, peeled, cored, and thickly sliced

¼ cup raisins or currants

2 teaspoons Sucanat or date sugar

½ cup apple juice or water

½ teaspoon cinnamon

¼ teaspoon ground cardamom or pumpkin pie spice

ASPARAGUS

1 pound asparagus, trimmed of heavy ends of stalks

BROWN GRAVY

2 tablespoons olive oil

2 tablespoons whole wheat pastry flour

1 tablespoon Gravy Master

2 tablespoons red wine

1 tablespoon Worcestershire sauce

½ teaspoon onion powder

½ cup water

2 cups vegetable broth (homemade or canned, or water and vegetable bouillon)

1. Preheat oven to 350°F.

2. Tuck the garlic slices under the string tying the loin of pork together. Rub loin with ground sage and salt and pepper.

3. Place the roast on a rack in a shallow pan and roast for 30 minutes per pound, from 1½ to 2 hours. Test the internal temperature of the meat with a meat thermometer; it should register 163°F. Remove from the oven immediately and let stand, loosely covered with foil, for about 15 minutes, or until internal temperature reaches 170°F.

4. While the meat is roasting, prepare the spiced apples: Place all ingredients in a saucepan and simmer, stirring frequently, for 10 minutes, until apples are tender. Set aside.

5. Bring water to a boil in a deep skillet. Add asparagus and cook until it turns bright green. Drain and set aside.

6. To make gravy: In a skillet, whisk olive oil and pastry flour over medium heat to form a paste. Whisk in seasonings.

7. Add water and whisk to form a smooth paste. Slowly stir in vegetable broth, whisking continuously to avoid lumps. Simmer to bring to desired thickness, whisking occasionally.

8. Slice pork into serving portions and arrange in center of a platter. Gently reheat spiced apples and spoon along one side of the platter. Place asparagus on the other side of the platter. Spoon a little gravy over all, then pour the remainder in a gravy boat and pass separately at the table.

SERVES 6

Food for Thought:
VEGETARIAN, STRICTLY

For five long years I lived as a vegetarian. I didn't sneak so much as a bite of candy. I ate no meat whatsoever. No ham and eggs. Nary a milk shake. My school lunchbag contained invariably three whole-wheat sandwiches, three apples, three oranges. I was getting all my protein from nuts, legumes, and grains. In my fervor, I didn't mind that classmates laughed and called me "The Health Nut."

Of course I was wrong (which is why I detail my adventure for you). It was too radical. I was a victim of the worst sort of health faddism—the self-directed kind. I had no scientific training for what I was doing. For example, amino acids were lacking in this Spartan diet of mine. I was always bloated and sleepy. Frequently I had gas pains far worse than the headaches I was banishing.

—Jack LaLanne, eighty-four-year old athlete and fitness pioneer. (In January 1997, Jack performed more pushups than the entire Dallas football team starting lineup.)

~~◦◦◦~~

BEAU'S BEEF HASH

One Sunday, after we had popped a banana-date bread pudding into the oven for brunch, our teenage son, Beau, developed this recipe, inspired from a spinach, beef, and egg hash we had once eaten at Joe's Restaurant in San Francisco. While the hash cooked, we whipped up a cucumber-yogurt salad, and shortly thereafter sat down to a delicious feast that you could have for brunch, lunch, or supper.

2 bunches fresh spinach, or two 10-ounce packages frozen
1 tablespoon olive oil
1 medium yellow onion, chopped
½ pound lean ground beef
2 turkey or chicken Italian sausages

¼ teaspoon dried thyme
6 egg whites
Freshly grated Romano cheese
Salt and fresh ground pepper to taste

1. Trim stems from spinach, wash, rinse thoroughly, and blanch for 1 minute in a large pot of boiling water. Drain, squeeze out excess water, coarsely chop, and set aside.

2. Heat olive oil in a large skillet. Add onion and sauté until tender. Stir in ground beef and sausage, breaking up the lumps with a wooden spoon. Cook until meat loses pink color. Add spinach and cook briefly. Stir to combine all ingredients.

3. Add thyme and egg whites, tipping and rotating the pan to distribute egg evenly. Allow to cook, without stirring, for 1 minute, to set. Remove from heat. Stir hash and season to taste with Romano cheese, salt, and plenty of freshly ground pepper.

SERVES 3 TO 4

BOWL O'BARBECUE

Grill these meats and vegetables and toss them in a large ceramic or colorful plastic bowl for serving. Accompany with roasted corn on the cob.

RUB

2 tablespoons garlic powder

2 teaspoons chili powder

Sea salt and freshly ground pepper to taste

MARINADE

½ cup olive oil

1 tablespoon Worcestershire sauce

4 garlic cloves, pressed

4 shoulder lamb chops

4 chicken or turkey Italian sausages

4 halved chicken breasts

2 large red onions, thickly sliced

2 zucchini, thickly sliced on the diagonal

2 red bell peppers, seeded and cut in slabs

2 yellow bell peppers, seeded and cut in slabs

1. Mix together the rub ingredients in a small bowl. Coat the meats and chicken with rub and refrigerate 30 minutes to 1 hour.

2. Mix marinade ingredients in a bowl. Add the vegetables and marinate for 30 minutes to 1 hour.

3. Heat grill to medium intensity. Place meats and vegetables on grill and cook until done, brushing with reserved marinade as needed.

4. Cut chops, sausage, and chicken breasts in thirds and toss them with the vegetables in a bowl.

SERVES 6

QUICK BOLOGNESE SAUCE ON THIN LINGUINE

Prepare this delicious sauce in just 30 minutes. The protein can be lean ground sirloin or ground turkey. Serve with a big FITONICS House Salad. For a vegetarian version, substitute firm tofu for the ground meat and 2 vegetarian sausage patties for the poultry sausage.

¼ cup pure olive oil

6 large garlic cloves, minced

1 large onion, finely chopped

1½ pounds ground beef, turkey, or firm tofu, crumbled

1 chicken or turkey Italian sausage, removed from its casing and crumbled

1½ tablespoons tomato paste

One 8-ounce can tomato sauce

Three 14-ounce cans Italian-style chopped tomatoes

1 tablespoon dried basil

1 teaspoon oregano

¼ teaspoon red pepper flakes or cayenne to taste

2 teaspoons powdered beef-flavored broth, or 1 beef or chicken bouillon cube

Sea salt and pepper to taste

1 pound linguine

1. Heat oil, garlic, and onion in a large saucepan. Sauté over medium heat until onion is transparent.

2. Break ground meat and sausage into saucepan and sauté until it loses color completely.

3. Add tomato paste, sauce, and chopped tomatoes. Stir in basil, oregano, pepper flakes, and broth or bouillon. Mix well.

4. Bring sauce to a boil, reduce heat, and simmer, uncovered, for 10 minutes. Season with salt and pepper to taste.

5. Cook linguine according to package instructions. Drain and serve with sauce.

SERVES 6 TO 8

SUNDAY POT ROAST DINNER

If you use a very lean cut of beef for this recipe, the natural gravy can be served without skimming. This is an "ignore the rules" cozy Sunday night feast. Remember, combining food is a tool, not a do or die rule.

1 tablespoon pure olive oil
1 large garlic clove, crushed
1 medium onion, chopped
One 3-pound lean eye-of-round roast
6 garlic cloves, sliced
1 cup beef broth
1 cup red wine
1½ cups water
1 bay leaf

½ teaspoon dried thyme
1 teaspoon sea salt
¼ teaspoon freshly ground pepper
3 carrots, peeled and cut in chunks
5 small red-skinned or new potatoes, peeled and cut in chunks
10 ounces frozen artichoke hearts, thawed
10 ounces frozen pearl onions

1. Heat olive oil in large Dutch oven. Rub roast with crushed garlic. Add onion and roast and brown meat on all sides. Add garlic slices, liquids, bay leaf, thyme, salt, and pepper.

2. Preheat the oven to 325°F. Cover pan tightly and place roast in oven. Roast for 2 hours, basting occasionally.

3. Add vegetables to pan and return covered pan to oven. Roast an additional 1½ hours, or until meat and vegetables are tender.

4. Remove roast from pan to a serving platter. Slice in thick slices. Serve with vegetables and natural pan gravy.

SERVES 4 TO 6

BEEF TENDERLOINS STUDDED WITH ROASTED GARLIC

Serve this savory dish with Spinach and Endive Salad with Strawberries. For an elegant finish, top with Roasted Beet Relish.

Two 8-ounce beef tenderloin steaks
1 teaspoon freshly ground black pepper
1 teaspoon fresh thyme

1 whole head of garlic
Sea salt to taste

1. Preheat the oven to 400°F.

2. Sprinkle tenderloins with pepper and thyme. Set aside.

3. Place garlic in an ovenproof baking dish and roast for 1 hour. Leave the oven on.

4. Slice the tops off the garlic heads and squeeze the softened garlic into a small bowl. Discard outer membrane.

5. Make horizontal incisions into the center of each tenderloin, creating a cavity large enough to push 1 teaspoon garlic paste into each piece.

6. Sear the steaks in a hot sauté pan until golden brown on each side. Place in oven and roast 10 to 12 minutes for medium rare, 5 minutes longer for well done.

7. Season with salt immediately upon removing from oven and serve right away.

SERVES 4

SHREDDED BEEF FOR
TACOS, BURROS, AND ENCHILADAS

Traditionally, this dish would be prepared with chuck steak. Flank or round steak, the leanest cuts of beef, are used here instead.

2½ pounds flank steak or round steak

½ cup apple cider vinegar

3 cups water or beef bouillon

2 onions, sliced

2 tablespoons minced dried onion

3 garlic cloves, minced

1 teaspoon garlic powder

1 teaspoon ground cumin

1 teaspoon sea salt

1. Trim any visible fat from steak. Place in a Dutch oven or Crockpot with remaining ingredients and cover.

2. Cook all day in Crockpot on high (7 to 8 hours) or 2 to 3 hours in a 325°F oven. Beef is ready when it falls apart easily when tested with a fork.

3. Remove meat from broth and shred it with two forks. Cover and refrigerate. Refrigerate broth to allow fat to come to the surface. Skim solid fat off top of broth and save to use in Red Chile Sauce (recipe follows).

4. Prepare Red Chile Sauce. Reheat the meat in the Chile Sauce with beans for Red Chile Burros. Or use meat cold in tacos or taco salads (see recipes that follow).

SERVES 8 TO 10

RED CHILI SAUCE

Powdered red chiles vary in intensity of heat. The New Mexican chile is the most intense. California chile powder is milder.

3 tablespoons all-purpose flour

3 tablespoons olive oil

1 teaspoon ground cumin

2 to 4 tablespoons chili powder (from California or New Mexico)

2 cups water or broth from beef plus water to equal 2 cups

1 teaspoon garlic powder

½ teaspoon salt

½ teaspoon oregano

1. In a small saucepan over medium heat, mix flour and oil. Stir until smooth.

2. Add cumin and chili powder, stir briefly, then add water or beef broth.

3. Add remaining ingredients.

4. Reduce heat and simmer uncovered, stirring frequently, until thick enough to coat a spoon.

5. Mix with shredded beef and/or beans.

SERVES 8 TO 10

How to Assemble a Burro

When beans, shredded beef, and Red Chili Sauce are prepared and you're ready to eat, it's time to assemble the burro. You will need the large-size flour tortillas, normally used for burritos. Lie a tortilla flat on your work surface. In the center of the tortilla, place ¼ cup of shredded beef, 3 tablespoons of Red Chili Sauce, and ¼ cup of beans. Fold sides of tortilla in toward filling and then roll envelope-style. Place on a hot skillet over medium heat for 30 seconds to 1 minute per side to toast. Watch carefully to avoid overtoasting. Serve with a big salad.

SHREDDED BEEF TACOS

If you are going to mix proteins with starches, this combination is a good choice. Because the taco shells are made from corn, they're far less heavy than bread.

6 taco shells
1 cup shredded beef (page 147)
Grated longhorn or jack cheese

Shredded lettuce
Chopped tomatoes
Salsa

1. Heat taco shells in a 350°F oven for 5 to 7 minutes. Fill with beef, cheese, lettuce, and tomato. Add salsa to taste. Serve with Home-Style Refried Beans.

SERVES 2 TO 3

NEW YORK STEAK SUPER SALAD WITH GOAT CHEESE AND GRAINY MUSTARD VINAIGRETTE

Two 6-ounce New York strip steaks
Salt and pepper to taste
8 cups mesclun greens
2 tomatoes, roughly chopped
1 pear cut in ¼-inch dice
¼ cup chevre (goat cheese)
¼ cup chopped walnuts

1 tablespoon walnut oil
¼ cup extra-virgin olive oil
3 tablespoons grainy mustard
Juice of ½ lemon
1 teaspoon cracked black pepper
¼ teaspoon sea salt

1. Sear steaks in a skillet over medium-high heat 4 minutes on each side. Sprinkle with a little salt and pepper, slice into ¼-inch strips, and set aside.

2. In a large bowl, toss together the greens, tomatoes, pear, cheese, and walnuts.

3. Make the dressing by combining the oils, mustard, lemon juice, pepper, and salt. Whisk or blend to emulsify. Drizzle vinaigrette over salad greens and toss well. Finally, toss in steak and serve.

SERVES 4

PART FOUR

Vegetarian
Power Meals

CHAPTER NINE
Tofu Entrees

NACHO CASSEROLE

A friend who's always far ahead of her time developed this recipe to serve to her vegetarian family back in the seventies. Today this economical dish is still a wonderful family option; children and husbands adore it, as do even the most reluctant eaters. It is also a fantastic party dish. Serve in a bowl with Jicama Slaw or steamed carrots tossed in olive oil and maple syrup. No one *ever* guesses this casserole contains tofu!

1 teaspoon olive oil

1 pound crumbled firm tofu

2 cups chopped onions

½ teaspoon ground cumin

½ teaspoon oregano

Dash of cayenne

10 ounces defrosted frozen or fresh corn kernels

One 15-ounce can black beans, drained (optional)

One 16-ounce jar hot or mild salsa

One 4-ounce can diced green chilies

1 dozen corn tortillas

1½ cups grated low-fat or soy cheddar cheese

2 tablespoons low-fat sour cream

2 tablespoons water

¼ cup sliced black olives

1. Heat the olive oil in a wide skillet over medium heat. When it's hot, sauté crumbled tofu with onions and seasonings for 5 minutes. Set aside. Preheat oven to 350°F.

2. Combine corn, beans, salsa, and chilies in medium bowl.

3. Cut tortillas in 2-inch wedges. In a 9-inch square overproof casserole dish, begin layering half the tortillas, then half the tofu mixture, then half the bean mixture, and half the cheese. Repeat layering, ending with the cheese.

4. In a small bowl, whisk together sour cream and water. Drizzle over top of casserole. Top with black olives. Bake for 25 minutes.

SERVES 4 TO 6

Food for Thought:

SOY FOODS

When the spirit moves you toward a vegetarian meal, replace animal proteins with soy foods, such as tofu.

• Soy foods are excellent sources of protein, calcium, magnesium, iron, zinc, copper, phosphorus, folic acid, and B vitamins.

• Soy foods contain negligible amounts of saturated fat, as opposed to animal protein sources.

• Soy foods have no cholesterol. When farmers wish to *lower* the cholesterol and saturated fat in livestock meat, they add soy to the feed.

• Soy foods lower the risk of heart disease and cancer.

• Soy foods are alkaline; they help bring the blood to the healthiest, slightly alkaline condition by neutralizing the acids that accumulate from meat, dairy, coffee, refined wheat, and sugar.

• Soy foods are inexpensive, 1 pound of tofu costs less than $2.00 and can feed a family of four.

• Soy foods come in many palatable and useful forms: soft, firm, and marinated tofu tempeh, okara and tofu burgers, tofu hot dogs, yogurt, cheese, and ice "bean."

• Soy foods are versatile in cooking: they can be the basis for soups, dips, sandwiches, and stir-fries, and they provide excellent substitutes for scrambled eggs and meat in spaghetti sauce, chili, and casseroles. (See Nuovo Bolognese Sauce and Nacho Casserole, pages 157 and 153.)*

For a wide variety of traditional American food preparations using tofu as a substitute for meat and dairy, see Marilyn Diamond, "Instead of Meat," The American Vegetarian Cookbook (New York: Warner Books, 1990), pp. 100–119.

SPICY TOFU AND RICE NOODLE "BOWL"

A light and satisfying "bowl" meal. Mirin, an Asian cooking sherry, is available in natural food stores and some supermarkets. Arrowroot is a natural thickening agent, which is also available in natural food stores.

½ pound firm tofu

1 bunch green onions (scallions)

4 cups coarsely chopped chard

3 cups bean sprouts

One 8-ounce package rice noodles

4 cups water

1 tablespoon vegetarian broth (powder)

One 1-inch piece gingerroot, pressed

2 garlic cloves, pressed

3 drops Chinese chili sauce, or ¼ teaspoon cayenne (optional)

½ teaspoon toasted sesame oil

1 tablespoon apple cider vinegar

1 tablespoon mirin

2 tablespoons miso paste

1 tablespoon arrowroot

2 tablespoons cold water

1. Cut tofu in ½-by-1-inch strips. Slice green onions, including 2 inches of green, and set aside, keeping the green separate. Set vegetables aside.

2. Cook rice noodles according to package directions. Drain, rinse under cold water, and set aside.

3. Combine water, powdered broth, pressed ginger and garlic, chili sauce, sesame oil, vinegar, and mirin in a wok or medium soup pan. Bring to a boil. Add tofu, onion (white part), chard, and bean sprouts. Return to a boil, reduce heat to medium, cover and simmer for 5 minutes.

4. Stir in rice noodles.

5. Remove ¼ cup broth from wok. Dissolve miso and set aside.

6. In a small cup, stir arrowroot in 2 tablespoons cold water to dissolve. Add to soup and boil briefly to thicken. Remove wok from heat and stir in miso mixture.

7. Serve in large bowls topped with reserved green onions.

Variation: For a delicious "Guru's Bowl," ladle soup into large bowls. Top Asian style with broccoli in Arame Sauce for Steamed Vegetables.

SERVES 4

NUOVO BOLOGNESE SAUCE

Some people love to cook a sauce for hours. This one doesn't require it, but will taste better if you do. This sauce easily passes for a meat sauce. Serve over fettucine or use in New World Lasagna.

8 large garlic cloves

1 medium carrot

1 large white onion

¼ cup olive oil

2 tablespoons dried basil, or ½ cup chopped fresh

1 teaspoon dried oregano

Scant ⅛ teaspoon cayenne

Dash of red pepper flakes

2 teaspoons vegetarian "beef broth" powder

2 vegetarian sausage patties

6 veggie burgers (tempeh or tofu burgers are preferable to grain burgers)

One 28-ounce can crushed tomatoes, including juice

Three 14-ounce cans diced tomatoes, including juice

1 vegetable bouillon cube

1 cup red wine

2 tablespoons onion flakes

1 tablespoon onion powder

Freshly ground pepper to taste

1. Mince garlic and carrot. Chop onion. Heat the oil in a wide skillet, and sauté the vegetables in hot oil with basil, oregano, cayenne, pepper flakes, and "beef broth" powder, stirring for 5 minutes. Add crumbled or coarsely ground veggie burgers and sausage and continue sautéing 5 more minutes.

2. Stir in remaining ingredients and bring to a boil. Simmer uncovered for 45 minutes to 3 hours, stirring occasionally. Adjust seasonings. (Do not add salt, since most veggie burgers contain plenty.)

MAKES APPROXIMATELY 8 CUPS

ᏜᎧ

NEW WORLD LASAGNA

With FITONICS House Salad, this is a fabulous meal. Add Oven-Roasted Rosemary Potatoes to create an exciting vegetarian dinner party.

1 recipe Nuovo Bolognese Sauce (page 157)
1 package lasagna noodles
2 tablespoons olive oil
1 bunch fresh spinach, washed and dried,
*   stems removed*
2 garlic cloves, pressed

BECHAMEL

3 tablespoons olive oil
3 tablespoons whole wheat pastry flour
3 cups soy milk, milk, or half-and-half
¼ teaspoon nutmeg
¼ teaspoon sea salt
Freshly ground white pepper
Freshly grated Parmesan cheese to taste

1. Prepare Bolognese Sauce. While it cooks, assemble other ingredients.

2. When sauce has 30 minutes cooking time left, boil lasagna noodles according to package directions for al dente.

3. Heat 1 tablespoon olive oil in large sauté pan. Sauté spinach and garlic until spinich is lightly colored and just wilted. Set aside.

4. To make bechamel: Heat 3 tablespoons olive oil in same pan. Whisk in flour to form a smooth paste. Add milk in a fine stream and whisk continuously until sauce has thickened. Season with nutmeg, salt, and pepper.

5. To assemble lasagna: Ladle 1 spoonful of bechamel into each of 4 plates. Top with 2 lasagna noodles, folded in half and arranged like ribbons.

6. Top noodles with some spinach and a generous ladle of Bolognese Sauce. Drizzle with bechamel.

7. Repeat the process using only one additional noodle, ending with bechamel.

8. Dust with Parmesan.

SERVES 4

TOFU "WRAP" FILLING WITH BROCCOLI, ONION, AND TOMATOES

A delicious filling for the "wrap" that goes down easily and satisfies you. Enjoy with a salad for a satisfying and cleansing meal.

16 ounces tofu, diced
2 tablespoons soy or teriyaki sauce
1 bunch broccoli
1 tablespoon olive oil

4 garlic cloves, minced
1 medium onion, diced
1 tomato, seeded and diced
3 tablespoons chopped fresh basil

1. Put the tofu in a bowl and pour soy sauce over, tossing to mix. Allow tofu to sit in soy sauce for 30 minutes.

2. Chop the broccoli in ½-inch pieces and drop into a large pot of boiling salted water for 1 minute. Drain and set aside.

3. Heat the oil in a wide skillet, and when it's hot, sauté garlic and onion until translucent.

4. Add the tofu and sauté until lightly browned. Remove from heat and immediately add remaining ingredients. Mix well and season to taste.

SERVES 5

෬ᩔᦙ

GARLICKY BROCCOLI AND TOFU
WITH THREE-GRAIN PILAF

8 ounces firm tofu

1 bunch broccoli, cut into long, thin florets

2 tablespoons safflower oil

2 garlic cloves, minced

4 green onions (scallions), cut into 1-inch slices

SAUCE

4½ tablespoons soy sauce

¼ cup mirin

2 tablespoons rice vinegar

2 tablespoons ketchup

¼ cup barbecue sauce

2 teaspoons toasted sesame oil

2 teaspoons Szechuan sauce or Chinese chili sauce

Three-Grain Pilaf and Peas (page 199)

1. Cut tofu into bite-size rectangular pieces, about ½ inch thick. Set aside.

2. Steam broccoli for 3 to 5 minutes until al dente. Set aside.

3. Heat 1 tablespoon oil in wok or heavy skillet. Add garlic, and immediately toss in broccoli. Stir constantly to prevent garlic from burning, about 1 minute, then remove from pan. Set aside in a holding dish.

4. Combine sauce ingredients in a small bowl and set aside.

5. Heat remaining tablespoon of oil in the wok. Toss in tofu and onions. Shake pan and toss to brown. Spoon in one-third of the sauce. Continue to stir-fry until tofu is cooked and coated.

6. Return broccoli to the wok and gently fold into tofu mixture. Fold in remaining sauce. Cook about 1 minute and serve over Three-Grain Pilaf.

SERVES 4

CHAPTER TEN
Legume Entrees

WHITE BEAN HUMMUS

An interesting departure from the traditional hummus made from garbanzo beans, this white bean hummus has a creamy consistency and flavor that lends itself to dips or sandwich filling. The amount of garlic you add should be determined by your palate. Love garlic? Here's a chance to load up on it. Serve with crudités and chips or pita toasts.

2 to 4 garlic cloves, according to taste

One 16-ounce can Great Northern beans, drained and rinsed

3 tablespoons fresh lemon juice

3 tablespoons tahini

½ teaspoon sea salt

¼ teaspoon cayenne, or to taste

Paprika for dusting

1. Using cutting blade in food processor, drop garlic through chute and process until finely minced.

2. Remove lid and add everything but the paprika. Process until smooth.

3. Scrape into a serving bowl, smooth with a rubber spatula, and dust with paprika.

YIELD 2½ CUPS

Variation: Substitute black beans for the white beans.

⟨∾⟩

HOME-STYLE REFRIED BEANS

This is a healthy version of refried beans, since no oil is used in the mashing step. This is an important staple to keep on hand for children who enjoy Toasted Bean and Cheese Burros.

2½ cups fresh pinto beans
6 cups water
2 bay leaves
3 garlic cloves
1 large onion

1 teaspoon garlic powder
1 tablespoon minced dried onion
1 tablespoon chili powder
½ teaspoon ground cumin
Sea salt and freshly ground pepper to taste

1. Spread beans on a cookie sheet and pick out any small stones or other debris. Place in a colander and wash thoroughly.

2. Put the beans in a large pot with water to cover. Bring beans to a boil. Boil 3 minutes, remove from heat, and allow to sit, covered, for 1 to 4 hours.

3. Drain, rinse, and cover with 6 cups of water. Add remaining ingredients. Return to a boil, cover (leaving lid slightly ajar), and simmer on low heat until beans are very soft, 1½ to 2½ hours. Stir beans occasionally and add additional water, if needed, to keep them covered in water. When they're cooked, set them aside to cool.

4. When beans are cool, remove bay leaves. Place 3 cups of beans and liquid in blender and puree. Return to pot over medium heat. Mash entire mixture with a potato masher to make a lumpy consistency. Adjust seasonings, adding salt and freshly ground pepper to taste.

SERVES 8

TOASTED BEAN AND CHEESE BURRO

6 to 8 tablespoons Home-Style Refried
    Beans (page 162)
1 flour tortilla

3 tablespoons grated Colby longhorn cheese

1. Spoon the beans in the center of the tortilla, then sprinkle grated cheese on top. Roll up envelope-style and toast on hot skillet over medium heat 30 seconds to 1 minute per side. Watch carefully.

SERVES 1

LENTILS AND MACARONI

Lentils are one of the most important components of a vegetarian diet because they supply the iron and zinc otherwise provided by beef. Vegetarian men should eat lentils as often as possible, since zinc is essential for healthy male sexual function. This easy soup is a delicious way to get your essential iron and zinc. It's a perfect choice to serve in Guru Bowls. Eat slowly with a spoon as you reflect on the blessings in your life.

1 cup lentils, rinsed and drained
10 ounces frozen petits pois
1 tablespoon pressed garlic
One 14.5-ounce can diced tomatoes,
    drained

3 cups cooked and drained macaroni or
    orzo
Sea salt and freshly ground pepper to taste

1. In a soup pot, bring water to a boil. Add lentils, peas, garlic, and tomatoes. Return to a boil, cover, and simmer over medium heat for 40 minutes or until lentils are tender.

2. Stir in pasta and season to taste.

SERVES 2

GREEK LENTIL STEW

Lentils are a high-protein legume used in abundance in Mediterranean, Greek, and Indian cuisine. These cuisines, especially the Greek, also rely on lemon for almost every dish. It's used on meats, salads, in soups and stews . . . Lemon is a vitamin C rich fruit, clean and purifying. It's the best natural alternative to strong vinegars. Using lemon frequently is one of the secrets to health in cooking. This dish will make a tasty lunch or dinner entree with a classic Greek salad (p. 169).

2 cups green lentils, rinsed

8 to 10 cups vegetable stock

2 teaspoons ground coriander

1 teaspoon ground cumin

1 tablespoon minced fresh oregano, or 1 teaspoon dried

1 teaspoon fresh thyme, or ¼ teaspoon dried

2 bay leaves

10 ounces frozen chopped spinach, defrosted

4 cups peeled and diced butternut squash, cut in ¼-inch cubes

1 white onion, diced

1 tablespoon olive oil

2 celery ribs, diced

2 tablespoons minced garlic

⅓ cup fresh lemon juice

Sea salt to taste

1. In a large stockpot, combine the lentils, stock, coriander, cumin, and herbs. Bring to a boil, then reduce heat and simmer, partially covered, for 30 minutes.

2. Add the spinach and squash. Cover and simmer another 10 minutes.

3. In a medium skillet, sauté the onion in olive oil until tender. Add the celery and garlic, and sauté until celery is tender. Add mixture to the soup. Season with lemon juice and sea salt and serve in warm bowls.

SERVES 4 TO 6

WHITE BEANS AND SPINACH IN THE WOK

A quick and pleasing accompaniment to grilled chicken or lamb, this dish also can be a main course with corn on the cob, Whole Wheat Sourdough Garlic Cheese Bread, and Grilled Portobello Mushroom Salad.

1 bunch fresh spinach

2 teaspoons olive oil

1 large garlic clove, pressed

*1 14-ounce can Great Northern beans,
    drained*

1 small tomato, diced

Freshly ground white pepper

1 Add spinach, olive oil, and garlic to a heated wok or skillet. Stir to coat spinach with oil.

2. Add beans, stirring to combine with spinach, and heat through. Stir in diced tomato. Season with pepper.

SERVES 4

CHAPTER ELEVEN

Super Salads

YUMMY SALAD FOR LOW-ENERGY DAYS

When you've been living it up or putting out a lot of energy for work, you may have a day when low energy reserves make you feel sour and acidic. This salad is an alkaline fix-me-up. I love to make a big bowl, from which I'll serve myself several times during the day. The energy comes back quickly and the acid feeling dissipates. This salad also makes a cleansing complement to any grilled fish or meat.

DRESSING

Juice of 1 orange

One 1-inch piece of gingerroot, pressed

2 teaspoons almond butter

2 teaspoons honey

2 teaspoons flaxseed oil

1 avocado, peeled, seeded, and diced

1 large navel orange, peeled and diced

3 kiwi fruit, peeled and sliced

6 strawberries, sliced

2 cups sunflower sprouts, chopped

1. Whisk dressing ingredients in the bottom of a large salad bowl until smooth, or combine them in a blender.

2. Add avocado, orange, kiwis, strawberries, and sprouts. Toss well.

SERVES 1

WARM ZUCCHINI AND SPINACH SALAD

Water-packed artichoke hearts in cans are preferable to those packed in oil. They interfere less with the flavors of your dressing and produce a cleaner, lighter salad, as you'll see in the recipe that follows.

8 sun-dried tomatoes

4 medium zucchini, sliced

1 bunch spinach, well washed, stems trimmed, coarsely chopped

1 cup quartered artichoke hearts, drained and coarsely chopped

1 avocado, peeled, seeded, and cubed

DRESSING

2 tablespoons olive oil

2 tablespoons fresh orange juice

¼ teaspoon dry mustard

1 garlic clove, pressed

1. Reconstitute sun-dried tomatoes by immersing them in boiling water for about 5 minutes. Remove and slice. Set aside.

2. Place zucchini in steamer in large pot over boiling water. Steam zucchini for 5 minutes and set aside.

3. Make dressing: Whisk olive oil, orange juice, mustard, and garlic together in bottom of a salad bowl.

4. Toss fresh spinach and steamed zucchini into dressing. Add sun-dried tomatoes, artichoke hearts, and avocado; toss well and serve.

SERVES 3

GREEK SPINACH SALAD

Serve this salad with chicken, use it as a main course with hot pita and black bean hummus, or serve it with steamed artichokes. We use spinach for this salad rather than lettuce to increase the fiber content.

8 cups spinach, stems removed and leaves torn into bite-size pieces

1 tomato, cut into thin wedges

¼ cup chopped fresh basil

1 unpeeled hothouse cucumber, sliced into paper-thin rounds

¼ cup thinly sliced red onion

2 ounces crumbled feta cheese

½ cup kalamata or oil-cured olives, whole or sliced off the pit

DRESSING

2 tablespoons extra-virgin olive oil

2 tablespoons water or chicken broth

2 tablespoons fresh lime juice

1 clove garlic, pressed

5 tablespoons buttermilk or plain yogurt

½ teaspoon Dijon mustard

1 teaspoon dried oregano

Salt and freshly ground pepper to taste

1. Place all the salad ingredients except the cheese and olives in a salad bowl. Top with feta cheese and toss gently.

2. Whisk dressing ingredients in a small bowl until creamy. Pour over salad and toss. Garnish with olives.

SERVES 2

FUSION SALAD OF SHIITAKE, SUN-DRIED TOMATOES, BASIL, AND ARAME

We're crossing Asian ingredients with Mediterranean ones here, and the Szechuan sauce is available in natural food stores.

1 tablespoon extra-virgin olive oil

8 ounces shiitake mushrooms, stems removed, caps sliced

¼ cup vegetable broth

1 large garlic clove, pressed

5 sun-dried tomatoes

¼ cup slivered red onion

⅓ cup reconstituted arame (page 269)

1 butterhead lettuce, washed and torn into bitze-size pieces

Large handful arugula, washed, stemmed, torn into bite-size pieces

½ cup minced fresh basil

DRESSING

¼ cup extra-virgin olive oil

1½ tablespoons apple cider vinegar

1 large garlic clove, pressed

½ teaspoon Dijon mustard

1 teaspoon vegetarian "chicken broth"

2 tablespoons water

1 teaspoon Szechuan sauce

1 tablespoon Bragg's Liquid Aminos

1. Heat oil in a medium skillet. Add mushrooms, broth, and garlic, and sauté over medium heat for 5 to 10 minutes, until mushrooms are tender.

2. Pour hot water over sun-dried tomatoes to cover, let sit for 5 minutes. Drain and slice. Set aside.

3. For the dressing: Whisk ingredients together in a large salad bowl. Add onion, sun-dried tomatoes, and arame.

4. Add greens and basil. Top with mushrooms and toss thoroughly. Serve.

SERVES 3

VEGETARIAN CHOPPED SALAD

With hot Skillet Corn Bread with Spicy Sweet Red Pepper Butter this salad makes a meal!

4 cups chopped romaine lettuce
6 cups chopped iceberg lettuce
2 vine-ripened tomatoes, diced
¼ cup pitted and chopped black olives
1 yellow bell pepper, diced
1 red bell pepper, diced
1 cup grated or cubed jack cheese
1 cucumber, peeled, seeded, and diced
2 cups cooked chick-peas, drained
¼ cup coarsely chopped fresh cilantro
½ cup chopped hearts of palm

THYME VINAIGRETTE

1 tablespoon apple cider vinegar
2 tablespoons fresh lemon juice
¼ cup extra-virgin olive oil
1 garlic clove, minced
¼ teaspoon dried thyme
Pinch red pepper flakes
Sea salt and freshly ground black pepper to taste

1. Combine salad ingredients in a large bowl.

2. Put the dressing ingredients in a blender, blend, and toss with salad.

SERVES 4

TACO SALAD

The yogurt lightens the guacamole here, and gives it a smooth texture and refreshing flavor. The mild salsa is actually the salad dressing. Include the jalapeño to add a kick to the salsa. Children and teens usually love this salad. It's a wonderful way to ensure that they eat their vegetables! This is a meal on its own, or serve with Toasted Bean and Cheese Burros or Red Chile Beef Burros.

4 cups shredded iceberg lettuce
4 cups shredded romaine lettuce
3 cups cooked black or pinto beans
1 cup fresh corn kernels, steamed
¼ cup minced green onions (scallions)
½ cup grated jack or cheddar cheese
    (optional)

SALSA

1 jalapeño (optional)
1½ cups chopped tomatoes
½ cup minced red onion
3 tablespoons minced fresh cilantro
2 tablespoons fresh lime juice
½ garlic clove, minced

GUACAMOLE

½ cup plain yogurt
1 avocado, peeled, seeded, and mashed
½ teaspoon ground cumin
¼ teaspoon dried oregano
¼ cup minced tomato
½ teaspoon chili powder (optional)
Sea salt to taste

4 cups tortilla chips
Chopped black olives for garnish

1. Combine salad ingredients in a large salad bowl.

2. Make the salsa: Cut seeds and core away from jalapeño pepper. Be sure to remove all seeds and ribs. Mince and combine with remaining salsa ingredients in a small bowl. Set aside.

3. Make the guacamole. Combine all ingredients in a small mixing bowl. Mix well.

4. Toss salad well with one-half the salsa, reserving remaining salsa to drizzle over top. Spoon salad onto serving plates and top each with a dollop of guacamole. Garnish with chips and olives and drizzle with remaining salsa.

SERVES 4

VEGETARIAN ANTIPASTO FOR TWO

The thin French green beans called *haricots verts* can usually be found in markets specializing in a wide range of produce—and they add a lovely touch to this healthy antipasto. To make this dish a light meal on its own, add some thick slices of hot whole-grain peasant bread or a thick slab of Italian cheese to each plate.

8 ounces button mushrooms, cut into quarters

1 teaspoon minced garlic

Olive oil

2 red bell peppers, quartered, seeds scraped out

2 Japanese eggplants, sliced on the bias into ½-inch thick pieces

1½ cups haricots verts *green beans, trimmed*

1 cup frozen lima beans or canned cannellini, drained

⅓ cup black Italian-style olives

1 medium tomato, sliced into wedges

1 cup marinated or water-packed artichoke hearts

¼ cup olive oil

3 tablespoons balsamic vinegar

Sea salt and freshly ground black pepper to taste

2 tablespoons minced Italian parsley

1. Preheat oven to 400°F.

2. Sauté mushrooms and garlic in a small skillet in 1 teaspoon olive oil until tender, about 4 minutes. Remove from flame.

3. On a lightly oiled baking sheet arrange peppers and eggplants. Roast for 20 minutes, turning over after 10 minutes to cook evenly. Remove each vegetable as it is cooked.

4. Bring a quart of water to a boil in a large saucepan. Add green beans and cook until they turn bright green and become tender. Drain under cold water and set aside.

5. Steam limas or cannellini 8 to 10 minutes until soft. Remove from heat.

6. Arrange the beans and all the vegetables in sections on a platter or individual plates. Drizzle separately with ¼ cup olive oil and the balsamic vinegar. Season with salt and pepper, garnish with fresh parsley, and serve.

SERVES 2 AS A MAIN COURSE, 4 AS A FIRST COURSE

PROVENÇAL THREE-BEAN SALAD WITH FRESH HERBS

It's easier to make this salad using prepared beans from a can or jar. There are many organic brands now available in natural food stores. The combination of fresh green beans, white navy beans, and red kidney beans makes a beautiful salad. The bay leaves add body to the flavor of the beans. Serve with Spinach Herb Orzo for a light dinner.

8 ounces green beans, trimmed and cut in 1½-inch pieces

3 bay leaves

½ teaspoon sea salt

One 14-ounce can navy beans

One 14-ounce can kidney beans

1 ounce firm goat cheese, crumbled

HERBES DE PROVENCE VINAIGRETTE

¼ cup extra-virgin olive oil

2 tablespoons tomato paste

1 teaspoon minced fresh rosemary, or ½ teaspoon dried

1 teaspoon minced garlic

1 teaspoon fresh thyme, or ½ teaspoon dried

1 tablespoon minced fresh basil, or 1 teaspoon dried

1 teaspoon dried savory

1 tablespoon apple cider vinegar

1 tablespoon fresh lemon juice

1. To cook green beans, drop into 3 cups boiling water with 1 bay leaf and ½ teaspoon sea salt. Boil 10 minutes. Strain and set aside. Discard bay leaf.

2. In a medium saucepan, heat canned beans in their liquid with remaining 2 bay leaves for 10 minutes.

3. Place dressing ingredients in a blender and puree until smooth.

4. Remove bay leaves from beans and discard. Toss beans together in a large salad bowl and coat well with dressing. Chill and serve with crumbled goat cheese.

SERVES 2 TO 4

GRILLED PORTOBELLO MUSHROOM SALAD

This easy-to-prepare yet exotic salad makes a pleasing complement to a grilled steak or simple chicken dish. The mushroom and cheese are strong in flavor and would tend to overwhelm fish.

GARLIC-YOGURT DRESSING

3 tablespoons olive oil

1 tablespoon fresh lemon juice

2 teaspoons apple cider vinegar

1 teaspoon Dijon mustard

1 garlic clove, pressed

1 tablespoon plain yogurt

6 cups cleaned and torn spinach or other fresh tender greens

¼ cup thinly sliced red onion

1 cup coarsely chopped sunflower sprouts

½ cup leek or clover sprouts

¼ cup diced smoked mozzarella cheese (optional)

2 portobello mushrooms

2 teaspoons olive oil

1. Make the dressing: Whisk ingredients together in a large salad bowl. Add greens, red onion, sprouts, and cheese. Toss well.

2. Brush mushrooms with olive oil and grill under broiler for 5 to 7 minutes depending on size.

3. Slice mushrooms on the diagonal, London broil–style. Add to salad and toss gently.

SERVES 4

$\sim$

PAINT BOX SALAD

Frozen vegetables can be used for this salad, but fresh are better. Canned organic beans are highly recommended. This is a popular salad with children. The mixture of colors and textures probably explains why.

DRESSING

1 tablespoon extra-virgin olive oil

1 tablespoon water

1 tablespoon fresh lemon juice

2 tablespoons yogurt or buttermilk

1 garlic clove, pressed, or ¼ teaspoon garlic powder

Salt and freshly ground pepper to taste

2 cups chopped romaine lettuce

1 cup chopped spinach

1 tomato, chopped

¼ cup cooked 1-inch pieces green beans

¼ cup cooked kidney beans or chick-peas

¼ cup cooked corn kernels

Several thin red onion rings (optional)

1. Combine salad dressing ingredients in a small bowl, and mix well with fork or whisk. Beat until smooth.

2. Add salad ingredients to bowl and toss well.

SERVES 1 TO 2

ROASTED VEGETABLE MELANGE

Serve this saucy roast vegetable salad on plates, arranging the vegetables whole or quartered, as you have cut them for roasting. Serve with Lime-Marinated Grilled Chicken with Avocado-Tomatillo Salsa.

DRESSING

¼ cup extra-virgin olive oil

1 tablespoon apple cider vinegar

2 tablespoons fresh lemon juice

2 teaspoons Dijon mustard

2 teaspoons salt

1 teaspoon minced garlic

⅛ teaspoon freshly ground black pepper

2 tablespoons minced chives

½ pound baby asparagus, trimmed

2 leeks, washed and quartered lengthwise

2 pounds small button mushrooms

2 plum tomatoes, quartered

1 zucchini, sliced in ¼-inch rounds

1. Make the dressing by combining ingredients in a blender. Puree and set aside.

2. Preheat oven to 400°F. Lightly oil a baking sheet and arrange vegetables on it. Bake, turning vegetables every 2 to 3 minutes to prevent burning. Remove with tongs as they are done. The entire process will take approximately 30 minutes.

3. Marinate warm vegetables in dressing for several hours before serving.

SERVES 2 TO 4

INDIAN VEGETARIAN PICNIC

The following three salads make a tasty summer lunch or supper. Serve with hot chapatis or nan, traditional Indian flat breads, available in Indian groceries or natural food stores, and Cucumber Raita.

MUNG BEAN AND ONION SALAD

2 cups mung bean sprouts
2 cups chopped tomatoes
½ cup chopped arugula

Juice of ½ lemon
2 tablespoons extra-virgin olive oil
¼ cup chopped red onion

1. Toss together all ingredients in a bowl, cover, and chill until ready to serve.

DILLED MUSHROOM CEVICHE

The mushrooms cook in the acidity of the vinegar as seafood does in the classic ceviche.

2 pints mushrooms, thinly sliced
1 small tomato, thinly sliced
1 tablespoon chopped fresh dill, snipped
2 tablespoons minced parsley
1 garlic clove, minced

2 tablespoons minced red onion
2 tablespoons balsamic vinegar
Dash of nutmeg
Sea salt to taste

1. Combine all ingredients in a bowl and toss gently.

⌒⌒

BASIC INDIAN-STYLE SALAD

This basic green salad with a simple raita dressing is one of our standard companions to the high-protein Power Lunch.

DRESSING

½ cup plain yogurt

¼ cup shredded carrot or cucumber

¼ cup minced cilantro, or 2 tablespoons finely chopped dill

1 tablespoon fresh lemon or lime juice

¼ teaspoon ground cumin

Sea salt and freshly ground pepper to taste

4 cups chopped salad bowl lettuce

½ cup thinly sliced hothouse cucumber

1 medium tomato, diced

1 cup alfalfa or clover sprouts

¼ cup thinly sliced red onion

½ lemon, quartered

1. Combine dressing ingredients in a large salad bowl.

2. Add lettuce, cucumber, tomato, sprouts, and onion, and toss well. Serve garnished with lemon wedges.

SERVES 2

PART FIVE

Soothing
Vegetarian Suppers

CHAPTER TWELVE

Pasta

CURRIED CHICKEN LINGUINE

Predominantly pasta, this marvelous dish is a crowd pleaser. Everyone always asks for the recipe. It combines well with a simple salad.

¾ pound linguine

1 bunch broccoli (approximately 4 cups florets)

2 tablespoons olive oil

2 teaspoons curry powder

1 teaspoon turmeric

1 teaspoon powdered chicken broth

¼ cup water

½ teaspoon onion powder

2 tablespoons green onions (scallions)

2 teaspoons dried basil

2 cups yogurt

2 poached chicken breasts halves, sliced

Salt and freshly ground pepper to taste

1. Cook pasta according to package directions. Drain and rinse under cold water to prevent sticking.

2. Cut heavy stems from broccoli, leaving approximately 2 inches of stem and the florets. Cut florets in thin lengthwise pieces. Steam for 3 to 5 minutes or just until tender. Remove from heat and set aside.

3. Using the pasta pot heat the olive oil. Add curry and turmeric and cook over medium heat for 30 seconds, whisking continuously. Add powdered chicken broth, water and onion powder. Whisk until smooth. Stir in green onions and basil, and cook for 1 minute. Stir in yogurt, remove from heat and whisk until smooth.

4. Add pasta, broccoli, and chicken to pot. Season with salt and pepper. Stir gently to combine with a rubber spatula or wooden spoon. Toss well, cover and chill until ready to serve, at least 1 hour.

SERVES 5

MEDITERRANEAN MACARONI SALAD

This is a pretty, delicious salad you could serve with crusty Italian bread dipped in peppered olive oil for a light evening meal.

8 ounces macaroni

2 teaspoons olive oil

1½ cups cooked cannellini beans

2 boxes frozen spinach, steamed and drained

¼ cup chopped marinated sun-dried tomatoes

¼ cup minced green onions (scallions)

¼ cup chopped fresh basil

2 tablespoons pitted and chopped Kalamata olives

DRESSING

2 tablespoons grated Parmesan cheese

¼ cup extra-virgin olive oil

2 tablespoons fresh lemon juice, or 1 tablespoon lemon plus 1 tablespoon balsamic vinegar

1 teaspoon dried basil

½ teaspoon dried oregano

½ teaspoon dried thyme

½ teaspoon dried chervil

2 garlic cloves

Sea salt and freshly ground black pepper to taste

1. Cook pasta according to package instructions. Drain well and put in a serving bowl. Toss well in olive oil to coat the pasta. Add beans, spinach, tomatoes, onions, basil, and olives, and toss well.

2. Combine dressing ingredients in blender and puree. Pour over salad and combine thoroughly.

SERVES 2 TO 4

PASTA SALAD WITH PESTO AND PEAS

This is a classic pasta salad. The source of the unusual taste is the brief blanching of the basil to make the pesto more flavorful. This makes a great supper with Perfect Tomato Salad with Feta Cheese.

8 ounces pasta shells
4 cups fresh basil
2 small garlic cloves
¼ cup pine nuts

1 tablespoon water
3 tablespoons extra-virgin olive oil
1 box frozen petits pois
¼ cup grated Parmesan cheese

1. Prepare pasta according to package instructions. While pasta cooks, prepare pesto.

2. Bring a small pot of water to a rolling boil. Immerse basil leaves in water for 10 seconds and remove immediately. Shock under ice cold water, then drain well.

3. In the work bowl of a food processor fitted with the metal blade or in a blender, mince garlic. Add pine nuts and water and process briefly. Add basil, and while you're processing, drizzle in olive oil in a fine stream until a thick paste forms.

4. Place peas in a steamer and steam 4 to 5 minutes, until bright green and tender.

5. Remove ½ cup pasta water from pot before draining. Blend the hot water into the pesto. Remove from machine and stir in Parmesan.

6. Drain pasta well and place in a large mixing bowl. Stir in peas and toss well with pesto. Chill briefly until the salad reaches room temperature, and serve.

SERVES 2

TWO PASTAS WITH SPINACH AND CHICK-PEAS

This savory pasta dish was inspired by a Punjabi vegetable dish for spinach and chick-peas from cookbook author Madhur Jaffrey. The sauce is marvelously innovative and bound to please adventurous lovers of pasta and fusion flavors. It makes a wonderful one-bowl supper served with hunks of crusty whole-grain bread to dip in the piquant sauce.

1 bunch fresh spinach

¼ cup olive oil

2 onions, peeled and chopped

One 3-inch piece gingerroot, peeled

4 large garlic cloves

¾ cup chicken or vegetable broth

2 teaspoons turmeric

1 teaspoon ground cumin

⅛ teaspoon cayenne

One 28-ounce can whole tomatoes with liquid

One 14-ounce can chick-peas, drained

1 serrano chile, seeded and minced

¼ cup raisins or currants (optional)

8 ounces spaghetti

1 cup orzo

Sea salt and freshly ground black pepper to taste

Juice of 1 lime

½ cup chopped fresh cilantro

1. Bring water to boil in two pasta pots.

2. Trim stems from spinach, discard any spoiled leaves, wash thoroughly, drain, and set aside.

3. Heat oil in a large saucepan over medium heat. Add onions and cook, stirring frequently until translucent.

4. Cut ginger into small pieces. Puree with garlic and broth in blender or food processor. Add to onions. Cook 5 minutes.

5. Stir in turmeric, cumin, and cayenne, and cook briefly over medium heat. Add spinach, tomatoes, chick-peas, chile, and raisins, and bring to a boil. Cover, reduce heat to medium-low, and simmer 30 minutes.

6. Prepare both pastas in separate pots of boiling water according to package directions for al dente.

7. Stir salt and pepper, lime juice, and cilantro into sauce. Cook 10 minutes.

8. Combine two pastas in a large bowl. Add sauce, and mix gently with rubber spatula, or place pastas in individual serving bowls and spoon sauce over tops of each.

SERVES 4

MILD SZECHUAN NOODLES IN PEANUT SAUCE

Another unusual pasta meal. The fresh julienned cucumber adds a lively taste and texture.

1 cup julienned carrots

½ cup bean sprouts

8 ounces thin asparagus, trimmed and blanched

2 cups julienned unpeeled cucumber

1 pound cooked buckwheat soba noodles

½ cup julienned green onions (scallions)

PEANUT SAUCE

1 teaspoon minced garlic

1 teaspoon minced fresh gingerroot

1 tablespoon minced green onions (scallions)

6 tablespoons smooth natural peanut butter

2 tablespoons soy sauce

2 teaspoons honey

1 tablespoon spicy barbecue sauce

1 tablespoon toasted sesame oil

1 teaspoon dry mustard

½ teaspoon salt

⅓ cup chicken or vegetable stock

2 teaspoons Szechuan sauce (available in natural food stores)

1. Blanch the vegetables by briefly immersing them in boiling water until colors brighten. Shock in cold water and drain well.

2. Julienne the cucumber by cutting it in scant ¼-inch rounds, which you then cut into matchsticks.

3. Combine all ingredients in a large mixing bowl.

4. Make the sauce: Combine ingredients in a blender and puree. Pour sauce over vegetables, and toss thoroughly to combine.

SERVES 2

SPINACH-HERB ORZO

The red pepper flakes give this orzo a nice bite. It's a lovely addition to a vegetable plate.

2 tablespoons fresh Italian parsley

½ teaspoon crushed red pepper flakes

1½ teaspoons dried basil

¼ cup extra-virgin olive oil

1 garlic clove, minced

1 package frozen chopped spinach, steamed and drained

1½ cups orzo, cooked according to package instructions

3 tablespoons grated Parmesan cheese

Sea salt and freshly ground pepper to taste

1. In the work bowl of a food processor, combine parsley, red pepper flakes, basil, olive oil, garlic, and spinach. Process until somewhat smooth.

2. Combine orzo and spinach mixture in a large mixing bowl. Season with Parmesan and salt and pepper to taste.

SERVES 2 TO 3

Food for Thought:

TIME OUT!

For physical stress release, skin rejuvenation, and sore muscles, try this bath sachet instead of bubbles. Listen to soft music. Light candles, let your mind relax, and breathe in warm herbs. You'll find the lavender leaves at a natural foods store.

6 ounces chamomile tea leaves

6 ounces lavender

3 ounces thyme

Use your hands to combine herbs in mixing bowl until well blended. Cut out a 12-inch square of cheesecloth and place a large mound of leaves in the center. Fasten with a rubber band or secure with a string, to create a loose bundle. Toss into a steaming hot bathtub and soak. Reserve remaining leaf blend in tight-fitting glass jar for other relaxing baths.

CAPPELLINI CAPONATA

If you love olives, you'll enjoy this light pasta.

8 ounces angel hair pasta

8 Roma (plum) tomatoes, peeled, seeded, and diced

2 teaspoons minced garlic

1 tablespoon dried basil, or ¼ cup chopped fresh

3 tablespoons extra-virgin olive oil

½ cup sliced Kalamata olives

3 tablespoons capers, drained

Freshly grated Parmesan cheese

Sea salt and freshly ground black pepper to taste

1. Cook pasta according to package instructions.

2. Combine tomatoes, garlic, basil, oil, and olives in a small saucepan. Cook over heat about 4 minutes, remove from heat, and add capers. Toss with pasta and add Parmesan cheese and salt and pepper to taste.

SERVES 2

FARFALLE WITH HERBED SAUCE OF SUMMER VEGETABLES

This rich sauce is full of vegetables and is bound to please healthy eaters. For those who shy away from vegetables but love pasta, they'll find it a pleasurable way to increase vegetable intake. A first course could be FITONICS House Salad.

2 tablespoons extra-virgin olive oil

1 cup chopped green onions (scallions)

2 garlic cloves, minced

½ teaspoon dried marjoram

½ teaspoon dried oregano

4 cups finely chopped broccoli

½ cup carrots, diced

½ cup frozen petits pois

½ cup vegetable broth

2 tablespoons tomato paste

4 cups peeled, seeded, and diced tomatoes, or one 28-ounce can plum tomatoes, drained and diced

Cayenne to taste

¼ cup chopped fresh basil, or 1 teaspoon dried

8-ounce package farfalle

1 teaspoon extra-virgin olive oil

Parmesan cheese to taste (optional)

1. In a wide skillet, heat the olive oil, and sauté the green onions and garlic in it. Add herbs and cook until onions and garlic are tender. Add the broccoli, carrots, peas, and broth, and continue to sauté, stirring frequently. Add the tomato paste, tomatoes, and cayenne to taste. Add fresh basil.

2. Cover and allow to simmer for 15 to 20 minutes. While sauce is simmering, cook the pasta. Stir olive oil into sauce. Drain pasta, transfer to serving bowl, and add sauce. Toss and garnish with Parmesan, if desired.

SERVES 4

෬෨

VERMICELLI WITH EGGPLANT CAPONATA

This is a fabulous simple pasta sauce that you will enjoy serving to guests. Start with Creamy Sorrel Soup and add hot Italian whole-grain bread dipped in olive oil and pepper with a FITONICS House Salad.

1 pound vermicelli or spaghetti

2 pounds (2 medium) eggplant, unpeeled, cut in ½-inch cubes

1¼ teaspoons salt

3 tablespoons olive oil

2 teaspoons minced garlic

2 bell peppers, yellow or red, seeded and diced

¼ teaspoon dried rosemary

¼ teaspoon dried oregano

1 teaspoon dried basil

2 pounds (about 5 large) tomatoes, peeled, seeded, and chopped, or one 35-ounce can Italian tomatoes, drained and chopped

10 Kalamata or other brine-cured olives, pitted and coarsely chopped

2 ounces capers, drained and rinsed

1. Prepare pasta according to package directions. Drain and keep warm.

2. Salt eggplant cubes and let sit for 15 to 30 minutes in a colander. Rinse under cold water and blot dry with paper towels.

3. Combine eggplant and oil in a large skillet with a lid. Cook over medium-high heat, stirring occasionally, until eggplant begins to soften. Reduce heat to medium-low, cover, and cook 10 to 12 minutes.

4. Add garlic, peppers, herbs, and tomatoes to eggplant in skillet. Mix well and cook, uncovered, for 7 minutes. Stir in olives and capers, and cook 2 to 3 minutes longer. If smoother texture is desired, puree half the sauce in a food processor. Serve tossed with vermicelli.

SERVES 6 TO 8

Food for Thought:
FOOD MYTHS

MYTH: FAT-FREE SUPERMARKET ITEMS WILL HELP YOU STAY/BECOME THIN

Fat-free supermarket items are not foods that prevent you from becoming fat. It is erroneous to think that they won't add fat to your body. A nonfat product simply has no "additional" fats or oils added to the recipe. Some other fat-free foods are basically laboratory experiments. The fat component has been removed and replaced with plasticlike chemicals or sugar (in the case of fat-free baked foods). Increasing the sugar to compensate for the chemical balance lost by removing the fat actually makes the product more toxic than it was with the fat left intact. More sugar and less butter is definitely not an improvement, just a change in cast members.

Remember: the closer a food is to its natural state, the more it will aid you in achieving a natural state of health, and a strong, beautiful body.

QUICK VEGETABLE MANICOTTI

A Greek Spinach Salad makes a pleasing first course. Serve with hot whole-grain or handmade Potato Foccacia.

8 ounces manicotti

1 large cauliflower

8 ounces part-skim ricotta cheese or tofu

2 tablespoons water

4 ounces Parmesan cheese, grated

½ cup finely chopped parsley

½ teaspoon Herbamare (page 27)

¼ teaspoon ground white pepper or lemon pepper

One 29-ounce can tomato sauce

1. Preheat oven to 350°F. Cook manicotti in a large pot of boiling water for 3 minutes only. Transfer to a colander and rinse under cold water. Drain and set aside.

2. Remove leaves from cauliflower. Cut cauliflower into small florets. Steam for 5 to 7 minutes or until tender.

3. In a large bowl, combine ricotta or crumbled tofu, the water, half the Parmesan, half the parsley, Herbamare, pepper, and cauliflower. Mix well.

4. Pour half the tomato sauce into a 14½-x-9¾-inch lasagna pan. Spread evenly over bottom.

5. Fill each manicotti shell with the cauliflower mixture. Arrange shells in the pan and top with remaining tomato sauce. Sprinkle with remaining parsley and Parmesan cheese. Bake until pasta is tender and sauce is bubbly, about 30 minutes.

SERVES 4 TO 6

CHAPTER THIRTEEN

Grains

CAULIFLOWER FAJITA WITH CORN SALSA

This healthy fajita recipe has a marvelous corn salsa that makes it ever-so-special. Make a large quantity and serve as a side-dish if any is left over.

CORN SALSA

¼ cup minced onion

1 garlic clove, minced

2 tablespoons olive oil

4 cups fresh corn kernels

3 cups diced red pepper (or tomatoes)

¼ cup coarsely chopped fresh cilantro

3 tablespoons fresh lemon or lime juice

1 teaspoon ground cumin

½ teaspoon sea salt or substitute

¼ teaspoon freshly ground black pepper

8 flour tortillas

2 large tomatoes, cut in wedges

CAULIFLOWER FILLING

2 tablespoon olive oil for sautéing (or ¼ cup broth)

1 small cauliflower, cored and sliced (or combination of 2 cups cauliflower and 2 cups cubed tofu)

1 red onion, sliced

1 yellow bell pepper, sliced

3 tablespoons fresh lime juice

1 teaspoon Herbamare (page 27)

¼ teaspoon cayenne

2 cups coarsely chopped lettuce, or 2 cups alfalfa sprouts

1. Make the salsa: In a wide skillet over medium heat, sauté onion and garlic in olive oil until translucent.

2. Add remaining ingredients in the order given, mix well, and cook briefly, approximately 5 minutes.

3. Make the filling: In a wide skillet, heat oil or broth over medium heat. When it's hot, add vegetables and seasonings, and sauté until crisp-tender, approximately 15 minutes.

4. To assemble: Heat tortillas one at a time on a hot, dry skillet, until just soft and heated through. Layer a line of corn salsa, cauliflower filling, coarsely chopped lettuce, and tomato wedges on each tortilla. Fold up one edge to catch juices and roll, envelope-style.

SERVES 4

Breakfast Cereal Supper:
The Simplest Grain Supper!

This is one of our favorite Soothing Suppers after a busy day that has included a substantial business lunch. We make it interesting by mixing several cereals, which we call the "designer" approach. Each of us designs our own blend, which can include mini-shredded wheat with bran, muesli, honey graham granola, shredded oats, brown rice puffs, or wheat flakes. The result always ends up being different and satisfying. Add the chopped dried fruit and banana for enzymes and fiber, and the cinnamon to relax your tired muscles, and choose vanilla soy milk for flavor and the healthful alkalinity it brings to the meal.

2 or 3 kinds of cereal, preferably those high in fiber and without refined sugar

Raisins, chopped black mission figs, or dates to taste

Cinnamon to taste

Sliced banana

Dairy milk, rice milk, or vanilla soy milk to taste

Design your favorite blend, mix well, and allow to stand 1 or 2 minutes for flavors to combine. Serve with a mug of hot cinnamon-flavored herbal tea or hot vanilla or carob soy milk.

The "Wrap" for Weight Loss and Health

Take any vegetable salad you enjoy, mix with steamed vegetables of your choice, and roll in hot whole wheat tortillas. Use condiments, such as salsa or mustard. Have two or three. You'll feel great, and

YOU'LL LOSE WEIGHT!

BROWN RICE "KOJI"

When your tummy wants a rest, turn to this old-fashioned winter stew. Our naturopathic doctor recommends eating this *Koji* (Japanese for stew) when you don't feel well. It's slow-cooked for hours so your digestive tract doesn't have to do any work; the fiber is broken down and the minerals are mostly in the broth. Include the broccoli leaves for added nutrients. Be sure to take your enzymes!

8 cups water

2 cups brown rice

2 carrots, scrubbed, but not peeled, and sliced

2 cups chopped green cabbage

2 celery ribs, sliced

4 garlic cloves, minced

4 green onions (scallions), sliced

1 onion, chopped

2 zucchini, sliced

2 broccoli stalks, peeled at heavy end and sliced on diagonal ⅛ inch thick

Kernels from 1 ear of corn

3 tablespoons powdered vegetable broth

1. Bring water to a boil in a large soup pot. Add all ingredients and stir to combine.

2. Cook over low heat for 2 to 3 hours to release the vitamins and minerals into the broth. Serve in warm soup bowls.

SERVES 4

QUICK AND CREAMY BROWN RICE RISOTTO

This healthy version of a traditional Northern Italian main course dish is simple to prepare. Try exotic mushrooms as a variation. Serve with steamed green beans or Curried Cole Slaw.

1½ cups instant brown rice
1 teaspoon olive oil
½ cup chopped onion
1 cup chopped mushrooms

½ cup tomato sauce
¼ cup grated Parmesan cheese
Sea salt and freshly ground pepper to taste

1. Cook rice in a saucepan according to package directions. When it's cooked, fluff with fork and cover.

2. While rice cooks, heat oil and onion together in a nonstick skillet. Sauté, adding 1 to 2 tablespoons water, for 3 minutes. Stir in mushrooms and cook, stirring occasionally for an additional 3 minutes.

3. Stir in cooked rice, tomato sauce, and Parmesan. Mix well and continue to cook several minutes, stirring, until rice becomes sticky and has a gluttony texture. Season to taste and cook through for 2 minutes.

SERVES 2

THREE-GRAIN PILAF AND PEAS

Delicious with Cucumber Raita and hot chapatis.

1 tablespoon olive oil

1 onion, minced

2 garlic cloves, minced

3 cups vegetable broth

½ cup bulgur

½ cup long-grain brown rice

½ cup pearl barley

Dash of cayenne or Tabasco

1 teaspoon ground coriander

¼ cup minced fresh parsley

½ cup frozen petits pois, defrosted

1. Place oil, onion, and garlic in a large skillet with a lid. Cook over medium heat 5 minutes, stirring occasionally.

2. Add broth, bulgur, rice, and barley, then bring to a boil. Add cayenne, coriander, and parsley, reduce heat to low, cover, and simmer 40 minutes.

3. Take the skillet off the heat and stir in the peas. Allow pilaf to stand, covered, for 10 minutes. Lift cover, fluff with a fork, and adjust seasonings.

SERVES 4 TO 6

TUSCAN RICE AND VEGETABLES

This delightful grain salad is perfect for a picnic buffet. Serve with Greg's Excellent Gazpacho and Chicken Breasts with Moroccan Spices.

2 cups water

1 cup short-grain brown rice or brown Basmati rice

Pinch of salt

1½ cups scraped and diced carrots

2 cups shelled fresh or thawed frozen baby lima beans

2 cups frozen petits pois

3 tablespoons olive oil

Sea salt and freshly ground pepper to taste

¼ cup finely chopped fresh basil

¼ cup chopped Kalamata olives

1. Combine water, rice, and salt in a heavy medium saucepan. Bring to a boil, stir once, cover, and simmer over very low heat until all of the water is absorbed, about 45 minutes. Remove from heat and fluff with a fork. Set aside.

2. Place carrots and lima beans in a vegetable steamer over boiling water and steam for 5 minutes. Add peas and steam an additional 3 minutes. Remove steamer tray with vegetables from steamer, and set aside while vegetables cool.

3. Combine olive oil and salt and pepper in a small bowl. Beat with a whisk or fork.

4. Combine rice and steamed vegetables in a large bowl. Add dressing and finely chopped basil. Stir in Kalamata olives and mix well. Adjust seasonings.

SERVES 4

Note: May be prepared one day in advance. Serve cold or bring to room temperature before serving.

TEX-MEX QUINOA SALAD

Great with Toasted Bean and Cheese Burros.

DRESSING

2 garlic cloves, crushed
2 tablespoons fresh lemon juice
¼ cup extra-virgin olive oil
2 tablespoons minced fresh cilantro
Sea salt and freshly ground pepper to taste

1 cup fresh or frozen cooked corn
1 cup quinoa, cooked according to package directions (yields approximately 2¼ cups after cooking)
½ cup cooked black beans, drained
¼ teaspoon ground cumin
1 large tomato, diced
¼ cup minced red onion
4-ounce can of minced green chilies (optional)

1. Make the dressing: Whisk dressing ingredients together in a small bowl. Set aside.

2. Combine corn, quinoa, and black beans in a medium serving bowl. Add remaining ingredients and dressing. Cover, chill for at least 1 hour, and serve cold.

SERVES 2 TO 3

Food for Thought:

QUINOA

Quinoa (pronounced Keen-wa) is actually a berry, though prepared and eaten as a grain. The fruit of a native Andean herb, it provides 9 essential amino acids, potassium, iron, and zinc. It has a mild nutty flavor and is frequently found on the menus of adventurous chefs, as an exciting substitute for rice. Quinoa needs to be very well rinsed, so be sure to follow the package directions.

COUSCOUS CONFETTI

Couscous, a staple in the Moroccan diet, looks like grain but is actually a tiny, rice-shaped pasta. Look for Fantastic Foods Whole Wheat Couscous. It's better tasting and higher in fiber and nutrients than refined couscous. This dish can be served hot as a side dish accompanied by steamed broccoli and Two-Minute Dilled Yogurt Sauce with cumin and garlic, or cold on a salad buffet including "Perfect" Tomato Salad with Feta, Provençal Three-Bean Salad with Fresh Herbs, and Potato-Leek Galette.

¾ cup couscous

1⅔ cups water

½ cup grated zucchini

½ cup grated yellow squash

½ cup grated carrot

2 tablespoons minced green onions
(scallions)

FOR THE HOT SIDE DISH VERSION

2 tablespoons butter or extra-virgin olive oil

½ teaspoon ground cumin

Sea salt

SALAD DRESSING

3 tablespoons extra-virgin olive oil

¼ teaspoon cinnamon

¼ teaspoon ground cumin

¼ teaspoon freshly ground white pepper

1 teaspoon apple cider vinegar

Sea salt and freshly ground pepper to taste

¼ cup coarsely chopped fresh mint leaves

1. Prepare couscous according to package directions: pour boiling water over couscous. Cover, then set aside for 20 minutes.

2. Blanch the grated vegetables one at a time by plunging into boiling water for 10 seconds, then immersing in a bowl of cold water to cool quickly. Drain well and place in serving bowl. Toss with couscous. At this point, add either the butter and seasonings in the hot version or the dressing for the salad.

3. To make the dressing: Combine all ingredients except mint in a small bowl and whisk until emulsified. Toss well with salad and garnish with chopped fresh mint.

SERVES 4

CHAPTER FOURTEEN

Potatoes

TWICE-BAKED NEW POTATOES WITH GARLIC AND PEPPER

An easy potato dish everyone loves. Great as a main course served with Baby Greens with Persimmon and Smoked Gouda, or as a side dish for those days when a steak or chicken-and-potatoes meal is appealing.

2 large new or Idaho potatoes, baked and cut in ¼-inch slices
2 tablespoons olive oil
1 garlic clove, pressed
½ teaspoon dried thyme

⅛ teaspoon chili powder
Seasoned salt to taste
Dusting of cayenne
Freshly ground pepper to taste

1. Preheat the oven to 375°F. Arrange sliced potatoes in shallow casserole with minimal overlap.

2. Combine remaining ingredients, except pepper and cayenne, and spread evenly over potatoes. Dust with cayenne and pepper.

3. Bake, uncovered, for 25 minutes, or until lightly browned.

SERVES 3

Food for Thought:

POTATOES

The ideal storage for potatoes is in a cool—not cold—dark place. Temperatures below 50°F will force the conversion of the potato starch to sugar, giving them an uncharacteristically sweet flavor. For this reason, unless you have cool storage space, it is best to buy potatoes as you use them and only keep a limited supply on hand.

Since onions and potatoes spoil each other, store potatoes away from onions.

When selecting potatoes, avoid old ones that are sprouting. They will be sweet since their starches will have turned to sugars.

Potatoes develop green patches when they have been exposed to light while they're growing. The green indicates the presence of a bitter chemical, solanine, which is poisonous in large quantities. Do not buy or use green potatoes.

Eat potatoes in their skins as often as possible. The skins contain the all-important fiber and nutrients.

OVEN-ROASTED ROSEMARY POTATOES

This rustic garlicky potato dish, with its crispy skins, disappears from the table like French fries. We love it as an accompaniment to Curried Cream of Pea Soup or Split Pea Soup with Garlic and Spinach.

¼ cup sweet butter

8 garlic cloves, minced

4 cups quartered red-skinned potatoes, skins on

1 cup water

3 tablespoons chopped fresh rosemary leaves, or 1 tablespoon dried

½ teaspoon sea salt

Freshly ground black pepper to taste

1. Preheat oven to 400°F.

2. Melt the butter in a medium skillet and add the garlic. Add the potatoes and sear over high heat. Toss the potatoes to coat them and begin browning them.

3. When garlic has cooked and gives off a sweet aroma, but is not yet brown, add ¼ cup water. Stir in rosemary, and transfer the entire mixture to a baking dish.

4. Bake the potatoes 10 minutes, then stir briefly and add additional water if the dish is dry.

5. Repeat step 4 every 10 minutes until potatoes are tender and water has totally reduced. Be sure not to add so much water that you drown the potatoes, just a few tablespoons at a time to prevent potatoes from sticking and burning.

6. Remove baking dish from oven and season potatoes with salt and pepper to taste.

SERVES 3 TO 4

SAFFRON POTATO SALAD

Serve with Opa Schnell's Favorite Italian Vegetable Soup and Free-Form Zucchini Tart.

DRESSING

1 tablespoon minced garlic

1 teaspoon fresh lemon juice

1 tablespoon Dijon mustard

A pinch of saffron

¼ cup extra-virgin olive oil

Sea salt and freshly ground black pepper to taste

1 pound red-skinned potatoes, steamed (peeling is optional)

1 cup thinly sliced oil-cured sun-dried tomatoes

1 cup Kalamata olives, pitted

2 tablespoons rinsed and drained capers

1 cup thinly sliced fennel

4 cups curly endive

1. Make the dressing: Place garlic, lemon juice, mustard, and saffron in a small mixing bowl. Whisk in olive oil until dressing emulsifies. Season with salt and pepper. Set aside.

2. Cut potatoes into bite-size cubes. Place into a large serving bowl. Add sun-dried tomatoes, olives, capers, and fennel. Toss well with three-quarters of dressing until vegetables are coated. Place on beds of endive, using remaining dressing to drizzle over greens. Serve warm or chilled.

SERVES 2 TO 4

BUTTERMILK SCALLOPED POTATOES WITH CUMIN

This potato casserole couldn't be easier to make. The buttermilk makes a cheesy sauce. For a Soothing Supper, serve with Herbed Artichoke Soup and Kale and Maui Muffins.

¼ cup whole wheat or oat flour

1 teaspoon sea salt

Freshly ground black pepper to taste

¼ teaspoon cumin

4 russet potatoes peeled (optional) and
    thinly sliced

1½ tablespoons butter

1 tablespoon extra-virgin olive oil

1 medium white onion, thinly sliced

2 cups buttermilk

Paprika for dusting

1. Preheat oven to 350°F. Combine flour, salt, pepper, and cumin in a work bowl.

2. Dredge potatoes in flour mixture and set aside.

3. Heat butter and oil in a skillet, add onion, sauté over medium heat until translucent and soft, approximately 5 minutes.

4. Fold onion into potatoes and place mixture in a shallow 2-quart casserole. Pour buttermilk over top. Dust with paprika.

5. Bake 1 to 1½ hours, or until potatoes are tender.

SERVES 4

WINTER VEGETABLE STEW IN HEARTY BROWN GRAVY

Stews are even more saucy and irresistible the next day, reheated as leftovers. Peeling the vegetables is optional. Scrubbed, unpeeled vegetables give a more rustic quality to the stew. Serve in large bowls with steamed kale and hot bread for dipping into sauce.

1 tablespoon olive oil

6 garlic cloves, minced

1 large onion, cut in chunks

2 celery ribs, cut in chunks

4 medium carrots, cut in chunks

1 small red pepper, seeded and diced

3 cups white rose potatoes, or 3 cups potato chunks, peeling optional

2 cups cubed apples, peeled

1 cup dried shiitake mushrooms, soaked in 2 cups warm water for 30 minutes and drained (reserve soaking liquid)

1 small butternut squash, peeled, seeded, and cubed

1 teaspoon dried thyme

½ teaspoon dried marjoram

¼ teaspoon dried rosemary

2 bay leaves

2 tablespoons flour

1 cup red wine

Sea salt and freshly ground pepper to taste

2 cups cauliflower florets

GRAVY

Mushroom soaking water, strained

3 vegetable or chicken bouillon cubes

3 cups water

3 pitted dates

¼ cup soy sauce

¼ cup apple cider vinegar

2 tablespoons blackstrap molasses

1. In a Dutch oven or large saucepan, heat the oil. When it's hot add the next 5 ingredients, and sauté briefly. Stir in potatoes, apples, mushrooms, and squash. Add the herbs. Add the flour and stir to coat vegetables. Add red wine. Cook over low heat while you prepare gravy.

2. In a blender, puree all gravy ingredients until smooth. Pour over the stew, bring to a boil, and season with salt and pepper to taste. Reduce heat to low, cover, and simmer for 30 minutes. Stir in cauliflower florets. Cover, and continue simmering for 30 more minutes. Taste for seasoning.

SERVES 6 TO 8

⌒⌒

EASY POTATO KNISHES

These treats are well worth the effort, and actually they are surprisingly simple to make, though they take a little more than an hour of prep time. Serve with Asparagus Vichyssoise or Hearty Split Pea Soup with Beans and Barley for a Sunday night supper your friends and family will long remember.

DOUGH

1 cup peeled and mashed steamed potatoes

¼ cup safflower oil

1 teaspoon sea salt

3 cups sifted spelt* or whole wheat pastry flour

1 teaspoon baking powder

½ cup cold water

POTATO FILLING

¼ cup butter

½ cup chopped onion

1½ cups mashed potatoes

½ teaspoon sea salt

¼ teaspoon freshly ground white pepper

1. Make the dough: Combine potatoes, oil, and seasoned salt. Sift flour and baking powder together. Add to potato mixture. Mix well.

2. Make a well in the center of the potato and flour mixture and add cold water. Knead into a smooth dough. Let rest on a lightly floured board and cover with a bowl or cloth for 30 minutes.

3. Make filling: Heat butter in skillet, add onion, and sauté until tender.

4. Combine mashed potatoes with onion, salt, and pepper, and mix well.

5. To assemble knishes: Preheat oven to 350°F. Cut dough into four pieces. Roll each as thin as possible. Cut into rectangles about 3 by 3½ inches for 2½-inch knishes or smaller for bite-size appetizers.

6. Place 1 tablespoon filling in center of rectangle and fold the two shorter ends toward the center first. Then fold the two longer ends over each other. Bake on a well-oiled baking sheet, folded side down, until golden, about 30 minutes.

MAKES 24 SMALL KNISHES, OR 12 2½-INCH KNISHES

---

*Whole spelt, an ancient grain that is currently being newly marketed, can be used in any recipe that calls for whole wheat. It is highly beneficial for those with wheat allergies. Available at natural food stores.

MASHED SWEET POTATOES AND PEARS

The pears are a marvelous complementary flavor to the sweet potatoes. For a traditional dinner, serve with roast chicken and steamed greens. For a Soothing Supper, serve with Split Pea Soup with Garlic and Spinach. The dish can be prepared a day in advance and refrigerated, covered, prior to final baking.

*2½ to 3 pounds sweet potatoes or yams
(approximately 6 medium potatoes)*
6 tablespoons sweet butter
*6 medium-ripe Bartlett or Anjou pears,
peeled, cored, and sliced*
1 cup canned pear nectar

6 cloves
*¼ cup dry sweetener, such as Sucanat, date
sugar, or maple sugar*
½ teaspoon cinnamon
½ teaspoon ground cardamom
Sea salt and freshly ground pepper to taste

1. Preheat oven to 400°F. Place potatoes on baking sheet and bake until tender when pierced, approximately 1 hour.

2. While potatoes bake, melt 2 tablespoons of butter in skillet over medium heat. Add pears and sauté 5 minutes, stirring frequently. Add pear nectar and cloves, bring to a boil over medium-high heat, reduce heat to medium-low, cover, and simmer until pears are tender, approximately 5 minutes, adding more pear nectar if pears begin to stick. Remove and discard cloves, cool slightly, and process in food processor or puree in blender.

3. After potatoes are done, lower oven temperature to 350°F.

4. Peel sweet potatoes. Mash with potato masher, incorporating remaining 4 tablespoons of butter, or beat in electric mixer. By hand, beat in the pear puree, sugar, cinnamon, and cardamom. Season with salt and pepper.

5. Transfer puree to baking dish. Bake until heated through, 15 to 20 minutes.

SERVES 6

◦

BEAU'S "DROP DEAD" POTATO PIZZA

In spite of all the "experimentation" going on around him, my son Beau grew up coolly during the *Fit for Life* years, and he's still going strong. Today he's a proficient cook, whose creations include this exceptional pizza. Serve with a FITONICS House Salad, and if you have some strapping teens around, add a bowl of Hot Mama's Vinegar and Chile Chicken Wings.

CRUST

3 cups mashed potatoes (preferably peeled and steamed russets)

1 tablespoon butter

2 eggs, beaten

¼ cup whole wheat pastry flour

1 teaspoon extra-virgin olive oil

TOPPING

2 thinly sliced ripe red tomatoes

4 whole water-packed artichoke hearts, sliced

¼ cup sliced sun-dried tomatoes

2 cups shredded mozzarella cheese

½ cup crumbled goat cheese

1 tablespoon extra-virgin olive oil

2 tablespoons minced fresh basil

1. Make the crust: Mix dough ingredients, except oil, to a smooth consistency. Oil a pizza pan. Press dough in pan by hand. Place under broiler to crisp slightly. Remove from oven.

2. Top with sliced tomatoes, artichoke hearts, and sun-dried tomatoes. Sprinkle with mozzarella, and goat cheese and drizzle with 1 tablespoon olive oil.

3. Place under broiler again to melt cheese. Remove from oven. Sprinkle with basil.

SERVES 2 TO 3

PART SIX

Soups as Side Dishes or Main Courses

BASIC VEGETABLE STOCK

Use canned stocks and broths, or bouillon (see Sources recommendations) for soup bases, or if you have time, make your own. Remember, the quality of your broth will be determined by the freshness of the vegetable ingredients you use.

2 carrots

2 parsnips

1 leek, thoroughly cleaned

3 celery ribs

1 white onion

1 clove

2 shallots

3 garlic cloves

1 bay leaf

1 small bunch fresh Italian parsley

2 sprigs fresh thyme, or ½ teaspoon dried

1 tablespoon black peppercorns

2 quarts water

1. Coarsely chop carrots, parsnips, leek, celery, and onion. Insert the clove into a piece of parsnip.

2. Chop shallots and garlic.

3. Wrap bay leaf, parsley, thyme, and peppercorns in a piece of cheesecloth. Tie bouquet garni tightly with kitchen string.

4. Place vegetables and bouquet garni in a stockpot. Add water. Bring the stock to a boil, turn down heat, and simmer about 1 hour. Strain out vegetables and discard bouquet garni. Store stock, covered, in the refrigerator for up to a week. The stock can also be frozen.

MAKES APPROXIMATELY 8 CUPS

THYME-SCENTED BROTH WITH SPINACH, TOMATOES, AND PASTA SHELLS

This excellent Italian-style soup takes only a few minutes to make. It's a delicious first course when your entree is a Super Salad, such as a Chicken Caesar. For a light supper make it a main course with bread and grilled vegetables.

3 garlic cloves, minced

1 tablespoon olive oil

2 tablespoons fresh thyme leaves

4 cups chopped fresh spinach, or 1 package frozen

6 cups chicken or Basic Vegetable Stock (page 215)

2 medium zucchini, sliced into paper-thin rounds

2 cups cooked pasta shells

3 cups peeled and diced plum tomatoes

2 cups cooked chick-peas, drained

½ teaspoon white pepper

Sea salt to taste

1. In a soup pot, sauté garlic in hot oil until it gives off an intense aroma. Add thyme leaves, spinach, and stock. Simmer, uncovered, over medium heat about 5 minutes.

2. Add zucchini and remaining ingredients, bring to a boil, and serve in warm soup plates.

SERVES 4

HERBED ARTICHOKE SOUP WITH KALE

One cup cooked kale fulfills our daily requirements for vitamins A and C and 10 percent of our iron and calcium intake. This innovative and nutritious soup makes an excellent first course for any protein or starch entree.

1 tablespoon olive oil

6 garlic cloves, minced

1 small red onion, sliced

½ cup white wine

10 ounces frozen artichoke hearts

½ teaspoon dried tarragon

½ teaspoon dried thyme

½ teaspoon dried marjoram

3 cups finely chopped kale

8 cups chicken or vegetable stock

Juice of 1 lemon

Sea salt and freshly ground black pepper to taste

1. In a soup pot heat oil over medium heat and sauté garlic and onion until tender. Add wine and artichoke hearts.

2. Add herbs, kale, and stock, and bring to a boil over high heat. Cover and reduce heat to medium-low to simmer for 20 minutes. Add lemon juice and season with salt and pepper to taste. Serve in warm soup bowls.

SERVES 3 TO 4

SPICY THAI BROTH WITH NOODLES

Here's a piquant soup that takes only minutes to prepare, and is a wonderful accompaniment to Thai Lemon Chicken Super Salad.

1 lime

3 teaspoons soy sauce

2 teaspoons rice wine vinegar

1 tablespoon spicy sesame oil

1 small serrano pepper, seeded, and minced

2 garlic cloves, minced

6 cups chicken broth

4 ounces soba noodles

1 tomato, peeled, seeded, and diced

1 cup loosely packed cilantro

1. Cut lime vertically into thin slices. Stack slices and cut into the smallest dice possible. Place in a small bowl and add the soy sauce, vinegar, oil, pepper, and garlic. Set aside.

2. In a soup pot, bring the broth to a boil and stir in seasoning mixture. Let steep for 10 minutes with the heat off. Strain the broth and return to a boil. Add soba and cook according to package directions, about 7 minutes, until tender. Add tomato and cilantro and serve in warm soup bowls.

SERVES 2

OPA SCHNELL'S FAVORITE ITALIAN VEGETABLE SOUP

We serve this delicious Italian soup as a main course for supper with hot Maui Muffins. Use the freshest garden vegetables and good olive oil for the best flavor. The long cooking time is one of the secrets for success. A spoonful of grated Parmesan in each bowl adds a nice touch.

¼ *cup extra-virgin olive oil*

1 carrot, minced

2 leeks, quartered lengthwise and finely sliced

4 garlic cloves, minced

2 medium zucchini, quartered lengthwise and sliced crosswise

5½ cups water

4 cups finely chopped spinach

One 14-ounce can diced Italian-style organic tomatoes and juice

1 teaspoon dried basil

1 tablespoon powdered beef-flavored broth

1 tablespoon powdered chicken-flavored broth

1 cup finely chopped fresh basil

Sea salt and freshly ground pepper to taste

1. Heat olive oil in soup pot with heavy bottom. Add carrot, leeks, and garlic, and sauté over medium-low heat until aroma fills the kitchen, approximately 5 minutes.

2. Add zucchini and sauté briefly. Stir in water, spinach, tomatoes, dried basil, powdered broths. Bring to a boil over medium-high heat, cover, and simmer over medium-low heat for 1 hour.

3. Stir in fresh basil, and simmer another 15 to 20 minutes.

4. Season with salt and pepper.

SERVES 3

⟋⟍

VEGETABLE CONSOMMÉ WITH CELLOPHANE NOODLES

Cellophane noodles, the transparent, cappellini-type pasta made from rice, are used in Japanese and Thai cuisine. Look for them in natural food stores or Asian markets. This is a good complement to Sesame Chicken Salad.

6 cups Basic Vegetable Stock (page 215)
2 cups cooked cellophane noodles
1 cup matchstick carrot
1 cup matchstick zucchini
½ cup julienned spinach
¼ cup paper-thin slices shiitake
  mushrooms

¼ teaspoon white pepper
Sea salt to taste
1 teaspoon sesame oil
1 tablespoon minced green onions
  (scallions)

1. Bring the stock to a boil in a large saucepan. Add remaining ingredients except green onions and simmer, uncovered, 3 minutes.

2. Season to taste and serve in warm soup bowls. Garnish with green onions.

SERVES 3 TO 4

HIS AND HERS MISO SOUP LUNCH

This recipe is one of a number of variations on miso soup meals in this book. It's a quick lunch (or dinner) recipe, bound to please a woman who likes the alkaline, easily digestible nature of tofu and a man who prefers more traditional protein sources, such as chicken. At least, that's how it goes at our house. (See Food for Thought: Miso, page 56.)

3 cups water

2 cups finely cut broccoli florets

1 cup chopped cabbage

2 green onions (scallions), chopped, green part reserved

⅓ pound tofu, cubed

1 chicken breast, thinly sliced

2 heaping teaspoons miso

1 large garlic clove, pressed

1 tomato, diced

1 ear corn kernels, cut from cob

Tamari, soy sauce, or Braggs Liquid Aminos to taste

1. Bring water to a boil in a medium soup pot or wok. Add broccoli, cabbage, and whites of onions, cover, and simmer 4 minutes.

2. Now divide mixture in half, by transferring part to a second pot. Stir tofu into one pot and sliced chicken into the other. Cover each pot and simmer 4 minutes, or until chicken is cooked through.

3. Remove ¼ cup of liquid from each pot. Stir 1 teaspoon miso into each until it dissolves, then add the garlic. Remove pots from heat. Return miso mixtures to each pot.

4. Spoon each soup into a large bowl. Stir in diced tomato and raw corn kernels, dividing evenly between the two portions. Top with scallion greens and serve with tamari.

Variation: Add 2 cups fresh angel hair pasta to soup before adding miso. Cook approximately 2 minutes. Or serve your miso soup meals with toasted bagels with garlic butter, a real fusion of ingredients.

SERVES 2

MISO SOUP SUPPER WITH MUNG BEAN NOODLES

This light but filling soup is also a perfect "Guru's Bowl" meal. Use the wheat-free mung bean noodle (sometimes called *harusame*) which has a gelatinous, "cellophane" quality, as a pleasant change from typical pasta. The flavors in this soup are *fusion*—Asian vegetables combined with sun-dried tomato–miso broth.

1 ounce (½ typical package) mung bean
  noodles

3 cups water

2 medium tomatoes, peeled, seeded, and
  coarsely chopped (optional)

1 bunch green onions (scallions), sliced

1 small bok choy, coarsely chopped

4 large shiitake mushrooms, stemmed and
  sliced

¾ cup cubed tofu (optional), or thinly
  sliced loin of pork

2 tablespoons powdered chicken-flavored
  broth

2 tablespoons sun-dried tomato paste or
  regular tomato paste

1 large garlic clove, pressed

One 1-inch piece gingerroot, pressed

1 heaping tablespoon miso

1. Drop noodles in boiling water to cover for 4 minutes. Drain in a colander and rinse with cold water. Set aside.

2. In the same pot, bring 3 cups of water to boil for blanching tomatoes. Immerse tomatoes for 30 to 60 seconds. Remove from water, slide skins off, cut in half, squeeze or spoon out seeds, and coarsely chop. Set aside.

3. Bring the water back to a boil for soup. Add onions, bok choy, mushrooms, tofu or pork, tomato paste, and powdered broth, mix well, and simmer until vegetables are bright green. Stir in tomatoes and mung bean noodles and simmer briefly to heat through.

4. Remove soup pot from heat. Using a garlic press, squeeze garlic and ginger into soup.

5. Remove ½ cup water from soup pot. Dissolve miso in water, and return to soup, stirring in well. Ladle into large warm bowls.

SERVES 2

MELLOW MISO SOUP WITH GREENS AND SEA VEGETABLES

So rich in amino acids and minerals, this miso soup of cruciferous and sea vegetables is a great detoxifying meal in a bowl.

4 cups water

2 garlic cloves, minced

2 green onions (scallions), sliced

1 cup soaked and drained wakame (see Sources)

2 cups finely shredded bok choy

2 cups finely shredded Savoy cabbage

1 cup firm tofu cut in ½-inch cubes

3 tablespoons mellow white miso

One 1-inch chunk fresh gingerroot

1 sheet toasted nori, cut in thin ribbons

1. Bring water to boil in a medium saucepan. Add garlic, onions, wakame, and greens, and boil 5 minutes.

2. Remove ¼ cup water. Stir the miso into this broth.

3. Stir mixture into soup and remove from heat. Press ginger, in small segments, through garlic press, directly into miso soup. Stir well.

4. Ladle the soup into 2 warm soup bowls. Served topped with shredded nori.

SERVES 2

Food for Thought:

BUTTERMILK

The lactose, or milk sugar, in *buttermilk* is converted into lactic acid during the fermentation process. For this reason, it is often more digestible than other dairy products. Buttermilk is also naturally low in fat. Friendly bacterial cultures, similar to those found in yogurt, are added to buttermilk, giving it a slightly sour-sweet quality. It is also an excellent source of calcium.

Originally, buttermilk was derived from cream, but today it is actually made from low-fat milk, with active cultures added to it. It is an excellent creaming component for soups, dressings, and sauces and an indispensable baking ingredient.

BUTTERNUT SQUASH SOUP
WITH VEGETABLE VERMICELLI

A hearty winter soup with an elegant twist. If you have a kitchen mandoline, you can create long thin strands of "vegetable" vermicelli. Serve with Free-Form Zucchini Tart for a Soothing Supper.

1 butternut squash, seeded and quartered

1 teaspoon sweet butter

2 shallots, chopped

2 leeks, white parts only, rinsed and sliced

5 cups Basic Vegetable Stock (page 215)

2 large zucchini, peeled

2 yellow squash, peeled

2 medium carrots, peeled

3 tablespoons plus 1 teaspoon honey

1 teaspoon cinnamon

Pinch of cloves

1 cup buttermilk

Sea salt and white pepper to taste

1. Preheat oven to 350°F.

2. Dot each quarter of squash with butter and bake, skin side down, on a lightly oiled baking sheet about 45 minutes, or until tender. Scoop flesh from the skins and set aside. You should have about 4 cups.

3. Place shallots, leeks, and squash in a soup pot, add the stock, and bring to a boil. Reduce heat and simmer, uncovered, for 45 minutes.

4. While the soup is cooking, place the grating attachment in the food processor. Cut the ends off the zucchini, yellow squash, and carrots and push through the grater to create thin strands.

5. Puree soup in three batches in a blender or food processor until smooth. Return to soup pot. Stir in honey and spices and bring to a boil. Stir in buttermilk. Add vegetables, and immediately remove from heat, stirring gently to create a uniform texture. Season to taste and serve in warm soup bowls.

SERVES 4 TO 6

CREAMY SORREL SOUP

Sorrel has been used through the ages for many medicinal purposes, from healing headaches, acne, ulcers, and sore throats to curing food poisoning. It's a tart-flavored, very distinctive green that has a distinctive lemony flavor. Look for it in the farmers' market or try growing it yourself if you have a garden. Green chard or spinach can be substituted for the sorrel, but the soup will not have the same flavor. Like all leafy greens, sorrel is extremely high in beta carotene and calcium. Excellent as a first course before New York Steak Super Salad with Goat Cheese and Grainy Mustard Vinaigrette.

2 garlic cloves, minced

½ cup minced white onion

½ cup white wine

3 cups sorrel leaves

2½ cups vegetable or chicken broth

1½ tablespoons cornstarch

½ cup buttermilk

Sea salt and freshly ground pepper to taste

1. In a large soup pot, combine the garlic, onion, white wine, and sorrel and cook over medium heat until soft, about 5 minutes. Stir in 2 cups broth, cover, and simmer about 15 minutes.

2. In a blender, process the sorrel mixture until smooth. Return to the soup pot. In a glass measuring cup, dissolve the cornstarch in 3 tablespoons reserved broth. Add to soup, then stir in remaining ½ cup broth. Add buttermilk. Simmer, stirring constantly, until smooth. Remove from heat and season with salt and pepper to taste. Serve hot or chilled.

SERVES 2

ASPARAGUS VICHYSSOISE

Leeks add a sweetness to this soup, which gets its creamy character from potatoes and buttermilk, not heavy cream. It is a lovely chilled soup in summer as a first course to any grilled chicken or fish entree.

3 leeks, trimmed and chopped

2 tablespoons sweet butter

1 tablespoon fresh thyme, or 1 teaspoon dried

1 bay leaf

6 cups chicken or vegetable broth

8 ounces small white potatoes, peeled and quartered

1 pound asparagus, trimmed and cut in 1-inch pieces

¼ cup buttermilk

Sea salt and white pepper to taste

1. Place the leeks in a bowl of cold water for 10 minutes to clean. Drain.

2. In a large soup pot, melt the butter and sauté the leeks, thyme, and bay leaf. Add broth and potatoes and bring to a boil. Reduce heat and simmer, covered, for 20 minutes.

3. Meantime, in a separate pot, cook asparagus in water to cover until tender and bright green, about 4 minutes. Remove asparagus from water and shock in ice water to preserve color. Set aside asparagus tips for garnish. Add asparagus to the soup for 30 minutes.

4. With a slotted spoon or skimmer, remove asparagus from soup and transfer to blender along with 2 cups soup stock. Process until smooth, and set aside.

5. Remove bay leaf from remaining soup. Process leek-and-potato mixture in two batches in blender until smooth. Return to soup pot. Stir in reserved asparagus mixture and buttermilk. Season with salt and pepper and serve in warm soup bowls or chill two hours and serve in cold glass bowls. Sprinkle with reserved asparagus tips for garnish.

SERVES 4

CREAM OF WILD MUSHROOM SOUP WITH FRESH SAGE

Exotic mushrooms have become so popular that they even turn up in supermarkets. If you're using dried mushrooms, rehydrate them in hot water for 30 minutes prior to cooking. Excellent with Mediterranean Macaroni Salad or Capellini Caponata.

8 ounces fresh shiitake mushrooms, or 4 ounces dried, rehydrated

8 ounces fresh oyster mushrooms, or 4 ounces dried, rehydrated

1 teaspoon olive oil

1 small carrot, peeled and diced

1 celery rib, diced

1 white onion, diced

2 garlic cloves, minced

1 cup red wine

8 ounces button mushrooms, cleaned

1 tablespoon chopped fresh sage, or 1 teaspoon dried

5 cups beef or vegetable broth

¼ cup heavy cream or half-and-half

½ cup buttermilk

¼ teaspoon white pepper

Sea salt to taste

Fresh sage leaves, or 2 tablespoons minced chives for garnish

1. Wipe fresh mushrooms clean and remove stems. In a large soup pot, heat the oil and add shiitake and oyster mushrooms, carrot, celery, onion, and garlic. Sauté until mushrooms are tender. Add wine. Coarsely chop button mushrooms and add to the pot. Add the sage.

2. Pour broth into the soup and bring to a boil. Reduce heat and simmer 20 minutes, uncovered. Remove from heat. Puree soup in small batches in a blender. Return soup to the pot over medium heat and stir in cream and buttermilk. Add white pepper and salt to taste. Garnish with fresh sage or minced chives and serve in warm soup bowls.

SERVES 4

SUMMER CORN CHOWDER

Serve with Amazing Blues for a Soothing Supper or as a first course to a protein and salad meal. The blended corn and milk give the chowder a rich, smooth texture. Half-and-half, of course, makes it richer.

2 cups milk, plain soy milk, or half-and-half

2¼ cups corn kernels, fresh or frozen

4 teaspoons flour

½ cup diced celery

½ cup diced green bell pepper

1 cup diced onions

2 cups diced, peeled potatoes

1 tablespoon olive oil

½ teaspoon coriander

Pinch of cinnamon

¾ cup diced fresh or canned tomatoes, drained if canned

4 cups water

1 teaspoon dried basil

¾ teaspoon sea salt

Freshly ground white pepper to taste

1 teaspoon fresh lime juice

1. In a blender, process milk, 1½ cups of the corn, and the flour. Set aside.

2. In a large soup pot combine celery, green pepper, onions, and potatoes in the olive oil. Cook, stirring frequently, over medium heat for 2 minutes. Stir in coriander, cinnamon, and tomatoes, and cook an additional minute.

3. Add milk-corn mixture to vegetables in the pot. Add 4 cups water, and mix well. Bring to a slow simmer, and stir frequently for 15 minutes. Add remaining corn and basil; mix well. Continue simmering, stirring occasionally and not allowing soup to come to a rapid boil until vegetables are cooked and tender, about 5 minutes. Stir in salt, pepper, and lime juice, and serve in warm soup bowls.

SERVES 4

CURRIED CREAM OF PEA SOUP

This soup comes together in less than 20 minutes, but it tastes as if you'd been cooking for hours. A nice first course to serve with a pasta entree such as Curried Chicken Linguine.

2 teaspoons olive oil
1 medium onion, chopped
1 garlic clove, chopped
2 teaspoons curry powder
¾ teaspoon turmeric
½ teaspoon ground coriander
¼ teaspoon ground cumin

2 tablespoons fresh lemon juice
2½ cups frozen peas
5 cups chicken broth
½ cup buttermilk or plain yogurt
Sea salt and freshly ground pepper to taste
Zest of 1 lemon

1. In a medium soup pot heat oil, and sauté onion and garlic over medium heat. Add curry powder, turmeric, coriander, and cumin. Cook for 15 seconds, stirring constantly. Add lemon juice and peas. Mix well and remove from heat.

2. Stir in broth and return the pan to the heat. Bring to a boil over high heat, stirring constantly. Cover, reduce heat, and simmer 8 to 10 minutes, or until peas are tender.

3. Remove ¼ cup peas from the pot. Puree the remaining soup in a blender or food processor until smooth. Return soup to the pot with reserved peas, and reheat, stirring constantly. When soup is hot, stir in buttermilk or yogurt and season with salt and pepper to taste. Garnish with lemon zest and serve warm or chilled.

SERVES 4 TO 5

CRÈME DE LA CRÈME CAULIFLOWER SOUP

There are cauliflower soups and then there's this cauliflower soup. It's the *crème de la crème*! Especially as a part of a vegetarian feast including Tofu "Wrap" Filling with Broccoli, Onion, Tomatoes, and Olives.

1 teaspoon safflower oil

1 medium onion, chopped

1 green bell pepper, chopped

1 small celery rib, chopped

1 medium cauliflower, cut into 1-inch florets

¼ teaspoon dried thyme

¼ teaspoon dried marjoram

4½ cups water

5 teaspoons powdered vegetable broth

½ tablespoon butter

1 teaspoon olive oil

1 tablespoon flour

¾ cup soy milk or buttermilk

Sea salt and white pepper to taste

1. In a medium soup pot, heat oil with onion, green pepper, and celery. Sauté briefly. Add cauliflower and herbs. Sauté 2 minutes. Add water and vegetable broth powder. Bring to a boil, reduce heat to medium-low, and simmer for 10 to 15 minutes.

2. Remove ½ cup cauliflower florets and cut into small pieces. Set aside. In a blender or food processor, puree remaining soup to a smooth cream. In the empty soup pot, melt butter with olive oil. When it's bubbling, stir in flour, and whisk in milk to form a thick cream. Stir in cauliflower pieces and blended soup. Simmer, stirring constantly, to thicken, but don't let the soup boil. Add salt and white pepper. Adjust seasonings to taste and serve in warm soup bowls.

SERVES 4 TO 6

GREG'S EXCELLENT GAZPACHO

My son Greg returned from a trip to Spain with this recipe to add to the family collection. He prepared it for us as a first course at a Sunday Bowl O'Barbecue. It's an excellent warm-weather option when ripe, juicy tomatoes are in season. The sourdough bread gives this gazpacho an unusual, creamy quality.

1 green bell pepper, seeded and cut in
    chunks

6 large tomatoes, cored and quartered

½ red onion, coarsely chopped

2 garlic cloves, peeled

Juice of 1½ to 2 lemons

1 cucumber, peeled and seeded

Cayenne to taste

3 tablespoons white wine or apple cider
    vinegar

One 1-inch-thick slice sourdough bread,
    crust removed

GARNISH

1 tomato, seeded and diced

1 small bell pepper, seeded and diced

½ cucumber, peeled, seeded, and diced

½ red onion, peeled and diced

1. Combine soup ingredients in a medium bowl. Blend in two batches in food processor or blender. Set aside.

2. Combine garnish ingredients in a small bowl and mix well. Serve soup in glass goblets with a spoonful of garnish on top.

SERVES 6 TO 8

GAZPACHO ARIZONA

Gazpacho has many versions. Try this one if you like spicy flavors.

2 green onions (scallions), trimmed

2 jalapeños, halved and seeded

2 garlic cloves, minced

6 tomatillos, husked and quartered

2 tablespoons olive oil

4 large beefsteak tomatoes, cored and
    quartered

1 yellow bell pepper, seeded and quartered

1 hothouse cucumber, quartered

¼ cup chopped fresh cilantro

½ cup tomato puree

½ cup chicken broth

3 tablespoons fresh lime juice

2 teaspoons chopped fresh oregano

1 avocado, peeled, seeded, and diced

Sea salt to taste

1. In the work bowl of a food processor, mince the green onions and jalapeños. Place in a strainer and rinse briefly under cold water. Set aside.

2. Place the garlic and tomatillo in the food processor, and chop finely. In a small skillet, sauté the garlic with the tomatillo mixture in hot olive oil over medium heat until garlic is fragrant. Place tomatoes, bell pepper, and cucumbers in food processor. Pulse several times to chop vegetables into pea-size chunks. Place in a large mixing bowl and set aside.

3. Add the cilantro to the chopped vegetables. Stir in tomatillo mixture and the jalapeño mixture. Add tomato puree and chicken broth, then stir in lime juice, oregano, and avocado. Add salt and taste for seasoning. Chill and serve.

SERVES 3 TO 4

CHILLED BROCCOLI AND WATERCRESS SOUP WITH A DOLLOP OF CRÈME FRAÎCHE

Crème fraîche is a sophisticated, slightly cultured, slightly sweet thickened cream. It's available in most specialty food shops and some natural foods stores and supermarkets. If crème fraîche isn't available, substitute sour cream. The cashew puree adds a unique flavor.

1 tablespoon olive oil

1 medium onion, chopped

1 celery rib, chopped

5 cups vegetable or chicken broth

1 small bunch watercress, chopped

1 small bunch broccoli, chopped

⅓ cup cashew pieces

2 teaspoons honey

Sea salt and freshly ground pepper to taste

½ cup crème fraîche

1. In a large stock pot heat the olive oil, and sauté the onion and celery until tender. Add broth, bring to a boil, and add watercress and broccoli. Cover, and simmer for 10 minutes.

2. In a blender or food processor, puree cashew pieces with ¾ cup broth from the soup and the honey until smooth. Set aside. Puree the soup, about 3 cups at a time, then return to the pot. Stir in cashew puree and chill for 1 to 2 hours. Season with salt and pepper to taste and serve topped with a dollop of *crème fraîche*.

SERVES 4 TO 6

CHILLED CUCUMBER BISQUE WITH DILL

The marriage of cucumbers and yogurt is ancient and universal, from Greece to India, and to America. What a soothing, cooling warm-weather lunch! Serve as a first course to a Super Salad meal.

1 tablespoon olive oil
1 white onion, diced
1 large cucumber, peeled, seeded, and diced
2 cups chicken broth
2 tablespoons chopped fresh dill

½ cup plain yogurt
Juice of 1 lemon
Dash of Tabasco
Sea salt to taste

1. In a large saucepan, heat the oil and sauté the onion until soft. Add cucumber and broth and bring to a boil. Cover, and simmer 20 minutes. Remove from heat and process in a blender, in small batches, until smooth. Pour into a serving bowl, cover, and chill.

2. Just before serving stir in the dill, yogurt, lemon juice, Tabasco, and salt to taste.

SERVES 4

⟲

CHILLED GOLDEN TOMATO BISQUE

Yellow tomatoes are sweeter and supposedly less acidic than their red counter-parts, and they're appearing more often in supermarkets. Substituting them for red tomatoes adds excitement to ordinary dishes. Great with Spicy Shrimp Quesadillas.

1 tablespoon olive oil

1 garlic clove, minced

1 green onion (scallion), chopped

2 pounds chopped yellow tomatoes

¼ cup chopped yellow bell pepper

3 cups chicken or vegetable broth

¼ cup plain yogurt

Sea salt and freshly ground white pepper to taste

2 tablespoons julienned fresh basil

1. In a large saucepan heat the oil, and sauté the garlic. Add onion and sauté another minute. Add tomatoes and pepper. Sauté to soften, about 3 minutes, and then add broth. Bring to a boil, reduce heat, and simmer 15 minutes. Cool about 10 minutes.

2. In a blender or food processor, blend the soup, 2 cups at a time until totally smooth. Strain through a fine mesh sieve and discard any pulp or put through a food mill. Refrigerate soup until cold, at least 2 hours. Stir in yogurt, season with salt and pepper, then serve garnished with basil.

SERVES 2

⟨◦◦⟩

YELLOW SPLIT PEA *DAL*

In India, *dal* is the name used to describe all members of the dried bean and pea family, as well as the dishes based on them. *Dals* are soups, but they are also used as sauces or condiments over rice and vegetables. Serve this *dal* as a sauce for Three-Grain Pilaf and Peas for a hearty meal in your Guru's Bowl.

1 cup yellow split peas
5 cups water
1 teaspoon sea salt
1 tablespoon safflower oil
1 medium onion, diced
2 teaspoons curry powder

½ teaspoon turmeric
½ teaspoon ground cumin
½ teaspoon coriander, ground
1 tomato peeled, seeded, and chopped
2 tablespoons minced fresh cilantro
2 teaspoons lime juice

1. Drain and place split peas in a medium saucepan. Add water and salt. Bring to a boil and simmer 40 minutes over low heat, partially covered, until peas are soft and soup is a thick puree.

2. Heat oil in a small skillet. Sauté onion until tender. Stir in curry powder, turmeric, cumin, and coriander and sauté 1 minute over medium heat, until spices are fragrant.

3. Stir onion, spices, and tomato into soup. Simmer, uncovered, for 5 minutes, add cilantro and lime juice and spoon over rice and vegetables.

SERVES 4

SPLIT PEA SOUP WITH GARLIC AND SPINACH

This is one of our families' favorite suppers served with any potato dish, muffins, or a sweet potato pie.

6 cups water

Two 15-ounce cans chicken or vegetable
  stock

¼ cup chopped garlic

1 cup chopped celery

1 medium bell pepper, chopped

½ cup minced fresh parsley

2 cups split peas

½ teaspoon dried sage

2 tablespoons dried minced onions

1 bag fresh spinach, stems removed,
  coarsely chopped

Salt and freshly ground pepper to taste

1. Bring water and stock to a boil in a large soup pot. Add all remaining ingredients except spinach and seasonings. Return to a boil and skim the surface of the soup. Reduce heat to medium low and simmer, covered, for 2 hours.

2. Add chopped spinach and salt and pepper to taste. Cover and continue simmering for 20 minutes. Adjust seasonings and serve in warm soup bowls.

SERVES 6

HEARTY SPLIT PEA SOUP WITH BEANS AND BARLEY

For convenience you can substitute a package of Manischevitz or Streits Vegetable Soup Mix for the barley and beans. This soup freezes well so the large quantity can be used for several meals. The long cooking time ensures delicious aromas throughout your home and a robust bowl of soup on a cold winter day. Great with Handmade Potato Focaccia or Skillet Corn Bread with Spicy Sweet Red Pepper Butter.

14 cups water

2 cups diced onions

1½ cups diced carrots

2 cups diced celery

2 cups chopped cabbage

⅔ cup minced fresh parsley

4 green onions (scallions), thinly sliced

2 garlic cloves, minced

1 medium zucchini, quartered and sliced
  (optional)

⅓ cup green split peas

⅓ cup yellow split peas

2 tablespoons barley

¼ cup baby lima beans or tiny white beans

3 tablespoons powdered vegetable broth

Seasoned salt

Freshly ground pepper to taste

1. Bring water to a boil in a large soup pot. Add the ingredients in the order given, except for the salt and pepper.

2. Return soup to a boil, skimming off any foam that comes to the surface with a large spoon. (Repeat this skimming process several times in the first 30 minutes of cooking, until no more foam forms.) Cover and reduce heat to medium-low.

3. Simmer soup for 2½ hours, stirring periodically to ensure that the barley isn't sticking. When soup is done, add salt and pepper to taste, and serve in warm soup bowls.

SERVES 6 TO 8

FRENCH ONION SOUP WITH MELTED GRUYÈRE

A wonderful accompaniment to a Super Salad.

2 tablespoons sweet butter

2 tablespoons olive oil

1 pound white onions, thinly sliced
   (approximately 8 cups)

1 cup red wine

6 cups beef or vegetable broth

1 bay leaf

Sea salt and freshly ground black pepper to
   taste

4 thick slices sourdough or whole-grain
   bread

Olive oil for brushing

1 cup grated gruyère cheese

1. Heat butter and oil in a medium saucepan over medium heat. When it bubbles, add onions. Cook about 20 minutes, stirring constantly, until onions are caramelized, but not dark brown. Add the wine and cook another minute. Preheat oven to 375°F.

2. Add the broth and bay leaf. Bring to a boil, lower heat, and simmer, uncovered, for 20 minutes. Remove bay leaf and season with salt and pepper.

3. Brush bread with olive oil and toast under broiler. Ladle soup into 4 ovenproof bowls set on a baking sheet. Top with toast, then cheese. Pop into the oven about 5 minutes or place under broiler about 30 seconds to melt cheese. Serve hot from the oven.

SERVES 4

MINESTRONE WITH SOURDOUGH GARLIC TOAST AND FRESH MOZZARELLA

Who can resist this hot garlicky, chewy, totally satisfying one-dish meal?

8 cups beef broth

5 tablespoons olive oil

1 medium onion, chopped

2 celery ribs, diced

2 medium carrots, diced

2 medium zucchini, diced

2 medium potatoes, dried (peeling optional)

1 can white beans, drained and rinsed

1 cup ½-inch long sliced green beans

2 large tomatoes, peeled and diced, or one 15-ounce can diced tomatoes, drained

2 tablespoons tomato paste

½ cup cooked orzo

6 leaves fresh basil, chopped, or ½ teaspoon dried

Sea salt and freshly ground pepper to taste

2 garlic cloves, pressed

4 slices sourdough bread

8 ounces fresh mozzarella, sliced ¼-inch thick

1. In a large soup pot, bring the broth to a boil.

2. In a skillet, heat 2 tablespoons oil with onion, celery, carrots, zucchini, and potatoes. Sauté 5 minutes. Add the two kinds of beans, then stir the mixture into the boiling broth. Return to a boil, and stir in tomatoes and tomato paste. Boil 5 minutes. Add cooked orzo. Stir in basil and salt and pepper to taste.

3. Combine the garlic with 3 tablespoons olive oil in a small bowl. Brush sliced bread with oil mixture and toast until golden.

4. To serve, place 1 slice toast in the bottom of each ovenproof soup bowl. Ladle soup over the top, and finish with cheese slices to cover most of the surface. Place under broiler for 30 seconds to melt cheese.

SERVES 4

PART SEVEN

Simple Salads
and Vegetable Dishes

CHAPTER FIFTEEN
Simple Salads

FITONICS HOUSE SALAD

This basic salad will complement both protein and starch entrees. It is inspired by the French and Italian traditional green salads. Organic Bibb or Boston lettuce is the ideal main ingredient. The Europeans eat their salads after their entrees. We recommend salad be eaten *first*. Eating salad first gives you a chance to fill up on salad rather than cooked food! A great weight-loss secret!

DRESSING
3 tablespoons extra-virgin olive oil
1 tablespoon fresh lemon juice
1 teaspoon apple cider vinegar
½ teaspoon Dijon mustard
1 pressed garlic clove

1 tablespoon plain yogurt or buttermilk
Sea salt to taste and freshly ground pepper

SALAD
6 cups Bibb or Boston lettuce, washed, dried, and broken in bite-size pieces

1. Whisk dressing ingredients in a large salad bowl.

2. Add greens and toss well.

SERVES 2

CRUDITÉS AND YOGURT

This first course replacement for the traditional salad can be served as an appetizer before any protein or starch entree.

DIP

1 cup plain yogurt

1 garlic clove, crushed

2 tablespoons minced green onions (scallions) or chives

¼ teaspoon ground cumin

1 tablespoon Parmesan cheese

2 teaspoons apple cider vinegar

CRUDITÉS

Sliced red and/or yellow peppers

Sliced celery ribs

Sliced cucumber rounds

Sliced fennel

Trimmed green onions (scallions)

Radishes

Carrot "chips" (peeled and cut thinly on the diagonal)

Peeled and sliced jicama

1. Make the dip: Blend all ingredients well.

2. Arrange crudités attractively on a serving plate with a bowl of dip in the center.

SERVES 3 TO 4

⟋⟍

SPINACH AND ENDIVE SALAD WITH STRAWBERRIES

A perfect complement to proteins.

DRESSING

2 tablespoons extra-virgin olive oil

1 tablespoon fresh lemon juice

2 teaspoons apple cider vinegar

2 tablespoons plain yogurt or buttermilk

2 teaspoons honey

Sea salt and freshly ground pepper to taste

SALAD

1 Belgian endive

4 cups spinach

¼ cup thinly sliced red onion rings

½ pint strawberries, thinly sliced

1. Whisk dressing ingredients in a large salad bowl.

2. Separate endive leaves and soak briefly (15 minutes) in cold salt water to remove bitterness. Drain, dry, and thinly slice lengthwise.

3. Break spinach or chop into small pieces directly into salad bowl. Add endive, onion rings, and sliced strawberries. Toss well.

SERVES 2

CALIFORNIA "SALADE SANTÉ"

This salad has all of "Cali-cuisine's" most popular ingredients: seeds, sprouts, seaweed—is a nutritional analysis really necessary here? (*Santé* is French for health.)

1 romaine lettuce, washed and dried

1 cup chopped sunflower sprouts

1 cup alfalfa or clover sprouts

1 carrot, peeled and coarsely grated

2 cups steamed broccoli florets

2 sheets toasted nori* seaweed, snipped or
    torn into shreds

½ avocado, sliced

¼ cup pumpkin seeds

DRESSING

¼ cup safflower oil

2 tablespoons fresh lemon juice

1. In a large salad bowl, tear romaine leaves into bite-size pieces. Toss with sprouts, carrot, broccoli, and nori.

2. Whisk together dressing ingredients in a small bowl and pour over salad. Toss gently and arrange avocado on top of salad. Sprinkle with pumpkin seeds and serve.

SERVES 2 TO 4

Toasted nori sheets for sushi can be purchased in natural food stores or Asian markets.

∽

MESCLUN SALAD WITH
SUN-DRIED TOMATOES AND OIL-CURED OLIVES

Although yellow sun-dried tomatoes are not as common as the red, they are available and worth buying when you see them. They have a sweet flavor and bring a special touch to this salad. The fresh tomatoes enrich the flavor of the sun-dried tomatoes. Serve with a protein entree such as Sautéed Shrimp in Sweet Corn Puree.

1 cup sliced sun-dried tomatoes
2 cups mesclun (see below)
2 cups chopped romaine
¼ cup cilantro leaves
2 medium tomatoes, chopped
¼ cup oil-cured olives, whole or pitted

DRESSING

¼ cup reserved tomato soaking water
2 tablespoons flaxseed oil
1½ tablespoons cream or buttermilk
Pinch of salt
1 tablespoon fresh lime juice
½ teaspoon molasses or honey
½ teaspoon Dijon mustard

1. Reconstitute tomatoes by soaking them in boiling water for 30 minutes. Drain, reserving ¼ cup liquid for dressing.

2. Combine tomatoes with remaining salad ingredients in large bowl.

3. Make the dressing: Whisk dressing ingredients together in a small bowl and pour over salad. Toss well and serve.

SERVES 2

Mesclun

Mesclun is a blend of wild greens and delicate baby lettuces. You can find it in the produce sections of most supermarkets nowadays, often in prewashed, prepackaged cellophane bags or sold loose by the pound.

I especially love these mixes because they are ready-to-go salads, packed with enzymes and interesting flavors—and usually organic! Whip up your own FITONICS House Dressing, and voilà!

6~9

THREE OF HEARTS SALAD

At the mere mention of hearts of palm or artichoke hearts, most people's eyes widen and smiles appear. They are the delicacies of the vegetable kingdom. For a light and healthy vegetarian meal, serve with Braised Bok Choy with Garlic and Ginger, corn on the cob, and crusty hot bread.

6 hearts of romaine lettuce

8-ounce can hearts of palm, drained and diced

8-ounce can artichoke hearts, drained and quartered

DRESSING

2 tablespoons mayonnaise

2 tablespoons fresh lemon juice

2 tablespoons extra-virgin olive oil

1 teaspoon minced green onions (scallions)

¼ teaspoon minced garlic

1 tablespoon Dijon mustard

Sea salt and fresh ground black pepper to taste

1. Tear away outer dark leaves of the romaine lettuce and cut the core away from small inner leaves. Toss in a salad bowl with hearts of palm and artichoke hearts.

2. Make the dressing: Whisk dressing ingredients together in a small bowl. Pour over salad and toss well.

SERVES 4

CURRIED COLE SLAW

Try keeping this delightfully unusual salad on hand in the refrigerator, for light lunches or as a dinner accompaniment. Garam masala is an aromatic blend of dry roasted, ground spices, originating in Northern India. In colder climates of India, garam masala is used as an internally warming blend, and actually generates inner body heat. Garam masala is available in natural food stores and in Indian markets or make the blend yourself. Serve this delightful slaw with any simple grilled chicken or meat or as the vegetable complement to Potato-Leek Galette or Free-Form Zucchini Tart.

1 tablespoon safflower oil or canola oil
1 bunch green onions (scallions), minced
1 teaspoon curry powder
¼ teaspoon black mustard seeds
¼ teaspoon garam masala (page 250), or
*   nutmeg to taste*

½ head cabbage, shredded
Juice of ½ lime
2 tablespoons water
1 tablespoon currants
1 cup plain yogurt
Sea salt to taste

1. Heat the oil in a medium skillet. Add the green onions and sauté briefly. Add curry and mustard seeds, and sauté about 20 seconds. Add garam masala or nutmeg.

2. Add shredded cabbage to skillet and sauté until wilted. Remove from heat and add lime juice, water, and currants. Put the cole slaw in a bowl, cover, and serve at room temperature or chill for at least 1 hour.

3. Stir in yogurt just before serving and season with salt to taste.

SERVES 4

Garam Masala

Homemade garam masala adds an exotic and robust flavor to many dishes. The recipe here gathers classic ingredients from a variety of the regional versions of this spice blend. The procedure involves toasting whole spice seeds to lengthen shelf life before they are ground to a powder and mixed with other powdered spices. Equipment required: (1) heavy-bottomed skillet or cookie sheet, (2) electric coffee mill or spice grinder, (3) fine-meshed sieve. This recipe was inspired by Yamuna Devi's beautiful book, *The Art of Indian Vegetarian Cooking* (New York: Dutton, 1987).

⅓ *cup whole cloves*

¼ *cup fennel seeds*

¼ *cup black peppercorns*

4 *cinnamon sticks*

½ *cup green cardamom pods*

½ *cup cumin seeds*

½ *cup coriander seeds*

2 *tablespoons ground nutmeg*

1 *teaspoon ground ginger*

1. Pan toast everything but the nutmeg and ginger over low heat, stirring occasionally, for 15 minutes, or oven toast in a preheated 200°F oven for 30 minutes.
2. Crush cinnamon sticks with a rolling pin. Tap whole cardamom pods to release seeds. Discard pods.
3. In a spice grinder, grind small amounts of toasted spices, in increments, to a fine powder. Pass through fine sieve and mix well with powdered spices. Cool and store in sealed container for 4 to 5 months in a cool, dark place.

MAKES ABOUT 1 CUP

Food for Thought:

ANUTRIENTS

Did you know there are heroes in the plant world that can prevent carcinogens from reaching and reacting with the body's tissues? They're called anutrients and they act like the 300-pound center on a football team: they block to create a barrier between carcinogens and their intended target. These hero foods include: cabbage, kale, broccoli, cauliflower, garlic, onions, leeks, shallots, oranges, grapefruit, and lemons.

What if your cells are already exposed to carcinogens? Oranges contain a nutrient, D-limonene, an antioxidant that suppresses the development of cancer in a cell already exposed to a carcinogen.*

Other suppressive nutrients are vitamin C, vitamin E, and selenium, which are found in oranges, green fruits, and vegetables. Calcium is another suppressive nutrient found in figs, soy products, and all leafy greens.†

Are there any nutrients that will retard the growth of cancer?

Carrots and celery contain compounds such as phthalides and polyacetylenes, which indirectly decrease cell multiplication rates.

The Burton Goldberg Group, Alternative Medicine *(Puhalec, Washington: Future Medicine Publishing, 1993), p. 316.*

†*Ibid.*

JICAMA SLAW

Jicama, a super crispy and juicy root vegetable of Mexican descent, is usually eaten as a snack food, peeled and sliced. Try pairing this light slaw with lightly steamed fish or as a tangy partner to a yummy burro.

1 jicama, peeled and cut in matchsticks

½ hothouse cucumber, peeled, seeded, and julienned

1 tomato, seeded and finely chopped

½ carrot, grated

¼ cup chopped cilantro

Juice of 2 limes

1 tablespoon honey

½ teaspoon cayenne

Sea salt to taste

1. Gently toss together all ingredients in a large bowl to combine.

SERVES 4

FENNEL, MUSHROOM, AND SHAVED PARMESAN SALAD

Surviving Egyptian writings from around 1600 B.C. describe the use of fennel as a natural medicine. It is still used today in far Eastern medicine to treat digestive disorders. The people of India chew fennel seeds after a meal to facilitate digestion. For an interesting variation, "wrap" this salad in hot whole wheat tortillas.

½ bunch spinach

6 ounces button mushrooms

2 fennel bulbs, outer layers removed

3 ounces fresh Reggiano Parmigiano

3 tablespoons extra-virgin olive oil

2 teaspoons fresh lemon juice

Sea salt and freshly ground black pepper to taste

1 garlic clove

1 tablespoon chopped fresh Italian parsley

1. Wash and dry spinach, remove stems and set aside.

2. On a mandoline or by hand, slice mushrooms and fennel as thinly as possible. Shave half the Parmigiano into long ribbons, using a vegetable peeler. Grate the remainder.

3. Whisk together oil, lemon juice, and salt and pepper in a small bowl. Add pressed garlic. Stir in grated Parmigiano.

4. Cover two serving plates with a layer of spinach leaves.

5. Toss fennel and mushrooms with dressing and place in mounds over beds of spinach. Finish with Parmigiano shavings and garnish each salad with parsley.

SERVES 2

BABY GREENS WITH PERSIMMON AND SMOKED GOUDA

Serve with a grilled steak, chicken, or halibut. Fujus are the flat round variety of persimmon shaped like a tomato. They're eaten in a semicrisp stage of ripeness. Few Americans have ever eaten persimmons and yet, they are the most widely consumed fruit on earth because of their enormous availability and popularity in Asia. It's the contrast of the sweet persimmon and the smoked gouda that makes this a special salad. The colors are beautiful as well.

DRESSING

2 tablespoons olive oil
¼ cup apple juice
1 teaspoon apple cider vinegar
1 garlic clove, pressed
Herbamare to taste
Fresh ground pepper to taste

2 fuju persimmons, peeled
1 package organic baby greens, washed
¼ cup julienned smoked gouda
¼ cup thinly sliced red onion

1. Make the dressing: Whisk all the ingredients together in the bottom of your salad bowl.

2. Slice the persimmons across the fruit to reveal the lovely floral formation in their centers.

3. Combine salad ingredients in bowl with dressing and toss well.

SERVES 3 TO 4

"PERFECT" TOMATO SALAD WITH FETA

Assemble this salad only at the peak of tomato season, when they're absolutely "perfect." Store feta in the refrigerator, immersed in water, in a sealed container. The water helps preserve and desalinate the feta, making it more palatable. Lovely with poached eggs served over steamed spinach.

2 large red beefsteak tomatoes
2 large yellow beefsteak tomatoes
2 tablespoons extra-virgin olive oil
2 tablespoons balsamic vinegar
1 tablespoon chopped fresh tarragon

2 ounces feta or goat cheese
Sea salt and freshly ground black pepper to taste
Additional chopped tarragon for garnish

1. Cut a slice off the top and base of the tomatoes and discard. Slice tomatoes into ½-inch rounds from top to bottom. Layer in overlapping slices on a platter or individual serving plates, alternating yellow and red.

2. Put the oil, vinegar, tarragon, goat cheese, and salt in the workbowl of a food processor and process until smooth—or do this with a fork or in a blender.

3. Spoon dressing over tomatoes and finish with freshly ground black pepper and tarragon.

SERVES 2

SALAD CZAR

Unusual, elegant—this salad could be an Eastern European version of Caesar salad. Serve with Beef Tenderloins Studded with Roasted Garlic or as an accompaniment to grilled steak.

⅓ cup extra-virgin olive oil
½ tablespoon fresh lemon juice
1 teaspoon Worcestershire sauce
2 teaspoons Dijon mustard
2 egg yolks, or ¼ tablespoon yogurt
Dash of Tabasco

1 garlic clove
Sea salt and freshly ground black pepper to taste
12 cups coarsely chopped romaine leaves
1 ounce black caviar

1. Whisk together oil, lemon, Worcestershire, mustard, egg yolks or yogurt, and Tabasco in a salad bowl. Mash garlic with a fork into dressing and remove pulp. Season with salt and pepper.

2. Toss lettuce leaves well with dressing. Toss gently with caviar and serve.

SERVES 4

WARM CAULIFLOWER AND OLIVE SALAD

Sometimes you tire of lettuce and other greens. Who says a salad always has to include them? This is a favorite way to make an ordinary cauliflower interesting and "salady." It enhances any spicy dish, such as Hot Mama's Vinegar and Chili Chicken Wings.

1 large head cauliflower, cut in thin, small florets

½ cup sour cream

½ cup yogurt

1 bunch green onions (scallions), minced

2 tablespoons apple cider vinegar

Herbamare and freshly ground pepper to taste

½ cup sliced large pimento-stuffed olives (see Note)

1. Steam cauliflower until soft, but not mushy. This dish will not hold together as a salad if the cauliflower is too al dente.

2. Combine sour cream, yogurt, onions, apple cider vinegar, and seasonings in salad bowl with a whisk.

3. Add cauliflower and sliced olives and mix well. Adjust seasonings.

SERVES 4

Note: Olives packed in vermouth are truly delicious in this dish.

CHAPTER SIXTEEN

Vegetables on the Side

EASY ZUCCHINI RATATOUILLE

A pleasing complement to a scrambled egg lunch or supper. Also delicious with sautéed fish.

2 tablespoons olive oil

2 garlic cloves, minced

2 onions, finely chopped

3 zucchini, halved and sliced

One 28-ounce can Italian plum tomatoes, drained, liquid reserved

2 teaspoons dried basil

⅓ cup sliced Kalamata olives

Sea salt and freshly ground pepper to taste

1. Heat oil in a deep skillet and add garlic and onions. Sauté until wilted, then add zucchini. Sauté 5 minutes, adding a little tomato juice as necessary, to keep the vegetables moist.

2. Add plum tomatoes, basil, and olives. Bring to a boil, and simmer 10 minutes. Season to taste.

SERVES 2

GARLICKY BROCCOLI RAAB WITH PARMESAN

Broccoli raab or rapini is not broccoli at all, but a variety of foliage turnip. It has dark green leaves on a sturdy stalk with small flower clusters. It can be slightly bitter and sharp in flavor, and it is absolutely delicious prepared with a lot of garlic. This vegetable likes to be blanched before sautéing; otherwise it will be tough. It is a wonderful accompaniment to Quick Bolognese Sauce with Linguine.

1 pound broccoli raab

2 tablespoons olive oil

1 tablespoon minced garlic

1 tablespoon sweet butter

¼ cup grated Parmesan cheese

Sea salt and cracked black pepper to taste

1. Bring large saucepan of lightly salted water to a boil. Add broccoli raab and blanch for 3 minutes. Drain and refresh in a bowl of ice water to keep leaves a light green.

2. Add oil and garlic to a very hot skillet, and sauté about 30 seconds. Add drained broccoli raab, and cook 5 minutes.

3. Add butter and Parmesan. Immediately remove skillet from heat and season with salt and pepper. Spoon greens into serving dish and serve hot.

SERVES 4

BRAISED BABY VEGETABLES
WITH WHITE CORN AND GINGER

This dish stands alone as a vegetable meal, will nicely complement a creamy vegetable soup, and would even mix well with pasta or rice for an unusual "Guru's Bowl" meal.

½ tablespoon olive oil
4 heads Belgian endive
2½ cups water
4 baby bok choy
4 baby zucchini

DRESSING

1 tablespoon minced fresh gingerroot
¼ cup safflower oil
2 tablespoons fresh lime juice
1 teaspoon white miso paste
Sea salt to taste
1 tablespoon water

4 cups white corn kernels, steamed
½ teaspoon sea salt
¼ teaspoon freshly ground black pepper

1. Preheat oven to 375°F.

2. Add oil to an ovenproof skillet and sauté the endive until golden, about 5 minutes.

3. Add water, bring to a boil, and place skillet in oven for 5 minutes. Add the bok choy and zucchini and cook in the oven for about 8 minutes, or until vegetables are tender.

4. Cool vegetables while assembling dressing. Whip together dressing ingredients in a small bowl, using a fork.

5. Mix corn in a bowl with salt and pepper.

6. Arrange corn in mounds in the center of serving plates, top with vegetables, and drizzle with dressing.

SERVES 4

BRAISED BOK CHOY WITH GARLIC AND GINGER

Delicious with mashed potatoes for a simple Soothing Supper.

1 tablespoon safflower oil

2 teaspoons minced garlic

1 large carrot, peeled and cut in scant ¼-inch diagonals (optional)

1 teaspoon minced fresh gingerroot

1 cup sliced leek or green onion (scallions), cut in ½-inch diagonals

1 medium bok choy, cut in ½-inch diagonals, leaves coarsely chopped

1 cup rich vegetable stock

1 tablespoon tamari

1 teaspoon Dijon mustard

1. Preheat oven to 375°F. Heat a large ovenproof skillet. Add oil, garlic, and carrot, and sauté for 1 minute, until carrot begins to brown.

2. Add ginger and leek, sauté for 1 minute.

3. Add bok choy and sauté until slightly limp, a few seconds. Add stock, tamari, and mustard to skillet and bring to a boil.

4. Cover and place skillet in oven for 15 minutes. When done, simmer for 2 minutes longer on stove to reduce sauce, if necessary.

SERVES 4

Food for Thought:

GRILLED CORN ON THE COB

Grilled corn has an earthy, sweet, slightly smoky flavor. It is a fabulous addition to Bowl O' Barbecue, a meal of grilled meats, sausages, onions, and peppers. Allow 1 ear or more per person.

1. Peel husks down about halfway and remove corn silk, leaving the corn covered in its husk.
2. Soak corn in a deep bowl filled with lukewarm water for about 15 minutes.
3. Grill corn, still in its husk, for 15 minutes, turning frequently. Serve immediately with butter and salt or cut in half and toss into a big bowl of barbecued goodies.

> ### *Food for Thought:*
> ## FRUIT VEGETABLES
>
> Cucumbers, eggplants, and zucchini, nicknamed "fruit vegetables" by farmers, are best when picked young, before they have reached full maturity. At this stage, they're more tender and flavorful and have fewer seeds.
>
> The older and larger they get, the greater the chance they will be watery or slightly bitter.

CALABACITAS CON LECHE

In the summer when you have squash from your garden or the farmer's market, don't forget this one! It's a great item on a picnic buffet.

¼ cup sweet butter

4 medium summer squash, sliced thinly

1 medium onion, sliced thinly

1½ cups fresh corn kernels, or 1 package frozen, thawed, or one 15-ounce can whole-kernel corn, drained

One 4-ounce can chopped green chilies

Sea salt and freshly ground pepper to taste

1 cup milk (or plain soy milk)

½ cup grated cheddar cheese

1. Melt the butter in a wide skillet over medium heat. When it's bubbling, add squash and onion, and sauté until soft.

2. Reduce heat and add corn, green chilies, salt and pepper.

3. Mix well and add milk. Simmer until well blended.

4. Add cheese and cover, for a minute or two, until cheese is melted.

SERVES 2 TO 3

PART EIGHT

Sauces, Salsas, and Salad Dressings

Chapter Seventeen
Sauces and Salsas

ROASTED PEPPER AND CORN SALSA

Serve over grilled or seared fish, poultry, or vegetables, or add to fajita garnishes.

1 green bell pepper

1 poblano pepper

4 ears cooked corn (approximately 2 cups kernels)

½ diced red onion

½ cup chopped cilantro

Juice of 2 limes, according to taste

3 tablespoons extra-virgin olive oil

½ jalapeño pepper, seeded and minced

Sea salt and black pepper to taste

1. Preheat oven to 400°F.

2. To roast the green and poblano peppers, place them on a pie plate or a shallow baking dish and bake for 45 minutes. Place in a paper bag until cool enough to handle. Peel off outer skin, remove seeds, and dice peppers into ¼-inch pieces.

3. Place corn in a mixing bowl. Add onion, roasted peppers, cilantro, lime juice, olive oil, and minced jalapeño. Season with salt and pepper. Toss gently to combine. Store in a covered glass bowl for up to 1 week.

MAKES 3 CUPS

KIWI-MANGO SALSA

An exotic and colorful salsa designed to spruce up lightly steamed fish, and it's also great with chips.

2 kiwis
1 mango
3 big tomatoes, or 6 Roma (plum) tomatoes
1 red onion, minced
Canned jalapeño peppers to taste

Cilantro (optional)
Fresh lime juice to cover, juice of about 2 limes
Salt to taste

1. Chop everything except lime juice and salt and mix together in a ceramic bowl.

2. Cover with lime juice. Let sit for a couple of hours to blend flavors. Taste for salt and correct seasonings. This salsa will keep in the refrigerator for about 1 week.

MAKES 2½ CUPS

TOMATO-CAPER TAPENADE

This *salsa fresca* is a speedy solution for topping steamed, sautéed, or grilled chicken or fish. Prepare it first, before other dishes, so the flavors can blend.

2 medium tomatoes, seeded and diced
2 tablespoons capers, rinsed and drained
Juice of ½ lemon
2 tablespoons extra-virgin olive oil

1 teaspoon fresh thyme
1 tablespoon coarsely chopped fresh basil
¼ teaspoon sea salt
Pinch freshly ground black pepper

1. Combine everything in a small mixing bowl.

2. Stir gently, then chill while you prepare your meal. Spoon over cooked meats at the table.

MAKES 1 CUP

Food for Thought:

GARLIC AND ONIONS

Fresh garlic and onions are high in enzymes that lower "bad" LDL blood cholesterol and raise your "good" HDL count. Use them generously, raw as often as possible. Use a garlic press to add garlic to salad dressings and finish soups. Add pressed garlic to mayonnaise, mustard, cream cheese, butter, or avocado to use as spreads.

CUCUMBER-TOMATO RAITA

Unbeknownst to most Westerners is the exciting culinary scene in India. Many of its dishes can promote the radiant health Americans are seeking. Yogurt made from fresh unpasteurized milk is a staple, usually in the form of raita, or yogurt salad, used as an all-purpose sauce. Serve over steamed fish and vegetables.

1 cup plain yogurt, whole or nonfat
¼ cup minced red onion
¼ cup seeded and shredded cucumber
¼ cup seeded and minced tomato

⅓ cup chopped fresh mint
½ teaspoon ground cumin
Pinch salt

1. Combine and chill until ready to use or serve immediately.

MAKES 2 CUPS

෧๏

TOMATO CHUTNEY

Make a quantity of this chutney and store for up to 1 week in a glass container with tight-fitting lid. Serve over fresh fish, chicken, or vegetables.

5 medium tomatoes, chopped in ½-inch cubes
2 medium onions, roughly chopped
1 small jalapeño pepper, seeded and minced
1 tablespoon grated gingerroot

1 tablespoon honey
⅓ cup white wine vinegar
Sea salt and freshly ground black pepper to taste

1. In a medium saucepan, combine everything but the salt and pepper. Cook, uncovered, over medium-high heat for 45 minutes, stirring from time to time.

2. Strain off any excess liquid, then season with salt and pepper to taste.

MAKES 2 CUPS

ARAME SAUCE FOR STEAMED VEGETABLES

Arame is a fine black sea vegetable, vermicelli-like when hydrated. It is rich in nutrients and enzymes. Its mild ocean flavor adds interest to vegetable dishes. Szechuan sauce adds just the right kick to this flavorful and unusual topping. Serve Arame Sauce over hot broccoli—add buttered baked beets and Essene bread with almond butter.

½ cup dried arame (see Sources)
2 tablespoons Bragg Liquid Aminos
2 tablespoons apple cider vinegar

¼ cup olive oil
1 teaspoon Szechuan sauce (optional)

1. Soak dried arame in room temperature water for 15 minutes. Drain and rinse thoroughly.

2. In a small bowl, whisk together Bragg Liquid Aminos, apple cider vinegar, and olive oil. Add Szechuan sauce if desired. Pour over arame. Serve immediately or refrigerate for several days. Bring to room temperature before serving.

MAKES 1 CUP

TWO-MINUTE DILLED YOGURT SAUCE WITH CUMIN AND GARLIC

Impressive over spicy grills in the summertime, over steamed salmon, or as a healthy dipping sauce for fresh vegetables or chips.

1½ cups plain yogurt

1 tablespoon fresh lemon juice

1 garlic clove, minced

¼ cup minced red onion

¼ cup snipped fresh dill

½ teaspoon ground cumin

Herbamare to taste

1. Combine ingredients in a mixing bowl and stir well.

2. Chill for at least 1 hour and serve cold.

MAKES 2 CUPS TO SERVE 4 TO 6

CRANBERRY-RAISIN RELISH

Usually cranberry dishes at Thanksgiving take a backseat to all the other featured creations. Inspired from a recipe from *Bon Appetit* magazine, this relish can be made several days in advance, before you're knee-deep in preparations with no time to fuss with the cranberries.

1 orange

1 lemon

4 cups fresh or frozen cranberries

1½ cups Tawny Port or cranberry juice

¾ cup Sucanat or other dry natural
    sweetener

½ cup fresh orange juice

1½ teaspoons cornstarch

1 teaspoon dry mustard

1 teaspoon fresh lemon juice

¼ teaspoon ground cloves

¼ teaspoon ground ginger

¾ cup raisins or currants

Pinch of sea salt

1. Zest orange and lemon—grate the rind—before squeezing the juice. Set aside 2 tablespoons grated orange peel and 1 teaspoon grated lemon peel.

2. Combine all ingredients, including grated peels, in a large, heavy saucepan. Simmer, stirring occasionally, until berries burst, raisins plump, and sauce thickens, approximately 15 minutes. Cool, cover, and refrigerate. Serve at room temperature. Keeps for 7 to 10 days.

MAKES 2 CUPS

ROASTED BEET RELISH

A no-fuss accompaniment to meat, vegetables, or grains. Serve cold with salad and turkey cutlets.

6 beets, greens removed and reserved for steaming or soup

¼ cup extra-virgin olive oil

3 garlic cloves, minced

Sea salt and freshly ground black pepper to taste

¼ cup balsamic or apple cider vinegar

¼ cup minced fresh basil, or 2 teaspoons dried

2 tablespoons honey

1. Preheat oven to 400°F.

2. Peel beets and cut into ½-inch dice.

3. In a medium mixing bowl, combine the beets with 2 tablespoons olive oil, the garlic, and a pinch of salt and pepper. Add remaining ingredients and mix well.

4. Bake 30-40 minutes or until tender, turning occasionally.

MAKES 2 CUPS

Chapter Eighteen
Salad Dressings

FITONICS HOUSE DRESSING

Use this classic dressing on any green salad. Pour it over sliced beefsteak tomatoes, shredded carrots, or cucumber. Add to cold rice or pasta salads. Toss with cubed chicken. It's all-purpose!

3 tablespoons extra-virgin olive oil
1 tablespoon fresh lemon juice
1 teaspoon apple cider vinegar
½ teaspoon Dijon mustard

1 garlic clove, pressed
1 tablespoon plain yogurt or buttermilk
Freshly ground pepper and sea salt to taste

1. Whisk all ingredients together in salad bowl before adding greens.

MAKES APPROXIMATELY ⅓ CUP

Food for Thought:

OILS

Always store oils away from heat and direct sunlight. Otherwise they can easily become rancid, taste old, and possibly cause food poisoning. While olive oil prefers cool, dark storage in the cupboard, sunflower, safflower, and canola oil do well stored in the refrigerator.

Also, be sure to replace lids promptly on oils when you are through using them. Prolonged contact with air will cause oxidation, significantly lowering shelf life and minimizing flavor. For this reason, those cute little metal pitchers with open spouts or clear glass table servers are definitely not the healthiest way to go.

SOY-LIME VINAIGRETTE

Serve as a dressing for salad or as a sauce for steamed vegetables, or steamed or grilled fish.

½ cup chopped shallot

1 garlic clove, minced

1 teaspoon grated gingerroot

½ teaspoon freshly ground black pepper

1 tablespoon honey

2 tablespoons soy sauce

2 tablespoons fresh lime juice

¼ cup safflower oil

1. In a small bowl, whisk together all ingredients except the oil.

2. Then drizzle in oil, continuing to whisk, until you have an emulsion.

MAKES 1 CUP, TO SERVE 4

SPICY TOMATO DRESSING

A delicious dressing for salad greens or a sauce for fish and vegetables. Can also be tossed with pasta or rice.

1 tablespoon fresh lemon juice

1 tablespoon apple cider vinegar

2 tablespoons tomato paste

¼ teaspoon Worcestershire sauce

Sea salt and freshly ground black pepper to taste

1 Roma (plum) tomato, core removed and seeded

¼ cup extra-virgin olive oil

1. Place everything in a blender and puree until smooth.

MAKES ½ CUP, TO SERVE 2

NEW HERB VINAIGRETTE

We call this "new" because of the healthful addition of apple cider vinegar to replace the less healthful but more commonly used wine vinegar. Honey, as well, is a healthful touch. Lovely on steamed cauliflower or as a dressing for a salad of mixed greens, orange, and grapefruit wheels.

¼ cup Italian parsley

1 tablespoon chopped fresh rosemary

3 tablespoons cilantro leaves

3 tablespoons fresh thyme

¼ cup fresh basil

¼ cup apple cider vinegar

2 tablespoons honey

2 garlic cloves

½ cup extra-virgin olive oil

1. Place everything but the oil in a blender or food processor, and puree.

2. Drizzle in olive oil and blend to emulsify.

MAKES APPROXIMATELY 1½ CUPS TO SERVE 8

BUTTERMILK–WALNUT OIL DRESSING

1 tablespoon fresh lime juice

1 tablespoon balsamic or apple cider
   vinegar

½ teaspoon Dijon mustard

⅓ cup buttermilk

1 tablespoon walnut oil

1. In a small bowl, combine lime juice, vinegar, and mustard.

2. Whisk in buttermilk and oil until emulsified.

MAKES ½ CUP TO SERVE 3 TO 4

PART NINE

Breads, Savory Muffins, and Sweets

Food for Thought:

SUGAR

The twentieth century has brought us an unlimited supply of sugar, artificial and refined sweeteners, which is by far the most common addiction we now have. Reports indicate that the average person consumes nearly 170 pounds of refined sugar, corn syrup, and artificial sweeteners per year, which is over 3 pounds per week.

Dr. Abram Ber is a medical doctor who became a homeopathic physician in the '70s. A pioneer in homeopathic medicine, he shares strong opinions on the harmful effects of refined sugar. Dr. Ber strongly advises his patients *never* to eat refined sugar in any form, for several reasons. According to his research, sugar suppresses the immune system, making it less resistant to bacterial infections. He has also found that sugar affects children very negatively, contributing to learning difficulties and hyperactivity, as well as ear infections. In adults, sugar also has pervasive ill effects, contributing to a rise in triglycerides and cholesterol, mineral deficiencies, anxiety, and depression. Dr. Ber also sees sugar as a major cause of obesity and yeast infections, *Candidiasis* (antibiotics, cortisone, and birth control pills also contribute to this condition). He claims it can contribute to diabetes and cause hypoglycemia, and aggravates symptoms of arthritis. At the very least, according to his research, sugar increases fatigue and energy loss.

The use of sugar is associated with many of the diseases that have made in-roads this past century. Sugar is very harmful to your health, and you must avoid it in order to be able to have a healthy life. Any disease that you presently have will be made worse by eating sugar. We are forbidden to do things that harm our health, and there is precious little doubt about the consequences of eating 170 pounds of sugar per year.

Food for Thought:

WORKING WITH YEAST

If you're not used to baking with yeast, don't worry—it's easy and fun, as long as you remember these points.

1. You must *knead* for the specified time or your results will be dense and heavy, especially when you're using whole-grain flours.
2. *Proofing*, or rising, is the period when the yeast is being activated and releasing gases. Don't cut the rising time short and also be careful not to overproof your dough, or your bread will not rise adequately or it will be full of holes.
3. *Atmospheric conditions* have an enormous effect on bread baking. Variables, such as the mineral content in the water, altitude, and humidity alter the temperament of the dough. Be sensitive to climatic conditions in your kitchen and be ready to make some changes. Here are some troubleshooting solutions:
   - *If the dough has not doubled in bulk*, rising time needs to be adjusted.
   - *If the dough is too sticky or too dry to work with*, the ratio of wet to dry ingredients needs adjusting.

BUTTER

Sweet butter is usually fresher than salted butter because the added salt acts as a preservative, assuring a longer shelf life. Sweet butter, because of its shorter shelf life, "turns over" in the market more frequently. Salted butter can be stored a long time before it's restocked in the dairy case, but sweet butter goes straight from the dairy to the supermarket.

BAKING DISHES

Foods bake more quickly in glass bakeware than in metal dishes. If you use a Pyrex baking dish and the recipe does not specify to do so, lower your oven temperature 10 degrees for rectangular bread baking dishes, and 25 degrees for larger casserole-style dishes.

CHAPTER NINETEEN

Breads

HONEY WHEAT BREAD

This is an unusually high fiber bread thanks to the addition of the rolled oats, wheat bran, nuts, seeds and raisins.

3 cups hot water

1 cup rolled oats

1 cup wheat bran

2 tablespoons sweet butter

½ cup honey

¼ cup molasses

2 tablespoons fresh yeast

¾ tablespoons sea salt

½ cup yellow cornmeal

2½ cups whole wheat flour

3 cups unbleached all-purpose flour

¼ cup crushed walnuts (optional)

¼ cup sesame seeds or flax seeds or both

½ cup soaked raisins (optional)

Additional all-purpose flour for kneading and dusting

1. In a large bowl or in the bowl of an electric mixer, pour the hot water over the oats. Set aside to soak 15 minutes.

2. Add bran, butter, honey, and molasses. Mix well. Add yeast, salt, and remaining ingredients, and combine using additional all-purpose flour if necessary. Knead the dough until it pulls away from the sides of the bowl or forms a tight, sticky ball. Work in additional all-purpose flour to keep dough from sticking to bowl.

3. Place dough in a large, lightly oiled bowl. Cover the bowl with plastic wrap and allow to rise in a warm draft-free place until doubled in bulk, 45 minutes to 1 hour.

4. Punch dough down with your fist to deflate. Divide the dough into 4 pieces. Shape into tight balls by folding the dough over on itself, creating a smooth skin with the bottom seam. Pinch the bottom seam together and place, seam side down, on a generously floured or parchment-lined baking sheet. Cover with a damp cloth or plastic wrap to rise again until doubled in bulk, about 1 hour.

5. Preheat oven to 425°F. Lightly dust the loaves with a handful of all-purpose flour. Using a very sharp serrated knife, slice a ½-inch deep X in the center of each loaf. Allow loaves to rest another 10 minutes, then bake 25 to 30 minutes, until loaves are puffy and golden and sound hollow when tapped.

MAKES 4 SMALL LOAVES

HANDMADE POTATO FOCACCIA

This recipe originated in Italy and passed from one professional baker to another until it reached this page. The beauty of this recipe is that the dough requires no kneading so it's not labor-intensive at all. Although it's a white bread, it's not nutritionally "empty" because it contains a substantial amount of cooked potatoes. Although the fresh herbs add a more intense flavor to the focaccia, dried herbs work well if fresh are not available. Hot focaccia and a yummy salad make a lovely meal.

STEP 1

3 cups unbleached all-purpose flour

2 cups water

1½ tablespoons active dry yeast

STEP 2

6 large russet potatoes, peeled and boiled until soft

½ cup water

3 tablespoons olive oil

1 ounce sea salt

7 cups unbleached all-purpose flour

3 additional tablespoons olive oil for the bowl

STEP 3

1 cup water

2 tablespoons kosher salt

1 tablespoon cracked black pepper

½ cup chopped fresh rosemary, or 3 tablespoons dried

1 tablespoon fresh thyme, or 1 teaspoon dried

¼ cup olive oil

1. Step 1: In a large mixing bowl, combine all the ingredients listed. Now you have what's called a sponge. Cover the bowl with plastic wrap and place in a warm, draft-free place for 25 minutes.

2. Step 2: Drain and mash the potatoes, either by running them through a food mill or mashing them by hand. Combine them in a large mixing bowl with the water, olive oil, and salt. Mix to combine, then add to the sponge. Work the dough only until the potato mixture is incorporated. Add the 7 cups flour, mixing by hand until flour is incorporated, about 4 minutes.

3. Place the dough in a generously oiled bowl to rise. Cover the bowl with plastic wrap and place in a warm place for 45 to 55 minutes, until doubled in bulk.

4. Step 3: Preheat oven to 425°F. Being careful not to handle the dough too much, divide it into 6 pieces. Press each piece flat onto a generously oiled baking sheet. Brush with water, then dust with salt and pepper. Bake until golden brown, about 15 to 20 minutes. Sprinkle with fresh herbs and then brush with olive oil. Bake an additional 5 minutes. Cool slightly before serving.

MAKE 6 INDIVIDUAL FOCACCIAS

SKILLET CORN BREAD
WITH SPICY SWEET RED PEPPER BUTTER

With a "Guru's Bowl" of soup or stew or a Super Salad, this makes the meal.

SPICY BUTTER

½ cup (1 stick) sweet butter, softened to room temperature
½ teaspoon ground red pepper flakes
1 tablespoon roasted garlic
1 tablespoon honey
Pinch of salt

CORN BREAD

1 cup finely ground cornmeal
2 cups unbleached all-purpose flour
1 cup boiling water
1 cup cooked corn kernels
2 teaspoons baking soda
½ cup honey
1 teaspoon sea salt
2½ cups buttermilk
1 cup melted sweet butter
2 large eggs

1. Make the spicy butter: Whip the butter ingredients together in a small bowl until incorporated. (To roast garlic, bake a whole bulb on baking sheet at 325°F for 1 hour. Cool and squeeze soft garlic pulp from husks.)

2. Make the corn bread: Preheat oven to 350°F.

3. Combine cornmeal and flour in a mixing bowl. Pour boiling water over the mixture and stir. Beat in remaining ingredients and combine well.

4. Pour the batter into a large (12-inch) greased cast-iron or other ovenproof skillet, and bake for 45 to 50 minutes, or until a knife inserted into the center comes away clean. Cool slightly on a baking rack before slicing. Spread Sweet Red Pepper Butter on slices of corn bread.

MAKES ONE 12-INCH CORNBREAD TO SERVE 8

WHOLE WHEAT SOURDOUGH GARLIC CHEESE BREAD

Kids "chow down" on this tasty complement to soups and salads. Look for whole wheat sourdough bread in the bakery of your natural food store. It's delicious! Any good whole grain bread, unsliced, can be substituted.

1 unsliced whole-grain bread, cut in 8 thick slices
2 tablespoons butter
2 tablespoons olive oil

2 large garlic cloves, pressed
1 cup grated jack or cheddar cheese
1 teaspoon thyme

1. Heat butter and oil in small saucepan. Stir in pressed garlic.

2. Brush garlic-butter mixture on bread slices, arrange in broiler pan.

3. Top slices with cheese and dust with thyme.

4. Place under hot broiler 4 to 6 inches from heat, and broil until cheese melts and crust of bread is lightly browned, 3 to 5 minutes. Watch carefully to avoid burning.

SERVES 4 TO 6

POTATO-LEEK GALETTE

This easy savory tart completes any vegetarian soup meal in fine style. Yellow-Finn potatoes are a creamy sweet European potato, ideal for baking because they become buttery and smooth, not overly starchy.

1 recipe Basic Flaky Pie Pastry (page 316)

1 cup thinly sliced, thoroughly rinsed leeks (page 39)

4 cups peeled, quartered, and thinly sliced Yellow-Finn potatoes

1 tablespoon extra-virgin olive oil

1 cup vegetable stock

Sea salt and freshly ground white pepper to taste

2 tablespoons sour cream

Buttermilk for brushing crust

1. Preheat oven to 375°F.

2. Line a large baking sheet with parchment paper. Prepare pie pastry and divide into two pieces, one slightly larger than the other. On a well-floured surface roll the larger of the two into a 10-inch circle. Do not trim. Place on baking sheet. Roll out remaining portion into a 9-inch circle and place on baking sheet. Cover crusts loosely with parchment paper or plastic wrap and refrigerate while preparing remaining ingredients.

3. In a large skillet over medium heat, sauté leeks and potatoes in olive oil. When leeks begin to soften, add vegetable stock and continue to cook until potatoes are soft, about 12 minutes. Add salt and pepper to taste and sour cream.

4. Remove potato-leek mixture from heat and cool slightly.

5. Retrieve crusts from the refrigerator and spoon filling into center of larger disk. Top with smaller disk and fold bottom crust over edge of top crust, rolling inward and pressing with fingertips to seal. Make 8 incisions in a star design on top, then pierce a hole in the center. Brush lightly with buttermilk.

6. Bake on bottom rack of oven for 30 to 35 minutes, or until crust appears light golden brown. Allow to cool on a rack before slicing into six wedges.

SERVES 6

FREE-FORM ZUCCHINI TART

We tripled this recipe and served it chilled to 25 people at a summer vegetarian birthday celebration. Surrounded by an array of chilled simple salads, it was a huge hit.

PIE DOUGH

1 recipe Basic Flaky Pie Pastry (page 316)
2 teaspoons dried thyme
½ teaspoon freshly ground black pepper

2 tablespoons extra-virgin olive oil
1 tablespoon butter
2 cups sliced onions

1 tablespoon minced garlic
1 tablespoon minced fresh basil
2 cups grated zucchini
Sea salt and freshly ground pepper to taste
½ cup grated mozzarella cheese
¼ cup grated Parmesan cheese

1. Follow recipe for pie pastry, adding thyme and black pepper to the dough. Wrap and chill.

2. Preheat over to 400°F.

3. Heat oil and butter in a large skillet until they're bubbling. Add onions, garlic, and basil, and sauté about 3 minutes. Add zucchini, and sauté another 5 minutes. Add seasonings. Drain off any liquid, and set aside.

4. Roll out pastry to an 8-by-12-inch rectangle, about ¼ inch thick, on a floured baking sheet. Pinch edges with fingers to create a rustic, slightly elevated border. Prebake the crust for 15 minutes. Remove partially baked crust from the oven, turn the temperature down to 350°F, and spread zucchini mixture over crust. Bake 20 minutes. Sprinkle surface with mozzarella and Parmesan, and bake on top shelf of the oven for an additional 5 minutes.

5. Cool slightly on a rack. Slice into small pieces and serve.

MAKES 24 SMALL SLICES

Chapter Twenty

Muffins

THOSE A-MAIZE-ING BLUES

What could be more unusual? Blue cornmeal and blueberries. The result is simply "a-maiz-ing!" Serve with soup for a Soothing Supper.

½ cup blue cornmeal

½ cup buttermilk

½ cup apple juice concentrate

5 tablespoons pure maple syrup or honey

¼ cup sweet butter, softened, or ½ cup corn oil

1 large egg

1½ cups unbleached all-purpose flour

¾ teaspoon sea salt

1½ teaspoons baking soda

1 teaspoon baking powder

6 ounces frozen blueberries, tossed in 3 tablespoons all-purpose flour

1. Preheat oven to 400°F. Line a 12-cup muffin tin with paper liners.

2. Combine cornmeal and buttermilk in a bowl and set aside.

3. In a mixing bowl, cream together apple juice concentrate, maple syrup or honey, and butter (or oil), and beat in egg.

4. Sift into a bowl the flour, salt, baking soda, and baking powder.

5. Combine cornmeal mixture with creamed ingredients and fold dry mixture into wet, incorporating with as few strokes as possible. *Do not overmix.* Batter should be lumpy and still have pockets of dry flour. Stir in berries.

6. Fill muffin cups to the top (for jumbo muffins, fill only 8 cups.) Bake 25 to 30 minutes. Cool slightly on a baking rack before releasing.

MAKES 8 TO 12 MUFFINS

MAUI MUFFINS

Sweet and fruity, these are a delicious complement to a savory soup.

2½ cups whole wheat pastry flour

½ cup oat bran

Pinch of sea salt

1 teaspoon ground ginger, or 1 tablespoon grated fresh gingerroot

½ teaspoon ground cloves

½ teaspoon almond extract

2 large bananas, mashed

¼ cup safflower oil

2 large eggs

1 cup pure pineapple-coconut juice (no additives)

¼ cup honey

1 cup grated unsweetened coconut for topping

1. Preheat oven to 350°F. Line a 12-cup muffin tin with paper liners.

2. Sift together the first 6 ingredients.

3. In a separate bowl combine remaining ingredients, except the topping. Fold dry mixture into wet, being careful not to overmix.

4. Fill the muffin cups. Fill only 8 cups for jumbo muffins, 12 for regular size.

5. Top each muffin with shredded coconut and bake 20 to 25 minutes, or until golden brown. Cool for 5 minutes in muffin tin before transferring to a wire rack.

MAKES 8 TO 12 MUFFINS

CHAPTER TWENTY-ONE

Sweets

AMBROSIA BARS

These are delightful as a finale to a fruit meal.

DOUGH

¼ teaspoon sea salt

¾ cup unbleached all-purpose flour

¾ cup whole wheat pastry flour

½ cup cold butter, cut into small cubes

½ cup ice water

2 large eggs

⅓ cup silken tofu

¾ cup honey or brown rice syrup

1½ cups shredded, unsweetened coconut

1 teaspoon grated orange zest

½ teaspoon baking powder

1 teaspoon pure vanilla extract

1. Preheat oven to 350°F. Have ready an 8-by-12-inch baking pan lined with parchment paper.

2. In a large mixing bowl stir together salt and flours. Then, by hand, using a pastry cutter or two knives, cut butter through the mixture until it resembles coarse crumbs. You want to rub the butter through the flour until it's properly incorporated. If you overdo it, your dough will be heavy and gummy. Drizzle in cold water until mixture binds into a loose dough. Press into the prepared pan. Bake 10 minutes.

3. In the work bowl of a food processor fitted with the metal blade, combine remaining ingredients. Spread mixture over dough. Return to oven and bake 40 minutes, or until golden brown and set.

4. Cut into 2-by-2-inch squares, and cool bars on a baking rack.

MAKES 24 BARS

RAISIN BARS

These healthy bars can be a treat that you eat warm along with a hearty bowl of soup or as a complement to a fruit meal.

DOUGH

1 cup unbleached all-purpose flour

1 cup whole wheat pastry flour

¼ teaspoon sea salt

¼ cup Sucanat or other natural sweetener

¼ cup sweet butter, softened to room temperature

½ cup sour cream

1 large egg white

2 tablespoons ice water

¼ cup buttermilk for brushing

FILLING

1½ cups raisins

3 large egg whites

¾ cup Sucanat or other natural dry sweetener

4½ tablespoons unbleached all-purpose flour

1½ tablespoons light or dark rum (optional)

1. Make the dough: Preheat oven to 375°F.

2. Sift together flours and sea salt in a bowl. Add sweetener. In a large mixing bowl, combine the remaining ingredients.

3. Fold dry mixture into wet and work it into a manageable dough. Wrap tightly with plastic wrap and refrigerate for 30 minutes.

4. Make the filling: Using a blender or a food processor fitted with the metal blade, combine all ingredients to create a paste.

5. To assemble the bars: Divide dough into two equal parts. On a floured surface, roll out each piece of dough to a rectangle about 12 by 6 inches. It should be ⅛-inch thick.

6. Spread half the filling lengthwise down the center 3 inches. Fold the sides over the filling and overlap slightly. Pinch edges of dough together to seal. Place each roll on parchment-lined baking sheet, seam-side down, once it's finished. Brush with buttermilk.

7. Bake 25 minutes, or until bottoms are evenly golden brown. Remove from oven and slice while warm into 1-inch bars.

MAKES 2 DOZEN

MAPLE MUESLI REFRIGERATOR COOKIES

Muesli is a Swiss grain breakfast cereal, the sophisticated city cousin of country granola. Not overly sweet, these cookies can replace bread as companions to soup or salad.

1 stick sweet butter, softened to room
*   temperature*
¼ cup pure maple syrup
½ cup Sucanat or other natural dry
*   sweetener*
1 large egg
½ teaspoon vanilla

1¼ cups muesli
½ cup whole wheat pastry flour
½ cup unbleached all-purpose flour
½ teaspoon baking soda

1. Cream together butter and sweeteners. Beat in egg and vanilla.

2. Combine dry ingredients in a bowl and fold into butter mixture. With your hands, roll dough into about a 9-inch long cylinder and wrap tightly with plastic wrap. Refrigerate until ready to use.

3. To bake: Preheat oven to 350°F. Remove plastic wrap from dough, and on a lightly floured surface, slice cookies into ¾-inch rounds, using a sharp serrated knife. Place on a parchment-lined cookie sheet, and bake 10 to 12 minutes. Cool on a baking rack.

MAKES 1 DOZEN COOKIES

◠◡

PBJ SHORTBREAD BARS

Kids, good luck keeping these away from Mom or Dad. Another innovative accompaniment for a savory soup or salad.

SHORTBREAD

¾ cup whole wheat pastry flour

¼ cup cornstarch, or 2 tablespoons arrowroot

¼ teaspoon sea salt

¼ cup Sucanat or other natural dry sweetener

2 tablespoons honey

6 tablespoons cold sweet butter, diced

¼ cup raw, unsalted peanut butter

½ teaspoon vanilla

STREUSEL

4 tablespoons sweet butter, softened to room temperature

1 tablespoon honey

½ teaspoon ground cinnamon

½ cup whole wheat pastry flour

¾ cup coarsely chopped raw unsalted peanuts

¼ cup fruit preserves or jam

1. Preheat oven to 350°F.

2. Make the shortbread: Sift together flour, cornstarch, and sea salt in a bowl.

3. In a mixing bowl, lightly combine sweeteners with butter so that lumps of butter remain separate and visible. Add peanut butter and vanilla, and swirl together gently with a wooden spoon. Do not whip.

4. Fold dry ingredients into wet in short quick motions, stirring only until mixture begins to bind. Using your hands, press dough into a 9-inch square baking pan.

5. Make the streusel: Combine ingredients in a small bowl. Spread preserves or jam evenly over surface of dough and top with streusel.

6. Bake 30 minutes, or until a knife inserted in the center emerges clean. Remove from oven and cool slightly on a baking rack before slicing.

7. Slice into 1½-by-1½-inch bars, and cool completely before removing from baking pan.

MAKES 12 BARS

APPLE BUTTER SQUARES

Good with soup, good as a dessert. These bars are easy and fun to make and eat.

1 cup oat flour
1 cup whole wheat pastry flour
1 tablespoon ground cinnamon
1 cup whole oats
1 cup quick oats

8 tablespoons (1 stick) sweet butter
¼ cup maple syrup or honey
1½ cups apple butter
¾ cup chopped pitted prunes

1. Preheat oven to 375°F. Lightly oil and flour an 11-by-7-inch (or equivalent) baking pan, or line the pan with parchment paper.

2. Combine dry ingredients in a large mixing bowl. Cut in butter by hand until mixture resembles coarse crumbs. Add maple syrup and work into a manageable dough. Divide into 2 equal parts.

3. Press first half of mixture into baking pan. Spread apple butter evenly over surface, avoiding edges by about ¼-inch. Dot with prunes. Crumble remaining oat mixture as evenly as possible to cover the apple butter. Do not press it down.

4. Bake 25 minutes on center rack of oven. Remove, and cool 15 minutes before slicing. Cut into 2-inch squares.

MAKES TWENTY 2-INCH SQUARES

Food for Thought:

PARCHMENT PAPER

An important asset in the baker's pantry, parchment paper is often mistaken for wax paper even though it's not transparent. Parchment prevents baked goods from sticking to the baking surfaces. In some cases it even prevents edges and corners from caramelizing and thus burning. Cleanup is a snap when you use parchment paper, and it also creates a more refined finished product. There's no oily mess from the "greasing and flouring" of the baking surface, which gives you a cleaner finish. You can use parchment paper any time a recipe calls for "greasing, oiling, and flouring." It's available in some supermarkets, hardware stores, and kitchen shops, and though it seems expensive, a little goes a long way. You can usually use each piece several times—just wipe it clean.

NUTS

When shopping for nuts, always look for the raw, unsalted varieties. They have no added oils or flavorings, and have their nutritional values intact, unlike the roasted and salted snacking varieties.

If a recipe calls for roasted nuts, preheat your oven to about 300°F, and place the nuts on a baking sheet in the oven for about 10 minutes, or until they smell good.

CINNAMON

Cinnamon, the spice of love, is an enchanting aromatherapy as well as a cooking spice. Our sense of smell is linked more directly to the brain than any of the other senses. Scents have an enormous effect on the psyche, and subtle aromas powerfully affect our thoughts and emotions, sometimes without our even knowing it.

Keep cinnamon sticks on hand to steep in your tea mug to relieve muscle tension.

Place a small bowl of whole cinnamon sticks and a few whole cloves next to your bed. The ancient Egyptians used cinnamon as an aphrodisiac—guaranteed to add spice to your life!

THE CLASSIC ALL-AMERICAN COOKIE

This "modified" recipe yields such a delectably gooey cookie, you'd never know that half the butter and all the refined sugar have been omitted. Remember, while chocolate carries with it a lot of fat (52 percent), carob has practically none (2 percent). And carob is rich in vitamins and minerals and good for the colon.

½ cup sweet butter, softened to room temperature

⅓ cup honey

⅓ cup corn syrup or brown rice syrup

1 large egg

1 teaspoon vanilla

1 cup unbleached all-purpose flour

1 teaspoon baking powder

¼ teaspoon sea salt

1 cup naturally sweetened chocolate chips or carob chips

⅓ cup slivered almonds

1. Preheat oven to 350°F.

2. In a mixing bowl, cream butter and sweeteners. Beat in egg and add vanilla.

3. In a separate bowl, sift together flour, baking powder, and sea salt. Combine with chips and almonds and fold dry ingredients into wet.

4. Drop by heaping tablespoons onto a parchment-lined baking sheet (make smaller drops if desired).

5. Bake 18 minutes, or 10 minutes for minicookies.

MAKES 12 JUMBO COOKIES

BIG SOFT CHEWY SPICE COOKIES

For those who love 'em chewy and spicy!

1 cup unbleached all-purpose flour
1 cup whole wheat pastry flour
¾ teaspoon cinnamon
½ teaspoon ground ginger
½ teaspoon ground allspice
½ teaspoon ground cloves
½ teaspoon white pepper
½ teaspoon baking soda

½ teaspoon sea salt
½ cup sweet butter
⅔ cup Sucanat or other natural dry sweetener
⅓ cup maple syrup or honey
1 large egg
Cinnamon for garnish

1. Preheat oven to 375°F.

2. Sift together dry ingredients in a bowl. Set aside.

3. In a mixing bowl, cream butter and sweeteners until light and fluffy. Beat in egg and combine well.

4. Fold dry ingredients into wet and shape dough into twelve 1-inch balls. Place about 2 inches apart on an ungreased cookie sheet, sprinkle with cinnamon, and bake 12 to 14 minutes. Transfer cookies to a baking rack to cool.

MAKES 12 COOKIES

BUTTERSCOTCH PECAN SANDIES

½ cup sweet butter

½ cup brown rice syrup

½ cup Sucanat or other natural dry
   sweetener

1 teaspoon vanilla

1½ cups ground pecans

1½ cups whole wheat pastry flour

½ cup unbleached all-purpose flour

1. Preheat oven to 375°F.

2. In a saucepan, melt butter and stir in sweeteners. Bring to a boil, still stirring, and remove from heat. Stir in the vanilla. Stir in nuts and flour until well incorporated.

3. Roll dough into golf-ball-size nuggets, and place 2 to 3 inches apart on a parchment-lined baking sheet.

4. Bake 12 minutes. Cool for a minute or two on the baking sheet, then transfer to a cooling rack.

MAKES 12 COOKIES

LEMON-CHOCOLATE BREAD PUDDING

Bread puddings are an old-fashioned way to bake and they are one of the good ways to eat high-fiber foods if you use a whole-grain bread. The eggs are a fine source of protein. Truly a nutritious sweet!

3 cups whole wheat or oat bran bread cubes

3 cups low-fat milk, scalded

3 eggs, beaten

⅓ cup dry sweetener or Sucanat

3 tablespoons melted butter

1 tablespoon vanilla

¼ teaspoon ground allspice

¼ teaspoon cinnamon

1 teaspoon fresh lemon juice

½ teaspoon grated lemon rind

⅓ cup carob chips or semi-sweet chocolate chips

Vanilla ice cream (optional)

1. Cut bread into 1-inch cubes, toss onto cookie sheet, and allow to dry for several hours. Place bread cubes in a bowl and add the scalded milk.

2. Beat the eggs, sweetener, butter, vanilla, allspice, cinnamon, and lemon juice and rind until smooth. Pour over bread-milk mixture and stir to combine.

3. Stir in chocolate chips gently, reserving a handful to sprinkle on top of pudding. Some will melt and create a marbled effect.

4. Preheat oven to 350°F.

5. Butter a 1½-quart baking dish. Pour in pudding. Sprinkle with chips. Bake 1¼ hours, until knife inserted comes out clean. Serve warm with a small dollop of vanilla ice cream, as you sit in front of the fire.

SERVES 6 TO 8

FLOURLESS COCONUT CHIP MACAROONS

Even if you don't have a sensitivity to refined flours, you'll love this flourless, wheat-free cookie. It's so delicate, perfect with a cup of your favorite herbal tea.

¼ cup sweet butter

⅓ cup maple syrup or honey

1 large egg white

1 tablespoon vanilla

1 teaspoon baking powder

1 cup shredded unsweetened dried coconut

½ cup naturally sweetened chocolate chips or carob chips

1 cup quick oats

1. Preheat oven to 375°F.

2. In a mixing bowl, cream together butter and maple syrup. Beat in egg white and vanilla.

3. In a separate bowl, combine remaining ingredients and fold into butter mixture. Drop by heaping tablespoons onto parchment-lined baking sheet.

4. Bake 10 minutes. Use a spatula to transfer to wire rack for cooling.

MAKES 2 DOZEN COOKIES

SESAME-ALMOND DROPS

Recipes that call for brown rice syrup are some of the most special because of the subtle malted flavor the syrup imparts.

1 cup raw almonds, blanched
½ cup brown rice syrup
1 teaspoon almond extract
1 large egg white
2 tablespoons sweet butter

3 tablespoons honey
2 tablespoons whole wheat pastry flour
1 teaspoon arrowroot
¼ cup sesame seeds

1. Preheat oven to 325°F.

2. Grind almonds to a powder in a blender or Vitamix. Add everything but the sesame seeds and blend until smooth, stopping the machine occasionally to scrape down the sides with a rubber spatula. Fold in sesame seeds.

3. Drop by the teaspoon onto an ungreased cooking sheet. Bake 15 minutes. Remove the cookies from the pan while hot and let cool on wire racks.

MAKES 24 COOKIES

Food for Thought:

MILK AND EGGS

Organic whole milk products are produced without the use of antibiotics, pesticides, or hormones. The farmers of organic dairies practice ethical treatment to animals. Their dairy products are not from inhumane, unsanitary factory "animal sweatshops"—better for the environment, better tasting, better for you.

Organic eggs are the humanely produced, healthy alternative to antibiotic-laden factory-farmed eggs.

APPLE-FILLED PHYLLO BASKETS

Although this is a real restaurant-style dessert, you won't believe how uncompli-cated it is to make. Phyllo dough is found in the frozen food section in your super-market. This recipe has no butter or extra added fat, with the exception of a little oil used to season the muffin tins.

2 tablespoons safflower oil for muffin tins

3 tablespoons maple syrup or honey

2 tablespoons fresh lemon juice

¼ teaspoon cinnamon

¼ teaspoon ground nutmeg

½ teaspoon ground allspice

3 large Granny Smith apples, peeled, cored, and thinly sliced

5 sheets phyllo dough

6 cinnamon sticks

Vanilla ice cream (optional)

1. Preheat oven to 350°F. Oil a 6-cup muffin tin with the safflower oil.

2. In a heavy skillet, over medium heat, mix the maple syrup, lemon juice, and spices. Cook the apples in the syrup until soft but not mushy, about 5 minutes.

3. Layer 5 phyllo sheets on top of one another and slice into thirds, then cut each third in half so you have 6 equal squares. Press sheets into muffin tins to form crin-kled baskets. Bake 7 to 8 minutes, or until lightly golden.

4. Remove baskets from muffin tins and assemble the dessert. When ready to serve, spoon the apple filling into the baskets. Garnish each basket with a cinnamon stick and serve warm. Top with vanilla ice cream for a sweet indulgence.

SERVES 6

PANFORTE

Italian for "strong bread," panforte is a traditional Christmas confection; chewy and crunchy, it lasts for weeks.

½ cup raw almonds

½ cup raw hazelnuts

1 cup Thompson seedless raisins

1 cup dried black Mission figs, stems removed

Zest and juice of 1 orange

Zest of 1 lemon

½ cup whole wheat pastry flour

¼ cup cocoa or carob powder

2 teaspoons ground cinnamon

¼ teaspoon white pepper

⅛ teaspoon ground coriander

1 cup honey

1. Preheat oven to 300°F.

2. Combine nuts in a bowl and set aside.

3. In a food processor fitted with the steel blade, chop raisins, figs, and orange and lemon zests. Process until smooth.

4. Sift together in a bowl the flour, cocoa, and spices. Combine with the fruit mixture.

5. In a small saucepan, combine the honey with the orange juice. Bring to a boil and pour into dough. Mix well and add nuts.

6. Spread panforte into a parchment-lined 8-inch square baking pan. Bake 55 minutes to 1 hour, or until firm in the center. Remove from the oven and cool in the pan to room temperature.

7. Turn panforte out onto a cutting board and slice into 1-inch squares. Dust tops with additional cocoa powder if desired.

MAKES 64 SQUARES

GEORGIA PEACH COBBLER

Serve with a dollop of frozen yogurt or ice cream.

DOUGH

½ cup oat flour

½ cup unbleached all-purpose flour

1 cup whole wheat pastry flour

1½ teaspoons baking powder

1½ teaspoons sea salt

½ cup (1 stick) sweet butter, chilled

½ cup (1 stick) safflower margarine

¾ cup cold buttermilk

FILLING

5 large peaches, peeled and sliced ¼ to ⅙ inch thick, or 24 ounces frozen sliced peaches, defrosted

SAUCE

¼ cup maple syrup or honey

2 tablespoons sweet butter

2 teaspoons arrowroot

1 tablespoon vanilla

TOPPING

¼ cup Sucanat or other natural dry sweetener

¼ cup whole wheat pastry flour

1 heaping teaspoon cinnamon

1 tablespoon sweet butter

¼ cup finely chopped pecans or rolled oats

1. Preheat oven to 350°F.

2. Make the dough: Sift the first five ingredients together into a bowl. Cut in the fats, using a knife or pastry blender, until mixture is lumpy, with pieces of fat varying from ¼ to 1 inch. Add buttermilk, and stir until mixture barely sticks together and is still lumpy. *Do not knead.* Divide cobbler dough in two pieces and refrigerate one of them.

3. Line an 8-inch square Pyrex, or other pretty baking dish of about that size, with half of the cobbler dough by pressing it into the bottom of the dish gently. Prebake about 12 minutes. Remove from oven and set aside.

4. Make the sauce: In a small bowl, mix all ingredients well. When cobbler dough has finished its prebaking, top it with the prepared peaches and the sauce. Crumble the chilled half of the cobbler dough over the top. Bake 30 minutes, leaving the oven on.

5. Make the topping: Combine topping ingredients and sprinkle over top of cobbler. Bake for an additional 5 minutes. Serve piping hot.

SERVES 6

⚭

BLUEBERRY COBBLER

½ cup yellow cornmeal

1 cup cold buttermilk

3 tablespoons Sucanat or other natural dry sweetener

1 cup plus 1 tablespoon whole wheat pastry flour

½ cup unbleached all-purpose flour

1½ teaspoons sea salt

1 teaspoon baking soda

¼ cup sweet butter, softened to room temperature

¼ cup corn oil, chilled

24 ounces fresh or frozen blueberries

HONEY SAUCE

½ cup honey

2 teaspoons cinnamon

1. Combine cornmeal, buttermilk, and sweetener in a mixing bowl. Set aside for 45 minutes to 1 hour, or until moisture is absorbed and cornmeal has softened.

2. Preheat oven to 375°F.

3. In a separate bowl sift together both flours, salt, and baking soda. With a sharp knife, cut in the butter and corn oil. Add the buttermilk mixture, continuing to use knives to incorporate.

4. Divide the dough in half and gently press first half into a 6-inch square Pyrex baking dish. Bake until lightly browned, about 20 minutes. Remove from oven and fill dish with the berries.

5. Make the honey sauce: Combine honey and cinnamon and drizzle over blueberries. Decorate top of cobbler with remaining dough by creating a lattice design. Gently criss-cross thick pieces of the dough, allowing the rough, nubby quality of the cobbler dough to remain intact. Bake 30 minutes. Serve warm.

SERVES 4 TO 6

LEMON BERRY LINZERTORTE

This delectable Bavarian sweet is traditionally made with a hazelnut-studded crust. Here we've used lemon zest instead for a lighter version but you can also add hazelnuts if you like.

½ cup (1 stick) sweet butter, softened to room temperature
½ cup maple syrup
1 large egg
Zest of 1 lemon (about 2 tablespoons)

1 cup unbleached all-purpose flour
1 cup whole wheat pastry flour
⅔ cup raspberry preserves
½ cup ground hazelnuts (optional)

1. In a bowl, cream together butter and maple syrup until fluffy. Beat in the egg and add lemon zest. Sift together flours and fold into butter mixture (simultaneously with nuts, if desired). Work in dry ingredients only until incorporated; do not over-mix or dough will become tough. Refrigerate for 1 hour.

2. Preheat oven to 350°F.

3. Divide dough into two equal pieces. On a smooth floured surface roll out first portion into a ¼-inch thick circle and gently press into a 10-inch springform or cake pan. Allow for a ½-inch lip around the foundation. Cut away and reserve any scraps.

4. Prick dough in several places with a fork to keep the bottom flat during baking. Spread evenly with raspberry preserves. Roll out remaining half of dough and cut into ½-inch strips. Lay half the strips evenly across the top of the preserves, then add another layer diagonally of the remaining strips.

5. Bake 35 minutes and release the bottom of the pan immediately. Cool the torte on a baking rack. Serve in thin wedges.

SERVES 8 TO 10

WALNUT OIL PIE CRUST

An entirely whole-grain pie crust that's easy to work with and versatile.

½ cup whole wheat flour

2 tablespoons date sugar

½ teaspoon sea salt

¼ cup walnut oil

3 tablespoons milk

6 tablespoons ice water

1. In a medium bowl, combine flour, date sugar, and salt. Using a fork, slowly stir the oil into the flour mixture until crumbly. Stir in milk, then water to bind. Press dough into a flat disk, wrap in plastic wrap, and chill at least 1 hour before rolling out.

2. To roll out the dough, follow the directions below.

MAKES ONE 10-INCH PIE CRUST

How to Roll Out Pastry Dough

You will need a rolling pin, ½ cup of unbleached all-purpose flour for dusting, and the chilled pastry dough.

Always begin with a clean, smooth, and level work surface. Dust the work surface with a small handful of flour. When dough is not too cold to manipulate, in about 5 minutes after it comes out of the refrigerator, press firmly onto the floured surface with the palm of your hand, flip over, and flatten the other side, again using the palm of your hand. Use more flour if you need to—the work surface should always be well floured. With the rolling pin, begin to roll out the dough from the center, always moving the pin away from you. Turn dough 90 degrees rolling dough 2 to 3 times between turns. Continue rolling and turning until dough has reached desired thickness and dimensions.

SWEET POTATO PIE

What a delicious option to keep on hand to top off a soup or salad meal! Watch left-overs disappear the next morning at breakfast!

4 medium sweet potatoes
1 recipe Walnut Oil Pie Crust (page 311)
½ cup date sugar
¼ cup sweet butter, softened to room temperature
2 large eggs

1 teaspoon vanilla
1 teaspoon cinnamon
1 teaspoon baking powder
½ teaspoon ground allspice
½ teaspoon ground mace
⅓ cup evaporated milk

1. Bake sweet potatoes at 350°F until tender, about 1 hour. Meanwhile, prepare crust and roll out to ⅙-inch thickness. Transfer to a 10-inch pie plate and chill.

2. Let potatoes sit until cool enough to handle. Leave oven on.

3. Peel sweet potatoes and mash them in a large mixing bowl until smooth. Add everything but the evaporated milk and mix thoroughly. Stir in the milk to form a thick puree.

4. Pour filling into prepared crust. Bake for 40 minutes. Cool to room temperature, and chill 1 hour before serving.

SERVES 6 TO 8

BASIC TART PASTRY

Using cold butter for tart pastry is one of the secrets to its light, flaky texture. The creaming of the cold butter and sweetener is a bit tricky. Start with your mixer on slow to keep bits of butter from flying from your work bowl.

1½ cups whole wheat pastry flour
½ cup unbleached all-purpose flour
½ teaspoon sea salt

½ cup cold sweet butter
½ cup maple syrup or honey
1 large egg, beaten

1. Sift together the first three ingredients into a bowl.

2. Cream together butter and sweetener in a mixing bowl, or use an electric mixer.

3. Beat egg into butter mixture.

4. Fold in flour mixture but do not overmix. Once flour has been added, handle dough as little as possible or it will become tough.

5. Form the pastry into a flat disk, wrap with plastic wrap, and refrigerate until ready to use, at least 30 minutes. Follow directions for rolling out on page 311.

MAKES ONE 9-INCH CRUST

GINGERED PEAR CUSTARD TART

Ginger complements the mellow pear without overpowering it.

1 recipe Basic Tart Pastry (page 313)
*3 pears, peeled, cored, and sliced
    lengthwise, about ¼ inch thick*

CUSTARD

¾ cup milk (soy or nonfat)
1 tablespoon honey
½ vanilla bean (page 40)
*3 tablespoons coarsely chopped fresh
    gingerroot*
1 large egg
¼ cup maple syrup or honey

1. Preheat oven to 350°F.

2. Roll out pastry dough and press into an 8-inch tart pan.

3. Arrange pear slices in tart shell in an attractive pattern.

4. In a small saucepan, bring milk, honey, vanilla bean, and ginger to a boil. Remove from heat and cover. Steep for 5 to 10 minutes. Strain milk and set aside to cool.

5. In a separate bowl combine egg and sweetener. Whisk in milk until mixture is thoroughly combined and frothy. Pour over pears. Bake on top shelf of oven until top begins to brown and caramelize, about 1 hour.

SERVES 6

HARVEST TART

Serve this elegant dessert in late autumn when it's difficult to find a variety of fresh fruits.

¼ cup fresh tangerine or orange juice

1 cup water

2 teaspoons whole cloves

1 vanilla bean, including pod, cut open

2 cinnamon sticks

1 tablespoon minced fresh gingerroot

½ cup coarsely chopped dried apples

½ cup coarsely chopped dried apricots

¼ cup coarsely chopped pitted prunes

¼ cup coarsely chopped dried peaches

4 Calimyrna figs, coarsely chopped

½ cup Thompson seedless raisins

3 tablespoons Courvoisier (optional)

1 recipe Basic Tart Pastry (page 313)

4 ounces mascarpone or cream cheese

¼ cup maple syrup

1. In a medium saucepan, combine orange juice, water, cloves, vanilla bean and seeds, cinnamon sticks, and ginger. Bring to a boil, simmer 2 to 3 minutes, and remove from heat. Cover and steep 10 to 15 minutes.

2. Place the six dried fruits in a mixing bowl. Stir in Courvoisier, if desired.

3. Strain the steeping liquid and discard the whole spices. Cool the liquid completely, then pour over the fruit mixture. Let stand for 1 hour to reach room temperature.

4. Roll out dough to ¼-inch thickness and press into a tart mold or pan, or use a 9-inch springform pan (see Note). Prick crust with fork. Bake at 375°F for 20 to 25 minutes, or until tart shell is a golden brown. Remove from oven but leave in tart mold several minutes. Carefully release from tart mold and set aside to cool on baking rack.

5. Spread cheese in bottom of cooled tart shell. Pile fruit mixture onto filling, using a spatula or spoon to cover the surface evenly. Drizzle with maple syrup.

SERVES 8

Note: If you use a 9-inch springform pan, build up the sides of the dough about 1 inch or so. A Pyrex pie plate will work too, for a more rustic look.

BASIC FLAKY PIE PASTRY

Pie pastry must always be made by hand to prevent the gluten from developing. Gluten, a protein found in wheat flours, gives bread dough great elasticity when it is kneaded or mixed. In breadmaking, the development of gluten is what gives a loaf its structure and volume. In pastry making, developing gluten is not the goal. Rather, you want to develop as little gluten as possible, so that your pastries will have a light, flaky quality.

1 cup unbleached all-purpose flour
1 cup whole wheat pastry flour
½ teaspoon sea salt

¾ cup sweet butter, chilled and cut in small pieces
¼ cup ice cold water

1. Sift flours and salt together into a large mixing bowl and set aside. *By hand,* rub the butter into the flour, using your palms in the beginning to soften the large pieces. When the mixture resembles coarse crumbs, drizzle in ice water and continue using your hands to shape a disk. Do this lightly; you don't want to overhandle the dough.

2. Seal the pastry tightly in plastic wrap and refrigerate immediately. Wait at least 40 minutes before rolling out (page 311).

3. Always roll out pie pastry when it is cold. Work quickly. If the butter melts, the dough will become sticky and hard to handle. Return dough to the refrigerator for 20 minutes or so if it becomes too warm and unmanageable.

MAKES 9- OR 10-INCH PIE CRUST

APRICOT-DATE LATTICE PIE

1 cup chopped pitted dates
⅓ cup unbleached all-purpose flour
2 tablespoons cold sweet butter
½ cup fresh orange juice
¼ cup maple syrup or honey

1 tablespoon arrowroot
6 cups thinly sliced fresh apricots
1 recipe Basic Flaky Pie Pastry, chilled
  (page 316)

1. Preheat oven to 350°F.

2. In a small mixing bowl, combine dates, flour, and cold butter. Use a fork or your hands to blend in the flour, evenly coating the dates and butter to create a crumbly mixture. Set aside.

3. In a small saucepan, whisk together orange juice, sweetener, and arrowroot over low heat, and continue whisking, about 3 minutes, until thick and gelatinous. Place apricots in a mixing bowl and pour the hot orange juice mixture over them, combining well. Stir in date mixture.

4. On a floured surface, roll two-thirds of pie pastry into a 10-inch circle. Gently place in a 9-inch pie plate. Do not cut away edges. Spoon filling into crust. With remaining pie pastry, make a lattice top by rolling out dough about ⅛-inch thick and cutting it into 10 strips. Lay in a lattice design over top of filling and fold over edges of bottom crust. Seal crust by pinching with your fingers.

5. Bake 30 minutes on bottom rack of oven. Move to top rack and bake another 30 minutes, or until the juices are bubbly and thick. Cool to room temperature and serve.

SERVES 6 TO 8

MILE-HIGH SPICED PEAR PIE

6 large pears, d'Anjou or Bartlett, peeled,
    cored, and cut into ¼-inch chunks
Juice of 1 lemon
¼ cup sweet butter
3 tablespoons maple syrup or honey
3 tablespoons whole wheat pastry flour
½ teaspoon ground ginger

¼ teaspoon ground cloves
¼ teaspoon ground mace
1 teaspoon cinnamon
½ vanilla bean, seeds scraped (page 40)
1 recipe Basic Flaky Pie Pastry (page 316)
Buttermilk for brushing crust

1. Preheat oven to 350°F.

2. Toss pears in a bowl with remaining ingredients except pastry and buttermilk.
Set aside.

3. Roll out pie pastry ¼-inch thick into a circle 16 to 18 inches in diameter. Gently
place in 9-inch pie dish. Do not cut away pastry scraps.

4. Spoon pear filling into pie dish, piling high in the center. Fold exposed crust over
filling, tucking it under in places, as though you were arranging fabric. A portion
of the filling will remain exposed in the center. Pour remaining juices over the top
of exposed pears. Brush top crust with buttermilk. Bake 50 to 60 minutes on bottom
rack of oven. Cool slightly on a baking rack and serve warm.

SERVES 6 TO 8

A Glossary for the Beginning Cook

adjust seasonings: to taste before serving and increase seasoning as needed.

à la: French for "in the style of."

al dente: Italian for "to the tooth," used to describe pasta that is cooked to be tender but firm, rather than soft, and can also be used to describe vegetables.

bake: to cook in the oven with dry heat.

baste: to ladle or brush drippings, liquid, butter, or other sauce over food as it cooks. Adds flavor and prevents dryness.

beat: to whip briskly by hand with a spoon, whisk, rotary beater, or to use an electrical beater.

bisque: a cream soup, usually with a shellfish base.

blanch: to cook in boiling water briefly to loosen skins or to heighten color or flavor. Used for nuts or tomatoes or to bring vegetables to al dente readiness.

blend: to combine several ingredients together, by hand or with an electric blender.

boil: to heat a liquid until large bubbles break the surface.

braise: to brown in fat, then cook, covered, on top of stove or in the oven with liquid.

bread: to coat with bread crumbs.

brown: to cook on stove in fat at high heat or set under broiler.

burro: an oversized burrito or Mexican or Southwestern rolled tortilla, stuffed with beans, meat, or vegetables.

chapati: a round, plate-sized unleavened flatbread typical of the cuisine of India, made from whole wheat flour.

chill: to place in refrigerator or bowl of crushed ice until cold.

chop: to cut with a large blade chopping knife into small pieces.

coarsely chop: to cut with a large blade chopping knife into bite-size pieces.

coat: to dip in wet or dry ingredients to cover.

cool: to bring a hot food to room temperature.

core: to remove seeds and center stem structure from fruits.

cream: to beat a fat by hand or with an electric mixer until smooth and aerated.

crimp: to make a decorative seal around the edge of a pastry or pie with fingers or fork.

crumble: to break up with the fingers.

crush: to reduce to a crumblike consistency.

cube: to cut into small, square pieces.

dal: a spicy soup from India, made from legumes and vegetables and served as a sauce with curries and rice or for dipping of chapatis.

dice: to cut into fine square pieces smaller than cubes.

drain: to strain off all liquid.

drizzle: to add a liquid over the top of a dish in a fine stream.

drop: to use one or two spoons to place cookie or biscuit dough on baking sheet.

fajita: Tex-Mex grilled meats or vegetables, served with hot tortillas, salsa, and guacamole.

fold: to mix, using a gentle over-and-over motion without beating.

fold in: to mix a light ingredient (i.e., beaten egg white or cream) into a heavier ingredient with a light over-and-over motion so that no volume is lost.

flake: to break into small pieces with a fork.

freeze: chill until hard and icy.

fusion: an unorthodox mixture of ingredients from diverse cuisines.

garnish: to decorate a dish before serving.

glaze: to coat food with a glossy coating in the form of syrup or melted jellies; to brush pastry with milk or beaten egg to make it glisten.

grate: to shred food into small particles by passing through a grater.

grease: to rub or coat with butter or oil.

grill: to broil with heat source underneath the food.

grind: to reduce to fine particles or paste by putting through a grinder.

julienne: food cut into matchstick-size pieces.

koji: a macrobiotic term for a long-cooked stew that is easily digested.

macerate: to marinate fruit in juices, wine, or brandy.

marinate: to steep savory foods such as meat, fish, poultry, or vegetables in a spicy liquid for several hours until food absorbs flavoring.

mash: to press into a pulp, usually with a potato masher.

melange: French for a mixture of foods, such as several vegetables in the same dish.

melt: to liquefy by heating.

mince: to cut in extremely fine pieces, to finely chop.

mirepoix: French for a mixture of minced sautéed vegetables—traditionally carrots, celery, and onions used to flavor soups, sauces, stuffing, and stews.

mix: to stir together, using a circular motion.

moisten: to dampen by adding liquid.

mold: to place food in a shaped container and cook, chill, or freeze long enough for the food to take on that shape.

mull: to heat fruit juice, wine, or tea with spices.

pan-broil: to cook in a skillet on the stove with as little fat as possible. Fat is poured off as it accumulates.

pan-fry: to sauté or cook in a skillet on the stove with fat and without pouring off drippings.

peel: to cut off the skin.

pinch: the amount of seasoning (salt, sweetener, herb, or spice) that can be taken up between the thumb and forefinger, usually less than ⅛ teaspoon.

plumb: to soak dried fruits until soft with liquid.

poach: to submerge in simmering liquid—used for fish, fowl, and fruit.

pound: to flatten with a mallet—a useful preparation step prior to cooking chicken breasts.

press: to squeeze, as through a garlic press, to extract juice and soft pulp used for garlic and ginger.

prick: to make holes with the tines of a fork necessary to keep pie shells from wrinkling or shrinking when they bake and to free fat from fatty fowl (duck or goose) as it roasts.

proof: to set a yeast mixture in warm, dry spot to rise.

puree: to produce a paste by pulverizing in a blender or food processor or forcing through a food mill.

quesadilla: cheese melted on a tortilla that is then folded around stuffings of chicken, beans, or vegetables; also served plain with only cheese filling as an appetizer in Mexican cuisine.

rancid: a word describing the spoiled, rank aroma and taste of old fatty foods, such as nuts, seeds, oils, butters, or cheeses.

reconstitute: to restore moisture to dried foods by adding water.

reduce: to boil down rapidly until volume is less and flavors are more concentrated; sauces are reduced.

raita: a sauce or salad of yogurt and vegetables; used in the cuisine of India.

rib: one branch or stalk of celery.

roast: to cook uncovered in an oven with dry heat; no liquid is used during roasting.

roll out: to roll into a thin, flat sheet with a rolling pin.

roux: a butter and flour paste, rubbed or melted together and used as a thickener in soups or stews; sometimes a roux is browned.

salsa: Mexican for "sauce," traditionally made from tomatoes or tomatillos and chilies.

sauté: to cook in a skillet on the stove with small amounts of oil, broth, or water.

scald: to heat milk or cream until tiny bubbles begin to form around the edge of the pan.

score: to make cuts in a food surface with a knife or the tines of a fork; unpeeled cucumber can be scored before slicing for a decorative effect.

sear: to brown meat quickly to seal in juices, in either a skillet or a very hot oven.

season: to add salt, pepper, herbs, spices, and other seasonings.

season to taste: to add the flavorings of your choice in an intensity that pleases your palate.

seed: to remove seeds from produce.

shave: to cut a thin, fine slice for cheese or chocolate.

shred: to cut in small thin strips by pressing through a grater or using a food processor.

simmer: to heat foods or liquids until small bubbles just begin to break the surface of the liquids; just below the boiling point.

skewer: to thread meat, vegetables, or fruit onto wooden or metal sticks.

skim: to remove froth or fat from the surface of a liquid with a spoon.

slice: to cut food with a knife or food processor.

sliver: to cut or snip food into extremely thin, fine pieces that are only an inch or so long.

soak: to let stand in water or other liquid.

steam: to cook, covered, over boiling water so the steam from the boiling water does the cooking. The level of boiling water should be far below the food that is cooking.

steep: to allow tea leaves, herbs, or spices to stand in any hot liquid until they have flavored the liquid.

stem: to remove the stem of a vegetable or mushroom.

stew: to cook, submerged in simmering liquid; a food that is cooked slowly.

stir: to mix with a spoon or whisk, using a circular motion.

stir-fry: popular Asian method of cooking meats, fowl, seafood, and vegetables by briskly stirring and tossing the foods in a small amount of oil over very high heat; usually done in a wok.

stock: the strained broth from boiled meats, fowl, seafood, or vegetables.

strain: to separate liquids from solids by passing through a sieve or colander.

stuff: to fill a cavity with a mixture of another food.

tandoori: a method using a clay oven to roast breads, meats, or seafood; used in the cuisine of India.

tenderize: to soften meats by pounding or by adding an enzyme tenderizer or soaking in an acidic marinade.

thicken: to concentrate a liquid by boiling down or adding flour or other starch thickener.

thin: to dilute by adding more liquid.

toast: to lightly brown by heating.

toast points: small triangular pieces of toast, a nice accompaniment to soup.

toss: to mix by flipping lightly over and over until food is uniformly seasoned for salads; it is important that tossing is thorough.

whip: to beat air into a substance, usually with a whisk, rotary, or electric beater.

wrap: a rolled sandwich for which the "wrapper" is a flour tortilla.

zest: the colored part of citrus rind, used for flavoring. A fine grater (zester) is used to "zest" oranges or lemons.

Sources

Products

Urban Organic
New York NY
718-499-4321
Home delivery of pesticide-free fruits and
vegetables.

Inside Out
New York Tri-State Area
800-394-6655
A comprehensive line of organic foods and
products. Delivery and mail order.

Diamond Organics
P.O. Box 2159
Freedom, CA 95019
800-922-2396
Organic mail-order produce, unsulphered dried
fruit, nuts, breads, oils, herbs, and sprouts.

Jaffe Bros. Inc.
P.O. Box 636
28560 Lilac Road
Valley Center, CA 92082-0636
619-749-1133
Organic mail-order products, including: grains,
unsulphered dried fruits, nuts, seeds, condiments, coffee and tea, pastas, oils, and more.

Krystal Wharf Farms
RD 2, Box 2212
Mansfield, PA 16933
717-549-8194
Organic herb, spice, fruit, and vegetable sup-
pliers and mail order.

Williams Creek Farm
188843 Williams Highway
Williams, OR 97544
503-846-6481
Mail-order organic fruits and vegetables.

Walnut Acres
Walnut Acres Road
Penns Creek, PA 17862
800-433-3998
Mail-order organic fruit, vegetables, juices,
grains, beans, nuts, and oils.

Mountain Ark Trading Company
120 South East Avenue
Fayetteville, AR 72701
800-752-2775
Mail-order grains, sea vegetables, miso, and
other Asian food items.

Gold Mine Natural Foods
1947 Thirtieth Street
San Diego, CA 92102
800-457-FOOD
Mail-order sea vegetables, Japanese noodles, miso, exotic mushrooms, and other Asian food items.

T & A Gourmet
P.O. Box 5179
Somerset, NJ 08875-5179
800-762-2135
Mail-order natural sweeteners, such as rice syrup, barley malt, sorghum, honey, conserves, and maple syrup.

Whole Foods Markets
National Corporate Office
601 N. Lamar
Austin, TX 78703
512-477-4455
The country's largest natural foods market chain, approximately 100 stores nationwide.

Spring Hill Music
P.O. Box 800
Boulder, CO 80306
Mail-order for spiritual music.

Organizations

California Action Network
P.O. Box 464
Davis, CA 95617
916-756-7857

Publishes a directory of organic products and produce, organic farmers, and wholesalers.

Mothers & Others
40 West 20th Street
New York, NY 10011
212-242-0010
National organization educating and working on food safety issues as they concern children.

Organic Food Production Association of North America
P.O. Box 1078
23 Ames Street
Greenfield, MA 01301
413-774-7511
Nonprofit organization linking consumers to organic growers, manufacturers, and retailers.

Center for Science in the Public Interest and Americans for Safe Food
1875 Connecticut Avenue, N.W.
Suite 530
Washington DC 20009
202-332-9110
Consumer organization for promoting information on food safety issues.

Coalition to Stop Food Irradiation (CSFI)
Los Angeles, CA: 818-353-2543
Berkeley, CA: 510-848-4424
Miami, FL: 305-672-8044
Boston, MA: 617-787-1542

Bibliography

Accairdo, Marcia. *Light Eating for Survival*. Fairfield, Iowa: 21st Century Publications, 1977.

Anderson, Jean, and Hanna, Elaine. *The New Doubleday Cookbook*. New York: Doubleday, 1975, 1985.

Baker, Elton and Elizabeth, *The Uncook Book*. Saguache, Colo.: Drelwood Publications, 1980.

Beutler, Jade, R.R.T., R.C.P. *Flax for Life!* Encinitas, Calif.: Progressive Health Publishing, 1996.

Bragg, Paul C., N.D., Ph.D., and Patricia Bragg, N.D., Ph.D. *Apple Cider Vinegar: Miracle Health System*. Santa Barbara, Calif.: Health Science, 1993, 1995.

Budwig, Dr. Johanna. *The Oil Protein Diet Cookbook*. Canada: Apple Publishing.

Cousins, Norman. *Head First*. New York: Penguin Books, 1990.

Cross, Pamela. *Kitchen Wisdom*. Altona, Canada: Camden House Publishing, 1991.

De Medici, Lorenza. *Tuscany: The Beautiful Cookbook*. San Francisco: HarperCollins Publishers, 1992.

Devi Yamuna. *Lord Krishna's Cuisine: The Art of Indian Vegetarian Cooking*. New York: E. P. Dutton, 1987.

Diamond, Marilyn. *The American Vegetarian Cookbook: From the Fit For Life Kitchen*. New York: Warner Books, 1990.

Erasmus, Uto. *Fats and Oils*. Vancouver, Canada: Alive, 1986.

Gisslen, Wayne. *Professional Cooking*. New York: John Wiley & Sons, 1989.

Hay, Louise L. *Heart Thoughts*. Los Angeles: Hay House, 1990.

Hom, Ken. *Asian Vegetarian Feast*. New York: William Morrow, 1988.

Hurd, Frank J., D.C., and Hurd, Rosalie, B.S. *A Good Cook . . . Ten Talents*. Chisholm, Minn.: Dr. and Mrs. Frank J. Hurd, 1968.

Kulvinskas, Victor P., M.S. *Sprout for the Love of Everybody*. Fairfield, Iowa: 21st Century Publications, 1978.

LaLanne, Jack. *Foods for Glamour*. Englewood Cliffs, N.J.: Prentice-Hall, 1961.

McManus, Timothy. *Bircher-Benner: Nutrition Plan for Raw Food and Juices*. New York: Nash Publishing, 1972.

Mishra, Dr. Rammurti S., M.D. *Fundamentals of Yoga*. New York: Harmony Books, 1969.

New Jerusalem Bible, The. Reader's Edition. New York: Doubleday, 1985.

Nishimoto, Miyoko. *The Now and Zen Epicure*. Summertown, Tenn.: Book Publishing Company, 1991.

Phillips, David A., Ph.D., N.D., B.E. *Recipes for Health and Pleasure*. Santa Barbara, Calif.: Woodbridge Press, 1983.

Roehl, Evely. *Whole Food Facts*. Rochester, Vt.: Healing Arts Press, 1988.

Rogers, Jean. *The Healing Foods Cookbook*. Emmaus, Penn.: Rodale Press, 1991.

Romano, Rita. *Dining in the Raw, Cooking with the Buff*. Florence, Italy: Prato Publications, 1993.

Rombauer, Irma S., and Becker, Marion Robauer. *The Joy of Cooking*. New York: Bobbs-Merrill Company, 1975.

Sahni, Julie. *Classic Indian Cooking*. New York: William Morrow, 1980.

Schiller, David. *The Little Zen Companion*. New York: Workman Publishing, 1994.

Sri Sathya Sai Baba. *Pathways to God*. Faber, Va.: Leela Press, 1991.

Sutphen, Dick. *The Oracle Within*. New York: Pocket Books, 1991.

SYDA Foundation. *Nectar of Chanting, The*. South Fallsburg, N.Y. 1978.

Tulku, Tarthany. *Gesture of Balance*. Boulder, Colo.: Dharma Publishing, 1977.

Walters, J. Donald. *Secrets of Bringing Peace on Earth*. New Delhi, India: UBS Publishers, 1993.

Wigmore, Ann. *The Sprouting Book*. Wayne, N.J.: Avery Publishing Group, 1986.

Subject Index

Recipe Index

୧ ୨